Hannigan and Prentice:
The Companies Act 2006 –
A Commentary
Second Edition

BPP College

' ihrarv & Information Service

68-70 Red Lion Street,
London WC1R 4NY
020 7430 7099
libraryholborn@bpp.com
bpp.blackboard.com

Hannigan and Prentice: The Companies Act 2006 – A Commentary
Second Edition

General Editor

Brenda Hannigan, MA, LLM
Professor of Corporate Law, University of Southampton

Consultant Editor

Dan Prentice
Barrister, Erskine Chambers and Fellow of Pembroke College, Oxford

Specialist Contributors

Ceri Bryant, MA, LLM
Barrister, Erskine Chambers

Alex Kay, MA
Partner, Herbert Smith LLP

Glynis D Morris, BA FCA

James Palmer, MA
Partner, Herbert Smith LLP

Carol Shutkever, MA
Partner, Herbert Smith LLP

LexisNexis®

Members of the LexisNexis Group worldwide

United Kingdom	LexisNexis Butterworths, a Division of Reed Elsevier (UK) Ltd, Halsbury House, 35 Chancery Lane, London, WC2A 1EL, and London House, 20–22 East London Street, Edinburgh EH7 4BQ
Australia	LexisNexis Butterworths, Chatswood, New South Wales
Austria	LexisNexis Verlag ARD Orac GmbH & Co KG, Vienna
Benelux	LexisNexis Benelux, Amsterdam
Canada	LexisNexis Canada, Markham, Ontario
China	LexisNexis China, Beijing and Shanghai
France	LexisNexis SA, Paris
Germany	LexisNexis Deutschland GmbH, Munster
Hong Kong	LexisNexis Hong Kong, Hong Kong
India	LexisNexis India, New Delhi
Italy	Giuffrè Editore, Milan
Japan	LexisNexis Japan, Tokyo
Malaysia	Malayan Law Journal Sdn Bhd, Kuala Lumpur
New Zealand	LexisNexis NZ Ltd, Wellington
Poland	Wydawnictwo Prawnicze LexisNexis Sp, Warsaw
Singapore	LexisNexis Singapore, Singapore
South Africa	LexisNexis Butterworths, Durban
USA	LexisNexis, Dayton, Ohio

© Reed Elsevier (UK) Ltd 2009

Published by LexisNexis Butterworths

A CIP Catalogue record for this book is available from the British Library.

ISBN 13: 978 1 4057 4449 2

Typeset by Letterpart Ltd, Reigate, Surrey

Printed and bound in Great Britain by Hobbs the Printers Ltd, Totton, Hampshire

Visit LexisNexis Butterworths at www.lexisnexis.co.uk

Preface

The second edition of this work marks the full commencement, finally, of the Companies Act 2006 on 1 October 2009. The origins of the Act lie in the Company Law Review launched in March 1998, so the process has been slow, but the end point has been reached and the piecemeal implementation of the Act since Royal Assent in November 2006 is now complete.

In this edition, all the Chapters have been updated to reflect that full implementation, noting especially the numerous statutory instruments (47 to date and counting) which give flesh to the statutory provisions. Other developments are also reflected, such as the implementation of the Shareholders' Rights Directive (effective 3 August 2009) which has necessitated significant changes to the law governing meetings and which is discussed in Chapter 7. A new Chapter on directors' conflicts of interest has been added in this edition to provide additional coverage of this important topic. Finally, the Department for Business, Enterprise and Regulatory Reform (BERR, previously the Department for Trade and Industry) has been renamed as the Department for Business, Innovation and Skills (BIS) and references to BERR in the text should be read accordingly.

The law is stated as of 1 May 2009.

Professor Brenda Hannigan

Professor Dan Prentice

24 June 2009

List of Contributors

General Editor

Professor Brenda Hannigan Professor of Corporate Law University of Southampton
Brenda Hannigan's principal research interests lie in company and insolvency law. She is the editor of *Butterworths Corporate Law Service*; Consultant editor of *Halsbury's Laws of England*, vols 7(1), (2) *Companies* (2009 re-issue) and the author of *Company Law* (2nd edn, 2009, OUP).

Consultant Editor

Dan Prentice
Dan Prentice is the Allen & Overy Professor of Corporate Law at Oxford, Fellow of Pembroke College and a tenant of Erskine Chambers. He is the General Editor of *Buckley on the Companies Act*, an Editor of *Chitty on Contracts* and the Assistant Editor of the *Law Quarterly Review*. He is a member of the Company Law Committee of the Law Society and also of a number of learned societies.

Contributors

Ceri Bryant
Ceri Bryant is a member of Erskine Chambers and has practised as a barrister in the field of company law in those chambers since 1986. She is a specialist in company law and corporate insolvency (contentious and non-contentious), and advises on all aspects of the operation of companies with a particular emphasis on advice on corporate and capital reorganisations, takeovers, members' and creditors' schemes of arrangement, schemes for the transfer of insurance business and capital reductions. She is a contributor to *Buckley on the Companies Acts* and to *The Law of Majority Shareholder Power* published in 2008 by Oxford University Press.

Alex Kay MA, Partner, Herbert Smith LLP
Alex Kay read law at Jesus College, Cambridge before joining Herbert Smith to undertake his articles. He qualified as a solicitor in 1997 and became a partner in 2003. Since qualification he has focused on corporate finance and mergers and acquisitions transactions for listed and non-listed UK and non-UK clients, including securities offerings, cross-border transactions, restructurings, joint ventures, private acquisitions and public takeovers. He has a particular experience in the financial institutions and real estate sectors. Alex writes regularly on company law, corporate governance and takeover regulation and participated in various of the City of London Law Society/Law Society working groups on the review of the Company Law Reform Bill, which became the Companies Act 2006. Alex is the editor of the European Community: Company Law Harmonisation chapter of *Tolley's Company Law*. Alex and James would like to thank Sharon Watters of Herbert Smith for her assistance in the writing of their chapter.

List of Contributors

Glynis D Morris, BA FCA
Glynis Morris graduated from the University of Manchester and then trained with KPMG, qualifying as a chartered accountant in 1979. She spent 20 years with the firm, working from their offices in Leeds, London and Cambridge with a wide range of clients in the business, charity and education sectors. She became a partner in the firm in January 1991 but left to set up her own practice near Cambridge in January 1996, providing accounting, audit and tax services to local clients as well as writing and lecturing extensively on accounting, auditing, company law and corporate governance issues. She relocated to mid-Wales in 2006 and now operates her practice from there. She is the author of *Finance Director's Handbook*, *Tolley's Manual of Accounting*, *UK Accounting Practice* and *An Accountant's Guide to Risk Management* and co-author of *Non-Executive Director's Handbook*. She also contributes to *Tolley's Company Secretarial Service*, *Tolley's Company Law* and *Butterworth's Corporate Law Service*, and writes regularly for professional websites, newsletters and magazines.

James Palmer MA, Partner, Herbert Smith LLP
James Palmer is a partner with Herbert Smith LLP, where he has been been since he joined as an articled clerk in 1986. He specialises in corporate law, mergers and acquisitions and securities law. He is a member of the City of London Law Society's Company Law Sub-Committee, which he chaired from 2002–2006. He has also led since 2002, the Takeovers Joint Working Party of the City Law Society and the Law Society of England and Wales. He is a contributor to *Butterworths Takeovers: Law and Practice* and has recently become a contributor to *Buckley on the Companies Act*.

Carol Shutkever MA, Partner, Herbert Smith LLP
Carol Shutkever read law at Sidney Sussex College, Cambridge. She has been a partner at Herbert Smith since 1998 where she focuses on providing technical advice on company and corporate finance law issues and analysing new law and regulation for the firm and its clients. She is a regular writer and speaker on company law issues and is a member of a number of the Law Society Company Law working parties on the Companies Act 2006 and has been involved in the discussions with Government on the Act and its implementation.

Contents

Chapter 5 The Derivative Claim – an Invitation to Litigate?

Chapter 6 Accounts and Audit

Contents

Contents

Contents

Commencement Timetable for the Companies Act 2006

This table is intended to provide guidance on the commencement timetable for the Companies Act 2006. It cannot however provide a definitive guide: you may therefore also wish to refer to the relevant commencement order, see the List of Statutory Instruments.

Following the final commencement on 1 October 2009, four provisions will not have been commenced. These are section 327(2)(c), section 330(6)(c), section 1175 as it applies in Northern Ireland, and Part 2 of Schedule 9.

1	General introductory provisions (1–6) *Section 2: 6 April 2007*	1 October 2009
2	Company formation (7–16)	1 October 2009
3	A company's constitution (17–38) *Sections 29 & 30: 1 October 2007*	1 October 2009
4	A company's capacity and related matters (39–52) *Section 44: 6 April 2008*	1 October 2009
5	A company's name (53–85) *Sections 69 to 74: 1 October 2008* *Sections 82 to 85: 1 October 2008*	1 October 2009
6	A company's registered office (86–88)	1 October 2009
7	Re-registration as a means of altering a company's status (89–111)	1 October 2009
8	A company's members (112–144) *Sections 116 to 119: 1 October 2007* *Sections 121 & 128: 6 April 2008*	1 October 2009
9	Exercise of members' rights (145–153)	1 October 2007

10	A company's directors (154–259) *Sections 155 to 159: 1 October 2008* *Sections 162 to 167: 1 October 2009* *Sections 175 to 177: 1 October 2008* *Sections 180(1), (2)(in part), & (4)(b), and* *181(2) & (3): 1 October 2008* *Sections 182 to 187: 1 October 2008* *Sections 240 to 247: 1 October 2009*	1 October 2007
11	Derivative claims and proceedings by members (260–269)	1 October 2007
12	Company secretaries (270–280) *Section 270(3)(b)(ii): 1 October 2009* *Sections 275 to 279: 1 October 2009*	6 April 2008
13	Resolutions and meetings (281–361) *Sections 308 & 309: 20 January 2007* *Section 333: 20 January 2007* *Sections 327(2)(c) & 330(6)(c) are not being* *commenced.*	1 October 2007
14	Control of political donations and expenditure (362–379) *Provisions relating to independent election* *candidates: 1 October 2008* *Part 14 came into force in Northern Ireland on* *1 November 2007, except for provisions* *relating to independent election candidates.*	1 October 2007
15	Accounts and reports (380–474) *Section 417: 1 October 2007* *Section 463: 20 January 2007 for reports and* *statements first sent to members and others* *after that date*	6 April 2008
16	Audit (475–539) *Sections 485 to 488: 1 October 2007*	6 April 2008
17	A company's share capital (540–657) *Section 544: 6 April 2008* *Sections 641(1)(a) & (2)–(6), 642–644, 652(1)* *and (3) & 654: 1 October 2008*	1 October 2009
18	Acquisition by limited company of its own shares (658–737) *Repeal of the restrictions under the Companies* *Act 1985 on financial assistance for acquisition* *of shares in private companies, including the* *"whitewash" procedure: 1 October 2008*	1 October 2009
19	Debentures (738–754)	6 April 2008
20	Private and public companies (755–767)	6 April 2008
21	Certification and transfer of securities (768–790)	6 April 2008

22	Information about interests in a company's shares (791–828) *Sections 811(4), 812, 814: 6 April 2008*	20 January 2007
23	Distributions (829–853)	6 April 2008
24	A company's annual return (854–859)	1 October 2009
25	Company charges (860–894)	1 October 2009
26	Arrangements and reconstructions (895–901)	6 April 2008
27	Mergers and divisions of public companies (902–941)	6 April 2008
28	Takeovers etc (942–992)	6 April 2007
29	Fraudulent trading (993)	1 October 2007
30	Protection of members against unfair prejudice (994–999)	1 October 2007
31	Dissolution and restoration to the register (1000–1034)	1 October 2009
32	Company investigations: amendments (1035–1039)	1 October 2007
33	UK companies not formed under the Companies Acts (1040–1043) *Section 1043: 6 April 2007*	1 October 2009
34	Overseas companies (1044–1059)	1 October 2009
35	The registrar of companies (1060–1120) *Section 1063 (in respect of England, Wales and Scotland): 6 April 2007* *Section 1068(5): 1 January 2007* *Sections 1077 to 1080: 1 January 2007* *Sections 1085 to 1092: 1 January 2007* *Sections 1102 to 1107: I January 2007* *Section 1111: 1 January 2007*	1 October 2009
36	Offences under the Companies Acts (1121–1133) *Section 1124: 1 October 2007* *Section 1126: 6 April 2008*	With relevant provisions
37	Companies: supplementary provisions (1134–1157) *Section 1137(1), (4), (5)(b) and (6):* *30 September 2007* *Sections 1143 to 1148: 20 January 2007* *Section 1157: 1 October 2008*	With relevant provisions
38	Companies: interpretation (1158–1174) *Sections 1161, 1162, 1164, 1165, 1169 and* *1172 : 6 April 2008* *Section 1167: 30 September 2007* *Section 1170: 6 April 2007*	With relevant provisions

39	Companies: minor amendments (1175–1181) *Section 1175 (in relation to England & Wales and Scotland): 1 April 2008* *Sections 1180: 1 October 2009* *Section 1181: 1 October 2009*	6 April 2007
40	Company directors: foreign disqualification etc (1182–1191)	1 October 2009
41	Business names (1192–1208)	1 October 2009
42	Statutory auditors (1209–1264) *Sections 1242 to 1244: 29 June 2008*	6 April 2008
43	Transparency obligations and related matters (1265–1273)	Royal Assent
44	Miscellaneous provisions (1274–1283) *Sections 1274 and 1276: Royal Assent* *Section 1275: 1 October 2009* *Sections 1277 to 1280: 1 October 2008* *Section 1281: 6 April 2007* *Section 1282: 6 April 2008* *Section 1283: 1 October 2009*	
45	Northern Ireland (1284–1287)	With relevant provisions
46	General supplementary provisions (1288–1297) *Section 1295: With relevant provisions*	Royal Assent
47	Final provisions (1298–1300)	Royal Assent

List of Statutory Instruments

Commencement Orders & Consequential Amendment Orders

The Companies Act 2006 (Consequential Amendments, Transitional Provisions and Savings) Order 2009	SI 2009/1941
The Companies Act 2006 (Part 35) (Consequential Amendments, Transitional Provisions and Savings) Order 2009	SI 2009/1802
The Companies Act 2006 (Commencement No.8, Transitional Provisions and Savings) Order 2008	SI 2008/2860
The Companies Act 2006 (Commencement No.7, Transitional Provisions and Savings) Order 2008	SI 2008/1886
The Companies Act 2006 (Consequential Amendments etc) Order 2008	SI 2008/948
The Companies Act 2006 (Commencement No. 6, Saving and Commencement No. 3 and No. 5 (Amendment)) Order 2008	SI 2008/674
The Companies Act 2006 (Commencement No. 5, Transitional Provisions and Savings) Order 2007	SI 2007/3495
The Companies Act 2006 (Commencement No. 4 and Commencement No. 3 (Amendment)) Order 2007	SI 2007/2607
The Companies Act 2006 (Commencement No 3, Consequential Amendments, Transitional Provisions and Savings) Order 2007	SI 2007/2194
The Companies Act 2006 (Commencement No. 2, Consequential Amendments, Transitional Provisions and Savings) Order 2007	SI 2007/1093
The Companies Act 2006 (Commencement No. 1, Transitional Provisions and Savings) Order 2006	SI 2006/3428

Articles of Association

The Companies (Model Articles) Regulations 2008	SI 2008/3229

The Companies (Tables A to F) (Amendment) Regulations 2008	SI 2008/739
The Companies (Tables A to F) (Amendment) (No.2) Regulations 2007	SI 2007/2826
The Companies(Tables A to F) (Amendment) Regulations 2007	SI 2007/2541

Accounts and Reports

The Companies Act 2006 (Accounts, Reports and Audit) Regulations 2009	SI 2009/1581
The Companies (Defective Accounts and Directors' Reports) (Authorised Person) and Supervision of Accounts and Reports (Prescribed Body) Order 2008	SI 2008/623
The Partnerships (Accounts) Regulations 2008	SI 2008/569
The Bank Accounts Directive (Miscellaneous Banks) Regulations 2008	SI 2008/567
The Insurance Accounts Directive (Miscellaneous Insurance Undertakings) Regulations 2008	SI 2008/565
The Large and Medium-sized Companies and Groups (Accounts and Reports) Regulations 2008	SI 2008/410
The Small Companies and Groups (Accounts and Directors' Report) Regulations 2008	SI 2008/409
The Companies Act 2006 (Amendment) (Accounts and Reports) Regulations 2008	SI 2008/393
The Companies (Summary Financial Statement) Regulations 2008	SI 2008/374
The Companies (Revision of Defective Accounts and Reports) Regulations 2008	SI 2008/373

Audit and Statutory Auditors

The Statutory Auditors and Third Country Auditors (Amendment) (No2) Regulations 2008	SI 2008/2639
The Statutory Auditors and Third Country Auditors (Amendment) Regulations 2008	SI 2008/499
The Statutory Auditors (Delegation of Functions etc) Order 2008	SI 2008/496
The Companies (Disclosure of Auditor Remuneration and Liability Limitation Agreements) Regulations 2008	SI 2008/489
The Statutory Auditors and Third Country Auditors Regulations 2007	SI 2007/3494

Other SIs

The Companies Act 2006 (Consequential Amendments) (Uncertificated Securities) Order 2009	SI 2009/1889
The Companies (Share Capital and Acquisition by Company of its Own Shares) Regulations 2009	SI 2009/2022
The Community Interest Company (Amendment) Regulations 2009	SI 2009/1942
The Overseas Companies (Execution of Documents and Registration of Charges) Regulations 2009	SI 2009/1917
The Limited Liability Partnerships (Amendment) Regulations 2009	SI 2009/1833
The Limited Liability Partnerships (Application of Companies Act 2006) Regulations 2009	SI 2009/1804
The Overseas Companies Regulations 2009	SI 2009/1801
The Registrar of Companies and Applications for Striking Off Regulations 2009	SI 2009/1803
The Companies (Shareholders' Rights) Regulations 2009	SI 2009/1632
The Company and Business Names (Miscellaneous Provisions) Regulations 2009	SI 2009/1085
The Companies (Shares and Share Capital) Order 2009	SI 2009/388
The Companies (Trading Disclosures) (Amendment) Regulations 2009	SI 2009/218
The Companies (Disclosure of Address) Regulations 2009	SI 2009/214
The Companies (Registration) Regulations 2008	SI 2008/3014
The Companies (Fees for Inspection of Company Records) Regulations 2008	SI 2008/3007
The Companies (Company Records) Regulations 2008	SI 2008/3006
The Companies Act 2006 (Annual Return and Service Addresses) Regulations 2008	SI 2008/3000
The Companies (Particulars of Company Charges) Regulations 2008	SI 2008/2996
The Companies (Reduction of Share Capital) Order 2008	SI 2008/1915
The Company Names Adjudicator Rules 2008	SI 2008/1738
The Companies (Authorised Minimum) Regulations 2008	SI 2008/729
The Companies (Late Filing Penalties) and Limited Liability Partnerships (Filing Periods and Late Filing Penalties) Regulations 2008	SI 2008/497
The Companies (Trading Disclosures) Regulations 2008	SI 2008/495

The Companies (Fees for Inspection of Company Records) (No.2) Regulations 2007	SI 2007/3535
The Independent Supervisor Appointment Order 2007	SI 2007/3534
The Company and Business Names (Amendment) (No.2) Regulations 2007	SI 2007/3152
The Companies (Fees for Inspection of Company Records) Regulations 2007	SI 2007/2612
The Companies (Political Expenditure Exemption) Order 2007	SI 2007/2081
The Companies Acts (Unregistered Companies) Regulations 2007	SI 2007/318
The Companies (Registrar, Languages and Trading Disclosures) Regulations 2006	SI 2006/3429

Table of Statutes

Paragraph references printed in **bold** type indicate where the Statute is set out in part or in full.

Table of Statutes

Table of Statutes

Table of Statutory Instruments

Paragraph references printed in **bold** type indicate where the Statutory Instrument is set out in part or in full.

Table of Statutory Instruments

Table of Cases

F

G

H

I

J

Table of Cases

Table of European Legislation

Paragraph references printed in **bold** type indicate where the Legislation is set out in part or in full.

Chapter 1

INTRODUCTION

Dan Prentice

1.1 In the Company Law Reform Bill 2005 the Government proposed replacing approximately two-thirds of existing company law legislation, principally the Companies Act 1985 ('CA 1985'). The Government initially did not see any need for consolidation of the Bill with what remained of the CA 1985.[1] Eventually, however, the Government agreed to consolidate the remaining provisions of the 1985 Act and provisions from other companies legislation and the Bill was renamed and became the Companies Act 2006 ('CA 2006') receiving the Royal Assent on 8 November 2006. The CA 2006 contains thirteen hundred sections and sixteen Schedules and when enacted had the dubious privilege of being the largest statute on the statute book. The company law provisions of the CA 2006 (Parts 1–39)[2] restate almost all of the provisions of the Companies Act 1985, the Companies Act 1989 ('CA 1989') and the Companies (Audit, Investigations and Community Enterprise) Act 2004 ('C(AICE)A 2004'). Certain provisions of existing company law legislation and related areas remain in force.[3] The Act extends to Northern Ireland.[4]

[1] 677 HL Official Report (5th series) cols GC94–97 (11 January 2006).
[2] See s 2(2) of the CA 2006 which defines 'company law provisions' of the Act.
[3] Paragraphs 9 and 10 of the DTI Explanatory Notes to the CA 2006 set out the provisions that have not been consolidated. See para 1.22.
[4] CA 2006, s 1299.

1.2 The CA 2006 is based on the recommendations of the Company Law Review ('CLR'). This was a review by a group of independent persons whose terms of reference required them to consider how core company law could be reformed 'in order to provide a simple, efficient and cost effective framework for British business in the twenty-first century'.[1] Launching the CLR, the DTI published an initial consultation paper in March 1998 entitled *Modern Company Law for a Competitive Economy* which noted that there were numerous difficulties with the then current legislation. The paper drew attention to the fact that the legislation is drafted in excessive detail, uses over-formal language, over-regulates some issues (such as capital maintenance) while other provisions are obsolete.[2] Equally, some matters are inadequately provided for or need legal underpinning such as the duties of directors and the conduct of meetings.[3] The Government's intention was that new arrangements should be devised to provide a more effective, including cost-effective, framework based on principles of consistency, predictability and transparency.[4]

[1] DTI Explanatory Notes to the CA 2006, para 4.
[2] See DTI, *Modern Company Law for a Competitive Economy* (1998), paras 3.2, 3.4.
[3] See DTI, *Modern Company Law for a Competitive Economy* (1998), para 3.7
[4] See DTI, *Modern Company Law for a Competitive Economy* (1998), para 3.1.

1.3 The process by which the CLR was conducted was that a Steering Group was set up to oversee the management of the project; there was also a widely-based Consultative Committee, and a project director. The project was divided into a number of discrete topics which were generally remitted to separate Working Groups which reported to the Steering Group. The issues for consideration and the recommendations of the Steering Group were then the subject of a series of consultation documents as follows:

- *Modern Company Law for a Competitive Economy: The Strategic Framework* (February 1999, URN 99/654).
- *Modern Company Law for a Competitive Economy: Company General Meetings and Shareholder Communication* (October 1999, URN 99/1144).
- *Modern Company Law for a Competitive Economy: Company Formation and Capital Maintenance* (October 1999, URN 00/1145).
- *Modern Company Law for a Competitive Economy: Reforming the Law Concerning Oversea Companies* (October 1999, URN 99/1146).
- *Modern Company Law for a Competitive Economy: Developing the Framework* (March 2000, URN 00/656).
- *Modern Company Law for a Competitive Economy: Capital Maintenance and Other Issues* (June 2000, URN 00/880).
- *Modern Company Law for a Competitive Economy: Registration of Company Charges* (October 2000, URN 00/1213).
- *Modern Company Law for a Competitive Economy: Completing the Structure* (November 2000, URN 00/1335).
- *Modern Company Law for a Competitive Economy: The Final Report, vols I, II* (July 2001, URN 01/943).

1.4 A central theme of the CLR proposals was 'think small first'. Previous company law reform had focused on the needs of the large publicly held company and adjusted the companies legislation, if at all, to deal with the needs of the small private company. The CLR considered that the starting point should be the small private company and it would be possible to build on this to deal with the needs of the public company.

1.5 When the Company Law Reform Bill was introduced, Part 31 of the Bill conferred on the Secretary of State powers to make a 'company law reform order' which could, *inter alia*, override primary legislation relating to company law. Because of concern at the scope of these powers, they were eventually withdrawn.[1] The CA 2006 does, however, vest extensive powers in the Secretary of State to make regulations and orders by statutory instrument.[2] Power is also given to the Secretary of State to make such provision as he considers necessary to amend repeal or revoke stipulated enactments where he considers this 'necessary or expedient in consequence of any provision made by or under the Act.'[3] The enactments[4] to which this amending power applies are enactments made before the passing of the Act, the Act itself or any subordinate legislation passed under it, and any enactment passed or made before the end of the session after that in which the CA 2006 is passed.[5] There is also a continuity of the law provision, s 1297, which importantly deals not only with the relationship between the CA 2006 and previous legislation but also applies to private transactions such as contracts and articles of association. The DTI Explanatory Notes to the CA 2006 explain the effect of the continuity of the law provision as follows:

'**CCA 2006, s 1297 Continuity of the law**

1722 This section provides that things done under the provisions in the 1985 Act that are repealed and replaced by the Act will continue to be legally effective. Similarly, references to the repealed provisions in enactments, instruments or documents are to be construed as including references to the corresponding new provision.

1723 Articles of association, company resolutions and contracts are all likely to refer to provisions of the Companies Acts or to rely for their effect on the way in which those provisions work. Except where a change is intended, those articles, resolutions and contracts should continue to have effect, not only with old references converted into new but also with their legal effect capable of continuing despite verbal differences between the old and the new.

1724 The section applies automatically in all cases in which it is capable of applying. It is in addition to any more specific transitional provisions, which may be included in commencement orders by use of the powering section 1296.'

[1] Also the Government introduced the Legislative and Regulatory Reform Act 2006 which contained some powers akin to those in Part 31: See Hansard, HL Deb GC 406 (30 March 2006).

[2] CA 2006, ss 1288–1292. For a list of the relevant provisions see *Implementation of Companies Act 2006: A Consultative Document* (February 2007) DTI, Annex B.

[3] CA 2006, s 1294(1).

[4] See the CA 2006, s 1293 for meaning of 'enactment'.

[5] CA 2006, s 1294.

1.6 The chapters in this collection deal with what are the most important reforms affected by the CA 2006. There have been other reforms, not of such significance as those dealt with at length, which are worthy of note.

1.7 In keeping with the think small first principle, the regime for private companies has been greatly simplified and the elective regime set out in s 379A of the CA 1985 has in substance become the default regime for private companies.[1] Thus where a private company has only one class of shares, the directors may exercise any power of the company to allot shares of that class or to grant rights to subscribe for or to convert any security into such shares[2] and a private company no longer has to hold an annual general meeting and the concept of an extraordinary general meeting has been abandoned.

[1] This has been repealed: see Sch 16.

[2] CA 2006, s 550. See para 8.4.

SHARE TRANSFER

1.8 Part 21 ('Certification And Transfer of Securities') of the CA 2006 restates some of the provisions of Pt 5 of the CA 1985 (ss 183–189). There is one important new provision. A company is required to register a transfer of shares or debentures or provide the transferee with reasons for its refusal to register as soon as reasonably practicable, but in any event within two months of the transfer being lodged with the company.[1] If the company refuses to register the transfer it must provide the transferee with such further information about the refusal to register the transfer as the transferee may reasonably request but this does not include minutes of the meetings of directors.[2] This alters the previous position where, if directors were vested with an absolute discretion to refuse to register a transfer, they did not have to provide reasons for their refusal. The section does not apply to a transfer of shares with respect to which the company has issued a share warrant or with respect to the transmission of shares or debentures by operation of law.[3] If the company fails to comply with the section the company and every officer of the company in default commits an offence.[4] Section 122 makes it clear that shares can be issued in bearer form and do not have to be first issued as registered shares and then strike out the name of the registered holder and issue share warrants.[5]

[1]   CA 2006, s 771(1). As to share registers and access to the register of members, see para 7.42.
[2]   CA 2006, s 772(2).
[3]   CA 2006, s 771(5).
[4]   CA 2006, s 771(3).
[5]   See the CA 1985, s 355.

CORPORATE DIRECTORS

1.9 A company must have at least one director who is a natural person but subject to this requirement any legal person, another company or a firm, may be a director.[1] Section 155(2) provides that the requirement to have at least one director who is a natural person is satisfied if the director is a corporation sole or someone appointed on the basis of the office that they hold.

[1]   CA 2006, s 155. For transitional arrangements which disapply the requirement to have at least one director who is a natural person until 1 October 2010 in some circumstances, see SI 2007/3495, Art 9, Sch 4, Pt 3, para 46.

EXPENSES OF WINDING UP

1.10 Section 1282 of the CA 2006 inserts into the Insolvency Act 1986 a new s 176ZA which reverses the rule in *Re Leyland Daf Ltd, Buchler v Talbot*.[1] Section 176ZA makes it clear that where the assets of the company available for payment of the general creditors are insufficient to pay the expenses of the winding up, such expenses will have priority over the floating charge holder and the preferential creditors. Expenses include the remuneration of the liquidator.[2] The assets of the company do not include any amount made available under s 176ZA(2)(a) of the Insolvency Act 1986 (the prescribed amount). Insolvency rules may restrict in prescribed circumstances the amount of expenses payable to expenses authorised or approved by the holders of debentures secured by a floating charge, preferential creditors, or the court.[3]

[1]   [2002] EWCA Civ 228, [2002] 1 BCLC 571; revsd [2004] UKHL 9, [2004] 1 All ER 1289.
[2]   Insolvency Act 1986, s 176ZA(4).
[3]   Insolvency Act 1986, s 176ZA(3); see the Insolvency (Amendment) Rules 2008 SI 2008/737.

COMPANY SECRETARY

1.11 Section 270 provides that a private company is no longer required to have a secretary (a company 'without a secretary').[1] A private company can continue to have a secretary (a company 'with a secretary').[2] In the case of a private company without a secretary, 'anything authorised or required to be given or sent to, or served on, the company by being sent to its secretary' may be given, sent to, served on the company, or if addressed to the secretary treated as being addressed to the company.[3] Anything else required or authorised to be done by or to the secretary of the company may be done by or to a director or a person authorised generally or specifically in that behalf by the directors.[4]

[1]   CA 2006, s 270(2).
[2]   CA 2006, s 270(2).
[3]   CA 2006, s 270(3)(a).
[4]   CA 2006, s 270(4). A document can be validly executed by a company if signed by a director in the presence of a witness who attests his signature (s 44(2)(b)). This deals with the situation where a private company does not have a secretary.

STRIKING-OFF – RESTORATION

1.12 The Act modifies the provisions relating to the dissolution of a company and its restoration to the register. Chapters 1 and 2 of Pt 31 deal with the striking off and the property of a dissolved company. Section 1003, replacing s 652A of the CA 1985, now extends the provision to allow a public company to apply for a voluntary strike-off. Section 1013 extends the period within which the Crown can disclaim property of a dissolved company vested in it to three years.

1.13 It is now possible to restore a company to the register by an administrative restoration procedure rather than court order. An application may be made to restore a company to the register that has been struck off under ss 1000 or 1001 (power of the registrar to strike off defunct company), and it can be made whether or not the company has been dissolved. The application can only be made by a former director or a former member and it may not be made after the end of a period of six years after the date of dissolution of the company.[1] The requirements which must be satisfied in order for the company to be restored are set out in s 1025:

(1)   the company was carrying on business or in operation at the time of the striking off;

(2)   where any property or right has vested in the Crown as *bona vacantia*, a Crown representative[2] consents in writing to the company's restoration, although this can be conditional on the applicant paying any costs incurred;

(3)   the registrar's records have been brought up to date and any outstanding penalties have been paid.

The application must also be accompanied by a statement of compliance (see para 1.21) that the applicant has standing to apply and that the requirements for administrative restoration[3] have been complied with.[4] The registrar must give notice to the applicant of his decision on the application and if it is positive it takes effect from the date of the notice.[5] Where a company is restored by the process of administrative restoration then generally the company is deemed to have been continued in existence as it had not been dissolved or struck off the register.[6]

[1]   CA 2006, s 1024.
[2]   'Crown representative' is defined in s 1025(6).
[3]   CA 2006, s 1025.
[4]   CA 2006, s 1026.
[5]   CA 2006, s 1027.
[6]   CA 2006, s 1028.

1.14 The different procedures for restoration under ss 651 and 653 of the CA 1985 have now been brought together in ss 1029–1035.[1] There are no changes of any great significance. The application must be made within six years of the dissolution,[2] and an application may be made at any time for the purposes of bringing an action with respect to personal injuries,[3] or where the registrar has refused an application to restore a company to the register an application to the court may be made within twenty-eight days of his notice of refusal even if this is outside the six-year period.[4]

[1]   See also Sch 2, para. 91.
[2]   CA 2006, s 1030(4).
[3]   CA 2006, s 1030(1). For the definition of personal injuries see s 1030(6).
[4]   CA 2006, s 1030(5).

COMPANY CHARGES

1.15 The Company Law Review initially consulted on the option of retaining the core of the registration requirements for company charges while updating and amending them to incorporate certain improvements.[1] By the time of its final report, the CLR had opted for a much more radical proposal, namely that the current scheme of registration should be replaced by a system of 'notice filing', that is a system which enables a charge holder to file a notice of a charge and from the date of registration to obtain priority.[2] The CLR recommended that the DTI refer the issue to the Law Commission to allow for proper consideration of possible reforms. The Law Commission published a Consultation Paper on registration of security interests[3] in 2002, followed by a Consultative Report[4] in 2004, followed by a Report[5] in 2005. The Government has not adopted these proposals. Company charges are dealt with in Pt 25 of the CA 2006 which replaces, with minor modifications, Pt XII of the CA 1985.[6] Part 25 contains a new provision, s 814, providing the Secretary of State with power to amend the provisions of Pt 25.[7]

[1]   CLR, *Modern Company Law for a Competitive Economy: Registration of Company Charges* (October 2000).
[2]   CLR, *Modern Company Law for a Competitive Economy: Final Report, vol 1* (July 2001), Chapter 12.
[3]   See Law Commission, *Registration of Security Interests: Company Charges and Property other than Land*, Consultation Paper No 164, July 2002.
[4]   See Law Commission '*Company Security Interests*', A Consultative Report (CP No 176) (2004).

5   Law Commission, *'Company Security Interests'* (Law Com No 296) Cm 6654.
6   *Implementation of Companies Act 2006: A Consultative Document* (February 2007) DTI, at para 2.206 ff.
7   See also The Companies (Particulars of Company Charges) Regulations 2008, SI 2008/2996.

AGE OF DIRECTORS

1.16 For the first time the legislation sets a minimum age for a director of 16 years (s 157(1)) and an appointment in breach of this requirement is void (s 157(4)), but the person appointed remains fully liable if he purports to act as a director or as a shadow director (s 157(5)). Regulations may allow for exceptional cases (s 158), for example, younger directors may be appropriate for a company operating as a youth charity. Under-age directors in office on 1 October 2008 automatically cease to be directors (s 159(2)). A previous restriction (CA 1985, s 293) on persons aged 70 or more acting as a director of a public company, save where the appointment was made or approved by the company in general meeting, has been repealed.[1]

1   Repealed as of 6 April 2007: see the Companies Act 2006 (Commencement No 1, Transitional Provisions and Savings) Order 2006, SI 2006/3428, Art 4(2)(c); for transitional provisions and savings see Art 8(1), Sch 5, Pt 3, para 7.

FOREIGN DISQUALIFICATION ORDERS

1.17 Part 40 of the CA 2006 (ss 1182–1191) provides for an important extension of the CDDA 1986 to allow for the disqualification of persons 'subject to foreign restrictions' from being a director, acting as a receiver or in any way being concerned, directly or indirectly in the promotion, formation or management of a UK company (defined in s 1183). Persons 'subject to foreign restrictions' are essentially persons who are disqualified under provisions of a foreign law equivalent to CDDA 1986 (see definition in s 1182). These disqualification powers will be implemented by regulations to be made under s 1184 which may provide for automatic disqualification or disqualification by order of the court or for the provision of disqualification undertakings. These provisions are necessary to close an identified gap in the law whereby persons disqualified in other countries are not within the scope of the CDDA 1986 and are able to act as directors etc of UK companies and even to act in the jurisdiction in which they are disqualified through the UK company.

REGISTER OF DIRECTORS

1.18 Every company must keep a register of its directors. A major change is that, from 1 October 2008, there is no longer a requirement for a director's usual residential address to be given in the register of directors (likewise for company secretaries, see s 277). Instead a service address may be given (s 163(1)(b)) and that service address may be stated as 'the company's registered office' (s 163(5)). This change was initially introduced in order to provide additional protection for directors who may be at risk of violence and/or intimidation from persons such as animal rights extremists but is now available to all directors.

1.19 The company is required to maintain a register of directors' residential addresses (s 165), but this register is not open to inspection. The details contained in the company's register of residential addresses must be notified to the registrar of companies on the appointment of a director (s 167). This information is then classified as 'protected information' (s 240) which cannot be disclosed by the company or by the registrar of companies (ss 241–242) save to the extent permitted by the CA 2006 (see ss 243–245) and the information must not be available on the public record (s 1087(1)(b)). Disclosure to public authorities will be permitted as will disclosure on the order of a court under s 244. The Act leaves many of these matters to be decided by regulations to be made under s 243 which will identify the categories of public authorities or creditors which will have access to protected information and will set out the conditions governing disclosures to them.[1]

[1] See Companies (Disclosure of Addresses) Regulations SI 2009/214.

1.20 As many directors are also shareholders, the protection afforded by the use of service addresses would be undermined without changes also to the annual return as another document of public record. Therefore, shareholders' addresses are required only in the case of public companies traded on an EU regulated market, and only in respect of holdings in excess of 5 per cent of any class of shares.[1] Access to the company's register of members is restricted by ss 116–117 which are discussed in at para 7.42.

[1] See CA 2006 ss 856A, 856B; Companies Act 2006 (Annual Return and Service Addresses) Regulations 2008, SI 2008/3000.

STATEMENT OF COMPLIANCE ON FORMATION

1.21 In filing returns to the registrar the CA 2006 may require a statement of compliance.[1] A statement of compliance on formation is a statement that the requirements of the Act as to registration have been complied with and the registrar may accept this as sufficient evidence of compliance.[2] The requirement of the CA 1985 for a statutory declaration or an electronic communication has been replaced in the CA 2006 with the requirement to make a statement of compliance. The statement does not have to be witnessed and may be made in paper or electronic form.[3]

[1] See, for example, CA 2006, s 9(1).
[2] CA 2006, s 13. See also s 1112 – the 'General False Statement Offence'.
[3] See DTI Explanatory Notes to the CA 2006, para 55. Section 1068 of the CA 2006 gives the registrar power to make rules about the form, authentication and manner of delivery of documents. Section 1068 does not empower the Secretary of State to 'require' documents to be delivered in electronic form but s 1069 empowers him to pass regulations requiring delivery in electronic form and such regulations are subject to the affirmative resolution procedure (see s 1290 for definition of 'affirmative resolution procedure').

PROVISIONS NOT CONSOLIDATED

1.22 The company law provisions that have not been consolidated into the CA 2006 are those on investigations that go wider than companies (Pt 14 of the CA 1985) and the provisions on community interest companies in Pt 2 of the C(AICE)A 2004.

The non-company law provisions that remain outside the CA 2006 are:

(a)   Part 18 of the CA 1985 (floating charges and receivers (Scotland);
(b)   Part 3 of the CA 1989 (powers to require information and documents to assist overseas regulatory authorities);
(c)   Sections 112–116 of the CA 1989 (provisions about Scottish incorporated charities);
(d)   Part 7 of the CA 1989 (provisions about financial markets and insolvency);
(e)   Schedule 18 to the CA 1989 (amendments and savings consequential upon changes in the law made by the 1989 Act);
(f)   Sections 14 and 15 of the C(AICE)A 2004 (supervision of accounts and reports); and
(g)   Sections 16 and 17 of the C(AICE)A 2004 (bodies concerned with accounting standards etc).

In non-company law areas the CA 2006 makes amendments to other legislation, in particular the Financial Services and Markets Act 2000, and also makes new provision of various kinds. The main areas in which provision of this kind is made are:

(a)   overseas disqualification of company directors (Pt 40);
(b)   business names (Pt 41) – replacing the Business Names Act 1985;
(c)   statutory auditors (Pt 42) – replacing Pt 2 of the CA 1989; and
(d)   transparency obligations (Pt 43) – amending Pt 6 of the Financial Services and Markets Act 2000.

1.23 Section 130 of the Act sets out a small number of sections that came into effect on the day the Act was passed. The remainder of the Act was brought into effect by a series of transitional orders the last of which was the No 8 Order.[1] The Act comes fully into effect on 1 October 2009.

[1]   The Companies Act 2006 (Commencement No 8, Transitional Provisions and Savings) Order 2008, SI 2008/2860.

Chapter 2

COMPANY CONSTITUTION

Dan Prentice

THE CONSTITUTION

2.1 Unlike its predecessor the 2006 Act defines what constitutes the company's constitution. Section 17 of the Companies Act 2006 ('CA 2006') defines a company's constitution as including its articles of association and any 'resolutions and agreements' affecting a company's constitution.[1] What constitute relevant resolutions and agreements is defined in s 29[2] and broadly these are agreements by all the members of a company or by all members of a class of shareholders which affect the company's constitution[3] or a special resolution. This definition applies to references to a company's constitution in the 'Companies Acts' as defined in s 2. The definition is not exhaustive as it applies 'unless the context otherwise requires', and the context could require a wider or narrower definition.[4]

[1] See also ss 30 and 36 which replace the Companies Act 1985 ('CA 1985'), s 380.
[2] The side note to the section refers to these as 'Resolutions and agreements affecting a company's constitution'.
[3] This would cover situations where the principle in *Re Duomatic Ltd* [1969] 2 Ch 365 applies.
[4] See s 257 which sets out a definition for the purposes of Pt 10. The certificate of incorporation (s 15) would also be a relevant constitutional document.

2.2 There are other provisions of the Act which contain information relating to a company's constitution. The 'registration documents' that have to be delivered to the registrar along with the memorandum of association contain details of the company's constitution.[1] Also, s 32 of the Act sets out the constitutional documents that have to be provided to a member who makes a request for such documents.

[1] CA 2006, s 9. This section is self-explanatory. Sections 10–12 itemise in greater detail the information required to be provided in the registration documents.

2.3 The Act effects a very fundamental reform with respect to the nature of the memorandum and of the relationship between the memorandum and the articles. The White Paper on *Modernising Company Law*[1] stated:

'2.2   The Government agrees with the Review (ie the Company Law Review) that neither "objects clauses" – the clause in a company's memorandum of association that defines its purpose – nor the split between the memorandum and articles in general serve a useful purpose any longer and should be removed. Instead companies should have a constitution in a single document. That constitution would be capable of containing an objects clause but, in the new structure, this would have only internal effect as between the directors and the members.'

Thus: (a) requirement to have an objects clause was to be removed, (b) the company should have a single constitution, (c) an objects clause was to be optional and could be included in the constitution but it would only have internal effect. These reforms have been put into effect.

[1]   Cm 5553–1, July 2002. See also *Company Formation and Capital Maintenance* Company Law Review, para 213.

2.4 The Secretary of State may by regulation prescribe model articles of association for companies and may prescribe different articles for different descriptions of companies, see para 2.33.[1] An amendment to the model articles does not affect the constitution of a company registered before the amendment takes effect.[2] Existing companies, that is, pre-2006 companies, are free to adopt all or any of the model prescribed for the purposes of the 2006 Act.[3]

[1]   CA 2006, s 19(1) and 19(2). See the Companies (Model Articles) Regulations 2008, SI 2008/3229, setting out model articles for private companies limited by shares or guarantee and for public companies.
[2]   CA 2006, s 19((4).
[3]   CA 2006, s 19(3).

FORMATION – MEMORANDUM OF ASSOCIATION (INCLUDING THE MEMORANDUM OF EXISTING COMPANIES)

2.5 It is now possible for a single person to form a public company. Section 7(1) provides that a company may be formed under the Act 'by one or more persons'. As in previous Acts, companies may not be formed to carry on an unlawful purpose.[1]

The memorandum of association has been made a much more limited document than its predecessor under the CA 1985 and is now predominantly historical in its focus. Section 8 provides that:

'(1)   A memorandum of association is a memorandum stating that the subscribers—
   (a)   wish to form a company under the Act, and
   (b)   agree to become members of the company and, in the case of a company that is to have a share capital, to take at least one share each.
(2)   The memorandum must be in the prescribed form and must be authenticated[2] by each subscriber.'

Given the contents of the memorandum, no provision is made or needed for its alteration. Also, in contrast with the old form of memorandum, no provision is made to add additional terms; s 8(2) requires the memorandum be in the prescribed form.[3] It is also important to note that a company's objects no longer appear in the memorandum.[4] A company still needs to have articles of association[5] unless it is a company that opts for the default model articles.[6]

Given this new structure, the issue arises as to what is to happen to companies incorporated under previous Companies Acts ('existing companies') where the memorandum was a significantly different document. Under the 1985 Act, it was possible, for example, to include provisions in the memorandum which otherwise could be included in a company's articles of association.[7] To deal with this, s 28 provides that provisions in an existing company's memorandum, other than those required by s 8,[8] are to be treated as 'provisions of the company's articles'.[9] This applies to substantive provisions and 'provisions for entrenchment (as defined in s 22)'.[10] This reform is to be welcomed as it results in pre- and post 2006 companies having a similar constitutional structure. The fusion of the memorandum does give rise to a number of issues.

1   CA 2006, s 7(2).
2   For the meaning of authentication see the CA 2006, s 1112.
3   See The Companies (Registration) Regulations 2008, SI 2008/3014.
4   See para 2.15.
5   CA 2006, s 18.
6   CA 2006, s 18(2) and 20. Default articles apply to all companies limited by shares and companies limited by guarantee, see para 2.4.
7   See the CA 1985, s 17.
8   Referred to as 'provisions of new-style memorandum', s 28(1).
9   CA 2006, s 28(1).
10 CA 2006, s 28(2). Where s 28 applies, there is no duty to give notice to the registrar of companies of the provision for entrenchment: see s 28(3). On provisions for entrenchment, see para 2.11.

Entrenched provisions in pre-Act memorandum

2.6 Under the CA 1985, it was possible to include in the company's memorandum provisions that could have been contained in the company's articles.[1] These provisions were made alterable by special resolution except where the memorandum provided that they were to be unalterable or they related to class rights.[2] These provisions will now be treated as 'entrenched provisions'.[3]

1   CA 1985, s 17.
2   CA 1985, s 17(2).
3   CA 2006, s 28(2). See para 2.11 on nature of entrenched provisions.

2.7 There is case law (mainly nineteenth century) that where there is a conflict between the terms of the articles and the terms of the memorandum, the latter prevails.[1] This is a rare event and the Act does not deal with it, leaving it to the courts to sort out the problem should it arise, which is remote.[2] This problem can no longer occur under the 2006 Act given that the form of the memorandum is prescribed and all other constitutional provisions will be found elsewhere.

[1] See, eg *Ashbury v Watson* (1885) 30 Ch D 376; *Re Runcorn Gilmore & Co Ltd* [1952] 2 All ER 871; 678 HL Official Report (5th series) col GC24 (30 January 2006).

[2] See *Paper seeking views on the application of the Companies Bill to existing companies* (2006) DTI, paras 25–28.

Effect of company's constitution

2.8 One of the issues on which the CLR (see para 1.2) sought opinions was on what should be the effect of the company's constitution and, in particular, should the structure of s 14 of the CA 1985 be maintained. This section, as interpreted by the courts, renders the articles and memorandum a contract between a company and its members and the members inter se. The language of s 14 is somewhat antique. Also, the contract constituted by s 14 was of a unique character: (1) a term can be implied in the articles but 'only if the term can be implied without recourse to extrinsic evidence',[1] the implication must be 'constructional', that is, 'purely from the language of the document itself',[2] (2) it is not subject to the doctrine of contractual rectification (the articles must be amended by a special resolution),[3] and (3) the court will not rescind the contract where there has been a misrepresentation relating to the contents of the articles.[4] There are also uncertainties as to who can enforce the s 14 contract, for example, directors or outsiders on whom the articles purport to confer rights.[5]

[1] *Dashfield v Davidson* [2008] EWHC 486 (Ch), [2009] 1 BCLC 220.
[2] *Bratton Seymour Service Co Ltd v Oxborough* [1992] BCLC 693 at 698.
[3] CA 2006, s 21.
[4] See *Bratton Seymour Service Co Ltd v Oxborough* [1992] BCLC 693.
[5] See *Modern Company Law for a Competitive Economy: Developing the Framework*, (March 2000) Company Law Review, para 4.83 ('*Developing the Framework*').

2.9 An alternative is to abandon the contractual model and make the company's constitution enforceable by statute. The articles would, as it were, become a statutory set of enforceable bylaws. The CLR favoured something along these lines but because of the opposition of the legal profession and other criticisms, it watered down its proposals and considered that 'Whether a modified contract, which we recognise may well be the best means of capturing the consensual character of relationships under the constitution, or explicit statutory powers and obligations are the best way of achieving the objective becomes a matter of drafting'.[1] Accordingly, s 33 in the CA 2006 which deals with the effect of a company's constitution mirrors, with some minor technical drafting changes, s 14 of the CA 1985. Section 33 provides:

'**CA 2006, s 33   Effect of company's constitutions**
(1) The provisions of a company's constitution, when registered, bind the company and its members to the same extent as if there were covenants, signed and sealed on the part of the company and of each member to observe those provisions.
(2) Money payable by a member to the company under its constitution is a debt due from him to the company.
   In England and Wales and Northern Ireland it is of the nature of an ordinary contract debt.'

This is a more modern drafting style.[2] Also, s 33 refers to a company's constitution and not the company's articles and memorandum, the language of s 14(1), an alteration which reflects the more limited role of the memorandum. More importantly, it makes it clearer than it was under s 14 that the company's constitution binds the company,[3] as well as the members, although this was always accepted to be the case under s 14.[4]

[1]   *Modern Company Law for a Competitive Economy: Completing the Structure* (November 2000) Company Law Review, para 5.69 ('*Completing the Structure*').
[2]   Any debt due under s 33 is an ordinary debt and not a speciality debt as was provided for in the CA 1985, s 14: see the CA 2006, s 33(4).
[3]   Section 14 provided that the articles would be considered to have 'contained covenants on the part of each member to observe all the provisions of the memorandum and of the articles'.
[4]   *Hickman v Kent or Romney Marsh Sheep-Breeders' Association* [1915] 1 Ch 881 is still relevant.

2.10 Section 33 does not affect any of the issues raised in para 2.8. In particular, although, as has been pointed out, there has been a slight alteration and a rewording of what was s 14. With respect to this drafting, Lord Sainsbury stated that:[1] 'We are not changing the law here: we are simply making it clear that it means what it has been recognised as meaning since at least 1915 and the celebrated *Hickman* case.'

[1]   686 HL Official Report (5th series) col 435 (2 November 2006).

ENTRENCHED PROVISIONS

2.11 The White Paper on *Modernising Company Law* stated as a result of its proposals[1]:

'2.3   The members of a company will be able to amend the constitution by special resolution. They will also be able – if they all agree – to make it more difficult to make changes, by requiring a higher majority or even unanimity. As now, anyone doing business with the company in good faith will not need to worry about the details of the company's constitution.'

The CA 2006 contains a power which enables a company to entrench a provision in its articles of association (a 'provision for entrenchment'). Section 22 provides:

'**CA 2006, s 22   Entrenched provisions of the articles**
(1)   A company's articles may contain provision ("provision for entrenchment") to the effect of which that specified provisions of the articles may be amended or repealed only if conditions are met, or procedures are complied with, that are more restrictive than those applicable in the case of a special resolution.
(2)   Provision for entrenchment may only be made—
    (a)   in the company's articles on formation, or
    (b)   by an amendment of the company's articles agreed to by all the members of the company.
(3)   Provision for entrenchment does not prevent amendment to a company's articles—
    (a)   by agreement of all the members of a company, or

(b) by order of a court or other authority having power to alter the company's articles.

(4) Nothing in this section affects any power of a court or other authority to alter a company's articles.'

[1] See para 10.

2.12 This is a departure from the pre-CA 2006 position under which a company could not contract out of the power to alter its articles of association by special resolution. A number of points need to be made:

(a) the provisions for entrenchment must be in a company's original articles or be inserted subsequently by an amendment to the company's articles requiring the agreement of all the members of a company.[1] Also, a provision for entrenchment does not prevent the amendment to a company's articles by agreement of all the members of a company,[2] or by order of the court or other authority having power to alter the company's articles.[3] The *Re Duomatic Ltd*[4] principle would apply both as regards insertion of an entrenched provision and its amendment. The agreement for entrenchment, or the agreement to delete a provision of entrenchment, must be by 'all the members' of the company and this would include voting and non-voting members and the holders of all classes of shares.

(b) a provision for entrenchment is one that provides that a company's articles or certain provisions in its articles can only be amended or repealed by a majority which is more restrictive than a majority needed for a special resolution, that is, 75 per cent of those attending and voting.[5] The terms of these more restrictive provisions will be set out in the articles.

(c) the provision for entrenchment must relate to 'specified provisions of the articles'.[6] This could cover all of the articles or only selected provisions, for example, those relating to a particular class of shares or a particular right. However, the insertion of, or amendment to, a provision for entrenchment must be agreed to by all of the members even though it may only relate to the rights of some of them.

(d) section 22 does not apply to contracts outside the articles, for example, an agreement by the company with a third party that it will not alter its articles.[7]

[1] CA 2006, s 22(2)(b).
[2] CA 2006, s 22(3)(a).
[3] CA 2006, s 22(3)(a). This could cover schemes of arrangement (Pt 26 of the Act) or orders under s 996 of the Act.
[4] [1969] 2 Ch 365.
[5] CA 2006, s 283.
[6] CA 2006, s 22(1).
[7] The type of agreement in *Russell v Northern Bank Development Corpn Ltd* [1992] 3 All ER 161.

2.13 Where a company has a provision for entrenchment in its articles, or its articles are amended so as to include such a provision or the articles are altered by court order or other authority so as to restrict or exclude the power of the company to amend its articles, notice of these must be given to the registrar.[1] Where a company amends its articles so as to remove a provision for entrenchment or the company's articles are altered by order of the court or other authority so as to remove a provision for entrenchment or any other restriction on, or any exclusion of, the power of the company to amend its articles, notice of this must also be given.[2] There must also be delivered to the registrar a statement certifying that the amendment has been made in compliance with the company's articles or any applicable order of a court or other authority.[3]

[1] CA 2006, s 23(1). This does not apply to a provision for entrenchment that arises by operation of s 28: s 28(3).
[2] CA 2006, s 23(2).
[3] CA 2006, s 24.

AMENDMENT TO ARTICLES

2.14 Articles can be amended by special resolution.[1] This will now apply to objects in the articles of association. No amendment can oblige a member to subscribe for additional shares or increase his liability.[2] In the Parliamentary debates the point was made that amendment referred to changes made to a company's constitution by its members whereas changes made by external intervention, for example a court order, were alterations.[3]

[1] CA 2006, ss 21 and 370. Notice of amendments must be sent to the registrar: s 21 (replacing the CA 1985, s 18).
[2] CA 2006, s 25, this is similar to s 16 of the CA 1985.
[3] HC Official Report SC D (Company Law Reform Bill) 4 July 2006, col 50.

OBJECTS 'CAPACITY'

2.15 A company no longer has to have an objects clause. Section 31(1) provides that 'unless a company's articles specifically restrict the objects of the company, its objects are unrestricted'. Thus where a company does have objects, the objects will appear in the company's articles and, as has been pointed out earlier, the objects of existing companies will now be treated as being part of their articles (see para 2.5).[1] Probably companies will continue to have objects clauses as, at minimum, they will be necessary for establishing the relationship between the members. Also, third parties will have an interest in a company having an objects clause. For example, banks in extending credit to a company will want to have a clear view of the type of business that they are lending to. Companies that are charities will still have to restrict their objects under charities legislation.[2] Where a company amends its articles to add, remove or alter its objects, notice must be given to the registrar and the amendment is not effective until it is registered by the registrar.[3] Any alteration to the objects does not affect any rights or obligations of the company or render defective any legal proceedings by or against it.[4]

[1] Also existing companies can delete their objects if they so wish.
[2] CA 2006, s 31(4).
[3] CA 2006, s 31(2)(c). Such conditional effectiveness does not apply to the amendment of other provisions in a company's articles.
[4] CA 2006, s 31(3).

CAPACITY

2.16 Section 39(1) provides that:

'(1) The validity of an act done by a company shall not be called into question on the ground of lack of capacity by reason of anything in the company's constitution.'

This replicates s 35(1) of the CA 1985 but substitutes 'company's constitution' for 'memorandum'. The other provisions in s 35 are not replicated because a company can now have unrestricted objects[1] and as directors are now under a statutory duty to comply with a company's constitution[2] they were accordingly considered unnecessary.[3] Where a company is a charity special provisions apply to ensure that the company can only act so as to carry out its charitable purposes.[4]

[1] CA 2006, s 31(1); para 2.15.
[2] CA 2006, s 171, see para 3.16.
[3] DTI Explanatory Notes to the CA 2006, paras 122–124.
[4] CA 2006, s 42: 'This section restates section 65 of the Charities Act 1993. It is a qualification to the rules in section 39 and 40' (DTI Explanatory Notes to the CA 2006, para 130).

POWER OF DIRECTORS TO BIND THE COMPANY

2.17 This is dealt with in ss 40 and 41 of the Act. Section 40 provides safeguards for a person dealing with a company where the directors exceed their authority and restates ss 35A and 35B.[1] Section 40(2)(b)(i), which replaces s 35B, simply provides that a person dealing with the company is not bound to enquire into any limitation on the powers of the directors to bind the company or authorise others to do so. There is no reference to a company's memorandum which is unnecessary in the light of the function that the memorandum plays under the CA 2006. Section 40(1) broadly replicates s 35A(1), but there is one difference of uncertain significance. Section 35A refers to 'the power of the *board of directors* to bind the company' whereas s 40 refers to 'the power of the *directors* to bind the company'. No reason has been given for this change in drafting style. It is clearer under the wording of section 40(1) that a decision by an inquorate board would be binding on the company, a conclusion which the court had already reached with respect to the wording of section 35A(1).[2]

[1] For cases dealing with s 35A see: *Smith v Henniker-Major & Co* [2002] 2 BCLC 655; *EIC Services Ltd v Phipps* [2004] 2 BCLC 589; *Wrexham Association Football Club Ltd v Crucialmove Ltd* [2006] EWCA Civ 237 at [47], [2008] 1 BCLC 508.
[2] *Smith v Henniker-Major & Co* [2002] 2 BCLC 655.

FORMALITIES AND EXECUTION OF DOCUMENTS

2.18 Formalities relating to contracts and execution of documents (ss 43–52) replicate the corresponding provisions of the CA 1985 (ss 36–40). There are some changes of substance. Section 47, which replaces s 38 of the CA 1985. now makes it clear that when appointing an attorney to execute deeds, a company should do so by a deed and this applies inside the United Kingdom as well as outside. Also s 44(2)(b) provides that a document may be validly executed by a director in the presence of a witness who attests his signature.

COMPANY NAMES

2.19 Part 5 of the Act deals with a company's name. Many of the provisions replicate those in the CA 1985. However, new important provisions are introduced with respect to company name adjudicators, see para 2.31.

2.20 Section 53 provides that a company cannot be registered by a name which in the opinion of the Secretary of State would constitute an offence or which is offensive.

2.21 Section 54 replicates s 26(2)(a) of the CA 1985 but it has been extended to cover a connection with any part of the Scottish administration or Her Majesty's Government in Northern Ireland.[1] Also new is the provision enabling the Secretary of State by regulations to extend the section to cover 'any public authority'.[2] 'Public authority' does not merely include Government departments but can apply to private sector bodies carrying out public functions, for example, Ofcom, Ofgem and the FSA.[3]

[1]   CA 2006, s 54(1)(a).
[2]   CA 2006, s 54(1)(c).
[3]   HC Official Report SC D (Company Law Reform Bill) 4 July 2006, col 456.

2.22 Section 55 enables the Secretary of State to pass regulations requiring approval of the use of certain sensitive words in a company's name. This replaces ss 26(2)(b), 29(1)(a) and 29(6) of the CA 1985.[1]

[1]   The current regulation is the Company and Business Names Regulations 1981, SI 1981/1685.

2.23 Section 56 empowers the Secretary of State to specify a 'Government Department or other body' from whom an application to register a name must seek approval. This section replaces s 29(1)(b) and (2) and (3) of the Act.

2.24 Section 57 is new. It enables the Secretary of State to specify in regulations to prohibit the use of specified characters, signs or symbols when appearing in a specified position, see SI 2009/1085.

2.25 Section 66(1) replaces s 26(1)(c) and (3) of the CA 1985 and prohibits a company from adopting a name that is already in the 'registrar's index of company names'. The index includes not only company names but also *inter alia* the names of LLPs, EEIGs and OEICs, and industrial and provident societies.[1] Section 66(1) and (3) replace s 26(3) of the CA 1985 and enable the Secretary of State to pass regulations as to matters to be disregarded and what words and symbols that are not to be regarded as the same when determining whether names are the same. Section 26(3)(d) of the CA 1985 treats only 'and' '&' as the same but the categories could now be extended to cover, for example, currency symbols '$' and 'dollar' or '%' and 'percent'. Where a name is the same as that on the registrar's index of company names, the prohibition is not discretionary, but s 66(4) enables regulations to be passed where a 'same' name may in specified circumstances or with specified consent be permitted, see SI 2009/1085.

¹   CA 2006, s 1099. This section replaces s 714 of the CA 1985. Section 1099(4) empowers the Secretary of State to pass regulations adding or deleting any description of body.

2.26 Section 67 replaces s 28(2) of the CA 1985 and empowers the Secretary of State to direct a company to change its name if the name is the same as or 'too like' a name already on the register;¹ this would cover a situation where the visual difference between the names is so small that third parties could be confused. A similar change of name direction can be made where 'a name should have appeared on the index' at the time the second name was registered. This covers the situation where, for some reason, for example, an overseas entity, the name has not been registered at the time the second name is registered. These powers will address those situations where the registrar did not have control of the circumstances relating to the first registration at the time of the second registration. Section 67(2) and (3), which replicate s 26(3) of the CA 1985, enables regulations to be passed similar to those on s 66 providing for what is to be disregarded or what words or symbols are to be taken as the same.

¹   CA 2006, s 67(1)(a).

2.27 Section 68 replaces s 28(4) and (5) of the CA 1985 as they applied to s 28(2). It provides that any direction to change a name under s 67 must be given within 12 months of the name being registered and the direction must be in writing. Failure to comply with the direction is made an offence.

2.28 Sections 69–74 are new and are designed to deal with the opportunistic registration of a name, for example where the name is chosen to extract money from a person who has an interest in the name.

2.29 Section 69 enables a person ('the applicant'), who need not be the company, to object to a particular registered name. The grounds for the objection is that the name is one which is associated with the applicant in which he has goodwill or it is sufficiently similar to such a name and its use in the United Kingdom could mislead by suggesting a connection between the company and the applicant.¹ The objection has to be made to a names adjudicator.

If either of the grounds on which an objection can be made is established, then it is for the respondent company to show one of the matters set out in (1)–(6) and if none of these factors is shown the objection will be upheld:

(1)   that the name was registered before the date on which the applicant can show goodwill in the relevant activities.

(2)   that the company is operating under the name.

(3)   that the company is proposing to operate under the name and has incurred substantial start-up costs, or was formally operating under the name but is now dormant.[2] There is no definition of what constitute substantial start-up costs. A proposal was made that substantial should be determined in relation to the annual revenue and assets of the company. This was not adopted.[3] As was pointed out,[4] many of the companies formed for opportunistic purposes will have low turnover and a small asset base or may have been bought off the shelf. For this type of company any costs as measured against annual revenue or assets would be substantial, and the adoption of this test would consequently delay the outcome of actions involving such companies when speed in removing the name from the register is of importance.

(4)   that the name was registered in the ordinary course of a company formation business and the company is available for sale to the applicant on the standard terms of that business. This only applies to companies formed by the incorporation agents for the purpose of sale and would not apply to a company which is not established for a third party.

(5)   that the name was adopted in good faith.

(6)   that the interests of the applicant are not adversely affected to any significant extent. As the applicant will have established one of the conditions in s 69(1) this ground will be difficult for the respondent to satisfy.

1   CA 2006, s 69(1).
2   CA 2006, s 69(4)(b).
3   678 HL Official Report (5th series) col GC58 (30 January 2006).
4   678 HL Official Report (5th series) col GC59 (30 January 2006).

2.30 Even if one or more of the facts set out in (1)–(4) above are satisfied, s 69(5) provides that the objection shall nevertheless be upheld if the applicant shows that the main purpose of the respondent was to obtain money (or some other consideration) from the applicant or to prevent him from registering the name.[1]

1   For obvious reasons factors (5) and (6) are not relevant to this subsection.

COMPANY NAMES ADJUDICATOR

2.31 Sections 70–73 set out provisions as to the office of company names adjudicators, enable the Secretary of State to establish procedural rules for adjudicating proceedings, provide that the adjudicator's decision must be made available to the public, set out the orders that the adjudicator is empowered to make, and provide for appeals from the adjudicator's decision.[1] An important feature of the adjudicator's powers is that if the respondent company fails to alter its name when ordered to do so the adjudicator may determine a new name for the company.[2]

¹   See The Company Names Adjudicator Rules 2008, SI 2008/1738.
²   CA 2006, s 73(4) and (5). The practice is to order the name of the company (the offending name) to be changed to its registered number.

TRADING DISCLOSURES

2.32 The obligation on the part of a company to disclose its name and the manner of disclosure are dealt with in ss 82–85¹ and are implemented in greater detail by regulation.²

¹   These replace ss 348, 349 and 351 of the CA 1985. Business names are dealt with in Pt 41 of the CA 2006. There is no longer any liability on a director, section 349(4) has been repealed.
²   See the Companies (Trading Disclosures) Regulations 2008, SI 2008/495; the Companies (Trading Disclosures) Regulations 2009, SI 2009/218.

MODEL ARTICLES

2.33 Section 19 of the Act enables the Secretary of State to prescribe by regulation model articles of association and different model articles may be prescribed for different companies. Different model articles have been introduced for public companies, private companies limited by shares and companies limited by guarantee.¹ The new articles are based on the principle that if the Act provides for something this will not be dealt with in the model articles.² Thus, for example, the articles will no longer provide for a default minimum number of directors as s 154 of the Act requires private companies to have one director and public companies to have two. The fact that private companies do not have to hold an annual general meeting (but may do so) is also reflected in the articles for private companies. Also, in keeping with the think small first principle, the articles of a private company do not provide for alternative directors as it was considered that such companies would not normally want such a provision to be included in the articles. Section 20 provides for default articles and the 'relevant model articles' for this purpose are the model articles prescribed for a company of that description at the time the company is registered.

¹   The Companies (Model Articles) Regulations 2008, SI 2008/3229.
²   Implementation of Companies Act 2006, Chapter 3 (February 2007).

Chapter 3

DUTIES OF DIRECTORS

Dan Prentice

INTRODUCTION

3.1 The core director's fiduciary duties have been judicially created.[1] The law precluding directors from making a secret profit from their office,[2] entering into a transaction where their interests conflict with those of the company,[3] or exercising their power for an improper purpose,[4] have been developed by the courts. In exercising their powers, the directors must act 'bona fide in what they consider – not what the court may consider – is in the interests of the company ...'.[5] It is generally considered that 'interests of the company' means interests of the shareholders of the company.[6] As the dictum from *Re Smith & Fawcett Ltd*[7] also highlights, it is for the directors and not the courts to determine what is in the best interests of the company. Existing side by side with the fiduciary duties are a director's duties of care and skill.[8] There has been little legislative intervention in formulating what are the director's core duties. The most important context in which directors' duties have been currently developed by the courts is in the context of the Company Directors Disqualification Act 1986 ('CDDA 1986').[9]

1   See generally, *Company Directors: Regulating Conflicts of Interest and Formulating a Statement of Duties* (1998) Law Com No 153.
2   *Regal (Hastings) Ltd v Gulliver* [1967] 2 AC 134n.
3   *Aberdeen Railway Co v Blaikie Bros* (1854) 1 Macq 461.
4   *Howard Smith Ltd v Ampol Petroleum Ltd* [1974] AC 821.
5   *Re Smith & Fawcett Ltd* [1942] Ch 304 at 306.
6   *Modern Company Law for a Competitive Economy: Developing the Framework*, (March 2000) Company Law Review, para 3.12 ('*Developing the Framework*').
7   [1942] Ch 304.
8   See Law Commission, *Company Directors: Regulating Conflicts of Interest and Formulating a Statement of Duties*, Part 12.
9   The reason why this is directly relevant to the development of the common law core duties is that, in disqualifying a director under s 9 of the Act, the court has to have regard to *inter alia* '1. Any misfeasance or breach of any fiduciary or other duty by a director in relation to the company' (Pt 1, Sch 1).

3.2 The CLR recommended that there be a clear statutory statement of the 'rules governing decision-making by directors'.[1] The justifications for this were that it would provide clarity and accessibility, enable defects in the current law to be rectified, and would deal with what the CLR referred to as 'scope', namely, in whose interests should companies be run.[2]

[1]   Company Law Review, *Final Report* (2001) Vol 1, paras 3.5 ff. This approach has its critics: see *Company Law Review – Developing the Framework*, Law Society Company Law Committee (August 2000, No 401). The main criticism being that it will constrict the flexibility of the common law by inhibiting development of the common law (including equity) by the courts.

[2]   *Final Report*, Vol 1, para 3.7.

3.3 Part 10 of the Companies Act 2006 ('CA 2006') ('A Company's Directors') deals with the duties of directors, in particular, Chapter 2 which sets out the 'General Duties of Directors'.[1] At the outset it is important to note that Pt 10 does not constitute a comprehensive codification of all aspects of a director's duties under the general law. As will become clear, the common law still has an important role to play in the development of the general duties of directors and, significantly, it remains applicable with respect to the remedies for breach of the statutory general duties.[2]

[1]   The government had clearly indicated its decision to adopt the recommendations of the CLR in its White Paper, *Modernising Company Law* (Cm 5553–I, 2002), Ch II, (4).

[2]   CA 2006, s 178. See para 3.37.

GENERAL DUTIES OF DIRECTORS

3.4 The scope and nature of a director's general duties are set out in s 170.

To whom duties owed

3.5 CA 2006, s 170(1) provides that:

'(1)   The general duties specified in sections 171 to 177 are owed by a director of a company to the company.'

This makes no alteration to the existing law. It is clearly established that a director owes his duties to the company and only to the company.[1] It follows from this that the proper plaintiff in any action to enforce a director's duties is the company.[2] To be recoverable, the loss from any breach of duty must be the company's loss, and any recovery will be in favour of the company. Section 170(1) refers to a 'director'. This obviously covers a *de jure* director, which includes a 'person occupying the position of director, by whatever name called'.[3] A *de facto* director[4] would also be subject to the general duties. Whether a *de facto* director is caught by a statutory provision is a matter of construction,[5] and it would be anomalous not to apply the general duties to such a director. The position of a shadow director is dealt with below.[6] Also, there have been significant recent developments where the courts have found that on the special facts of the case a director owes duties to the shareholders individually,[7] or to the creditors.[8] These principles will still be applicable and be capable of judicial development but they do not fall within Pt 10.

[1]   *Percival v Wright* [1902] 2 Ch 421.

[2]   See Chapter 5 'The Derivative Claim – an Invitation to Litigate?'.

3   CA 2006, s 250. This is a matter of nomenclature and covers situations where directors are not called directors but have titles such as 'governors' or 'managers' but it does not cover a *de facto* director, see *Re Lo-Line Electric Motors Ltd* [1988] 2 All ER 692 at 699.

4   See *Secretary of State for Trade and Industry v Hollier* [2006] EWHC 1804 (Ch), [2006] All ER (D) 232 (Jul), *Gemma Ltd v Davies* [2008] 2 BCLC 281 and *Re Paycheck Services* [2008] 2 BCLC 613 on the nature of a *de facto* directorship.

5   *Re Lo-Line Ltd* [1988] 2 All ER 692.

6   See para 3.14.

7   *Peskin v Anderson* [2001] 1 BCLC 372.

8   *West Mercia Safetywear v Dodd* [1988] BCLC 250.

Continuation of duties on cessation of office by director

3.6 CA 2006, s 170(2) provides:

'(2) A person who ceases to be a director continues to be subject—

(a) to the duty in section 175 (duty to avoid conflicts of interest) as regards the exploitation of any property, information or opportunity of which he became aware at a time when he was a director, and

(b) to the duty in section 176 (duty not to accept benefits from third parties) as regards things done or omitted by him before he ceased to be a director.

To that extent those duties apply to a former director as to a director, subject to any necessary adaptations.'

A little background to the understanding of this subsection is needed. Obviously where a director is in office he is subject to the full panoply of duties. Where a director ceases to hold office, the question arises as to the extent to which such duties remain applicable. This issue was addressed, as regards common law fiduciary duties, in *Ultraframe (UK) Ltd v Fielding*.[1] As regards the fiduciary duty of a director not to enter into a transaction where his interest conflicts with those of the company ('the no conflict rule'[2]), the court held that once 'a director resigns his office, the 'no conflict rule' ceases to apply to his future activities'.[3] However, as regards the 'no-profit rule',[4] namely, that a director is accountable for any profit which he has acquired because of his position as a director unless it is consented to by the company, the position is different. Ceasing to be a director does not immunise 'a director from being in breach of the no-profit rule' where, after ceasing to be a director, 'he uses for his own benefit, property of the company or information he has acquired while a director'.[5]

1   [2005] EWHC 1638 (Ch), [2005] All ER (D) 397 (Jul); for the appeal on costs, see [2006] EWCA Civ 1660, (2007) Times, 8 January.

2   On which see para 4.1.

3   [2005] EWHC 1638 (Ch) at 1309.

4   [2005] EWHC 1638 (Ch) at 1318.

5   [2005] EWHC 1638 (Ch) at 1309.

3.7 CA 2006, s 170(2)(a) applies the no-profit rule to an ex-director;[1] an ex-director is prohibited from exploiting for his benefit 'any property, information or opportunity of which he *became* aware at a time when he was a director'.[2] Actual awareness is needed, and it follows that an ex-director will not be liable where he profits from something of which he should have been aware but of which he is ignorant when acting as a director.[3] An ex-director will continue to be entitled to legitimate benefits such as pension payments where these will have been consented to.[4]

1   It refers to s 175 (duty to avoid conflicts of interest) but it is clear that it deals with the no-profit rule: see s 175(2).
2   CA 2006, s 170(2)(a) (emphasis added).
3   CA 2006, s 177(5).
4   HC Official Report SC D (Company Law Reform Bill) 6 July 2006, col 524.

3.8 By CA 2006, s 170(2)(b) an ex-director is also subject to the duty not to accept benefits from a third party with respect to things done or omitted which arose when he was a director.[1] There is no 'time limit' on the liability of an ex-director under s 170(2); no matter how long after his directorship has terminated provided the benefit arises out of his position as a director, he is liable.

1   See para 4.11.

Adaptations of general duties to ex-directors

3.9 The concluding sentence of CA 2006, s 170(2) provides that 'To that extent those duties [ie general duties] apply to a former director as to a director, subject to any necessary adaptations'. This is a somewhat opaque provision. It is clear that s 170(2) will only apply to directors who are in office at the time the Act is brought into effect and who resign subsequently. Directors who resign prior to the effective date of the Act's implementation[1] will be subject to the common law. However, as regards directors who fall within s 170(2), the circumstances that would justify 'adaptation' will very much depend on the facts. The justification for this possibility of 'adaptation' was said to deal *inter alia* with the situation where an ex-director no longer attends board meetings, or to recognise the fact that an ex-director does not have the same powers as a director or knowledge of the affairs of the company.[2] Situations are foreseeable where these factors might be relevant. For example, a company rejects an opportunity and a director subsequently resigns. The ex-director takes up the opportunity but unknown to him the company has altered its policy and decided to pursue it. In this situation adaptation would be appropriate. The policy underlying the power of adaptation was to preserve flexibility to the courts in applying the principal director's duties to persons who were no longer directors.[3] Exactly what 'adaptation' entails is unclear. It is probably not a waiver of the consequences of breach of the duty but an actual modification of the duty. How this would impact on a director's contract of service which specifically required a director to observe his statutory duties, the duty of loyalty to disclose a breach of duty,[4] or the application of Chap 7 of Pt 10,[5] again is unclear. 'Adaptation' is a judicial act. It is submitted that if the court 'adapts' the duties then it entails that there was no breach and therefore there was no duty that had been breached. Thus if the court adapts a director's duties then, for example, in the context of CDDA 1986 proceedings there would cease to be any breach that could found a disqualification order. It is unclear whether the court could find a breach of duty by the ex-director but 'adapt' the remedies. 'Adaptation' could theoretically appear to permit this. These various difficulties arise from the fact that 'adaptation' is a novel, untried concept. But the better reading of the provision is that 'adapts' addresses the nature of the duty and where adaptation takes effect it has consequential impact on remedies and that it also permits the court to adapt remedies without qualifying the underlying duty.[6] However, it will probably be very infrequently that a court will be faced with an issue involving the adaptation of a director's duties.

1 That is, when Pt 10 is brought into effect: see Chapter 1 'Introduction'.
2 HC Official Report SC D (Company Law Reform Bill) 6 July 2006, col 525.
3 HC Official Report SC D (Company Law Reform Bill) 6 July 2006, col 525.
4 *Item Software (UK) Ltd v Fassihi* [2004] EWCA Civ 1244, [2005] 2 BCLC 91.
5 A contract to indemnify a director may not cover a breach of duty but if the duty is 'adapted' so as to be found to be non-existent would the indemnity provision be enforceable?
6 For example, to order a director to return misappropriated corporate funds but not make provisions for the payment of interest.

Relationship between general duties and common law and scope of the rules

3.10 CA 2006, s 170(3) provides:

'(3) The general duties are based on *certain*[1] common law rules and equitable principles as they apply in relation to directors and have effect in place of those rules and principles as regards the duties owed to a company by a director.'

1 Emphasis added.

3.11 The general duties are based on *'certain* common law rules and equitable principles'.[1] Although not referred to in the Parliamentary debates, the adjective, as a matter of clear statutory interpretation, leaves open the possibility that common law rules and equitable principles not covered by the general duties are still applicable and that the courts are free to develop such rules. Although the use of the adjective 'certain' creates a penumbra of doubt, the general duties will substantially 'have effect in place of' most of the common law rules and equitable principles and given the scope of the general duties there will be little scope for the development of new common law duties.

1 Emphasis added.

Interpreting the general rules

3.12 CA 2006, s 170(4) provides:

'(4) The general duties shall be interpreted and applied in the same way as common law rules or equitable principles, and regard shall be had to the corresponding common law rules and equitable principles in interpreting and applying the general duties.'

3.13 The opposition sought to have this subsection deleted in that it appeared to conflict with s 170(3): sub-s (3) replaces the common law and equitable principles but sub-s (4) appears to preserve them. In the House of Commons the opposition observed:[1]

'To start the ball rolling, I shall give the views on subsections (3) and (4) of Patrick Mitchell and Carl Powlson, of the City law firm Herbert Smith:

> "These sections appear to us to be fundamentally inconsistent. On the one hand section 156(3) states that the general duties are to have effect 'in place of' the relevant common law rules and equitable principles. On the other hand, section 156(4) states that the new codified duties should be interpreted and applied having regard to the pre-existing common law rules and equitable principles. This, coupled with the fact that the codified duties are phrased using different terminology to the existing common law directors' duties, means that there is uncertainty as to the extent to which the new duties replicate, replace, or apply in addition to the pre-existing common law directors' duties, or whether they are to apply in conjunction with them. In reality therefore, it is perhaps difficult to see how the codified duties will be more accessible or comprehensible (indeed arguably they could prove to be more uncertain and more complex)." '

There is some plausibility to this criticism of the interrelationship of these subsections as at first glance they do appear to conflict. However, the subsections cover different issues. Subsection (3) goes to the *scope* of the general duties and operates to replace the common law whereas sub-s (4) goes to the *interpretation* of the general duties. Thus, for example, it would be proper to refer to the common law in deciding how to determine the 'purposes' for which a power has been conferred in applying s 171(b),[2] a matter of interpretation that would fall within sub-s (4) but which would not involve applying the common law proper purposes doctrine which has been superseded by s 171.[3] Also, in determining whether 'powers' had been exercised 'for the purposes for which they are conferred' presumably it would be proper to refer to the common law authorities on fused purposes, one proper the other not. Also, the duties of directors as developed by the courts are often informed by other equitable principles (eg the duties of trustees and other fiduciaries) and s 170(4) will enable the courts to have regard to these equitable principles in applying the interpretative rules mandated by sub-s (4).[4] As was stated by the Solicitor General in committee proceedings in the House of Commons, s 170(4)[5] 'also enables the court to have regard to developments in the common law rules and principles as they apply to other fiduciary relationships'. In a situation where the statutory duties and the common law duties overlap,[6] then the statutory duties would prevail. The common law rules on causation[7] with respect to breach of fiduciary duties will also apply to breach of the statutory duties and loss to be recoverable will have to be caused by the alleged breach of duty. The Act contains provisions on director's duties which have no common law counterpart[8] and to these the common law rules of interpretation would have no applicability.

---

[1] HC Official Report SC D (Company Law Reform Bill) 6 July 2006, col 528. For s 156(3) and (4) read s 170(3) and (4).

[2] See para 3.16.

[3] Although there does not appear to be any difference between the common law and the statutory provision. See paras 3.16 ff.

[4] HC Official Report SC D (Company Law Reform Bill) 6 July 2006, col 528.

[5] HC Official Report SC D (Company Law Reform Bill) 6 July 2006, col 537.

[6] The duties of nominee directors are an example of such overlap: see *Re Neath Rugby Club Ltd, Hawkes v Cudy* [2008] 1 BCLC 527 at paras [26]–[28].

[7] See *Lexi Holdings plc v Luqman* [2009] EWCA Civ 117, [2009] All ER (D) 269 (Feb).

[8] Section 175 (directors authorisation of director's conflict of interest).

28

Shadow directors

3.14 There is uncertainty as to the extent to which the full panoply of directors' duties apply to shadow directors.[1] In *Ultraframe (UK) Ltd v Fielding*[2] the court held that the law did not impose on a shadow director 'the same fiduciary duties ... as are owed by a *de jure* or a *de facto* director'.[3] However, it did not follow from this that a shadow director owed no fiduciary duties. On the facts of a particular case, a shadow director may owe fiduciary duties to the company where equity would impose fiduciary obligations on a person who had control of property belonging to another, or where there is a relationship of trust or confidence between the parties.[4] The indirect influence exercised by a shadow director who does not directly deal with the company's assets would normally not be sufficient to impose fiduciary duties particularly where the director had been acting in his own interests.[5]

1   See the CA 2006, s 251 on the definition of a shadow director. The wording has been slightly altered to the definition in the Companies Act 1985 ('CA 1985'), s 741 but there is no change of substance.
2   [2005] EWHC 1638 (Ch), [2005] All ER (D) 397 (Jul).
3   [2005] EWHC 1638 (Ch) at 1284.
4   [2005] EWHC 1638 (Ch) at 1285.
5   [2005] EWHC 1638 (Ch) at 1289.

3.15 As regards the applicability of the general duties to shadow directors, CA 2006, s 170(5) provides that:

'The general duties apply to shadow directors where, and to the extent that, the corresponding common law rules or equitable principles so apply.'

(a)   This does not clarify the law and this was accepted by the Government who reasoned that as the future development of the common law was unclear the position should not be set out definitively in statutory form but the legislation should allow for future judicial development.[1]

(b)   The penultimate word of s 170(5), the adverb 'so', is not intended to crystallise the 'corresponding' duties as of the date the Act comes into effect. It does not mean 'at this moment in time'; statutes are always 'speaking' and this requires the position to be examined at the time when the statute is being applied.[2]

(c)   The application of s 170(5) thus involves a complex two-stage process:
   (i)   the court will need to determine which common rules and equitable principles apply to shadow directors at the time the issue arises (these rules no longer applying to *de facto* or *de jure* directors as they will be subject to the general duties), and
   (ii)   then decide which of these correspond with the general duties. To the extent of the correspondence, the general duties apply to shadow directors. Where the general or equitable principle is not applicable to shadow directors, the statutory duty replacing that rule or principle does not apply.

1   678 HL Official Report (5th series) col GC248 (16 February 2006).
2   678 HL Official Report (5th series) col GC248 (16 February 2006). See Bennion, *Statutory Interpretation* (4th edn, 2002) Butterworths.

DUTY TO ACT WITHIN POWERS

3.16 The duty of directors to act within their powers is set out in CA 2006, s 171 which provides:

'A director of a company must—
(a)   act in accordance with the company's constitution, and
(b)   only exercise powers for the purposes for which they are conferred.'

Directors, as fiduciaries, must observe the scope of their mandate. Where a director breaches this duty he is obliged to restore any lost assets[1] and bona fides is not a defence.[2] In determining what are the purposes for which a power has been conferred, the case law on this topic will provide guidance.[3] What constitutes the company's constitution for the purpose of s 171 is set out in s 257. As s 171 imposes a duty on directors to act in accordance with a company's constitution it is now more arguable that a shareholder could bring a derivative action to oblige the directors to observe the terms of the company's articles which relate to his rights, or possibly which if enforced would benefit a third party.[4]

1   *Re Lands Allotment Co Ltd* [1894] 1 Ch 616.
2   *Charterbridge Corpn Ltd v Lloyds Bank Ltd* [1970] Ch 62.
3   This is because of s 170(4), see para 3.12. See, on how the purpose of a power is determined, *Howard Smith Ltd v Ampol Petroleum Ltd* [1974] AC 821; *Harlowe's Nominees Pty Ltd v Woodside (Lake Entrance) Oil Co (NL)* (1968) 121 CLR 483 (Aust HC). A company does not now have to possess objects and this may marginally make the exercise of determining what is the purpose of a power a little more difficult.
4   See Chapter 5 'The Derivative Claim – an Invitation to Litigate?'; 'Chapter 2, 'Company Constitution'.

DUTY TO PROMOTE SUCCESS OF THE COMPANY

3.17 CA 2006, s 172(1) provides that:

'(1)   A director of a company must act in the way he considers, in good faith, would be most likely to promote the success of the company for the benefit of its members as a whole, and in doing so have regard (amongst other matters) to—
(a)   the likely consequences of any decision in the long term,
(b)   the interests of the company's employees,
(c)   the need to foster the company's business relationships with suppliers, customers and others,
(d)   the impact of the company's operations on the community and the environment,
(e)   the desirability of the company maintaining a reputation for high standards of business conduct, and
(f)   the need to act fairly as between members of the company.'

This is one of the most contentious provisions of the Act. The CLR, see para 1.2, discussed at length whether the duty of directors to act in the interests of the company 'should be interpreted as meaning simply that they should act in the interests of the shareholders, or whether they should also take account of other interests, such as those of employees, creditors, customers, the environment, and the wider community'.[1] There were those who argued that these wider interests should be treated as independent purposes and should not be subordinate to, or be treated as simply a means of promoting, the interests of shareholders.[2] The CLR did not recommend this 'pluralist' approach but recommended that director's duties be framed in an inclusive way so that the directors, in exercising their powers for the 'success of the company for the benefit of its members', should give due recognition to the interests of others (customers, employees, suppliers, the community).[3] The Government adopted the CLR recommendation, referred to as constituting 'enlightened shareholder value'.

[1]   *Modern Company Law For a Competitive Economy* (1998), para 3.7. Employees' interests had to be taken into consideration under the CA 1985: see s 309. Also on liquidation, the directors could benefit employees: see the CA 1985, s 717. This provision is replicated in s 247 of the CA 2006.

[2]   *The Strategic Framework* (1999), para 5.1.12.

[3]   *Developing the Framework*, paras 2.11, 3.20–3.36; see also *Completing the Structure*, Chapter 35; *Modernising Company Law*, Cm 5553 (2002), para 2.8.

Success of the company for benefit of members as a whole

3.18 A director's primary duty is to promote the 'success' of the company for the 'benefit of the members as a whole'. This is to be contrasted with the common law duty of the directors to act 'in the best interests of the company'. 'Success' replaces 'interests'. It was argued that what constitutes success is far from clear, whereas interests was a concept that is supported by an existing body of case law.[1] Success probably means, for a commercial company, long-term shareholder value.[2] Examples were raised where the criterion of success could pose difficulties; for example, a proposal to wind up the company, or the recommending of a lower takeover offer because the directors were more confident that this would come to fruition than a higher alternative.[3] Decisions of this nature already have to be made by directors and they are not made any more difficult by s 172. These are essentially commercial decisions and the courts will defer to the commercial judgment of the directors provided they act in good faith and their decision is not manifestly unreasonable. The director's decision also has to be for the 'benefit of ... the members as a whole'. The members of a company may often have different views as to what is in their interests, for example, some may want dividends while others may want capital gains.[4] However, it is for the directors, and not the members, to decide what is in the interests of the members and, provided they act fairly as between members,[5] and act with competence their decision will be difficult to impeach.

[1]   See Law Society, *Company Law Reform White Paper*, Cm 6456 (June 2005) at p 6.

[2]   678 HL Official Report (5th series) col GC256 (6 February 2006).

[3]   See *Company Law Reform White Paper* Cm 6456, The Law Society, June 2005, para 33.

[4]   See this divergence in the context of schemes of arrangement: *Re Hellenic & General Trust* [1975] 3 All ER 382.

[5]   Section 172(1)(f); see also *Mutual Life Insurance Co of New York v Rank Organisation* [1985] BCLC 11.

In what the director 'considers, in good faith'

3.19 This makes it clear that the primary duty is subjective. It is for the directors, and not the court, to decide in good faith what will promote the success of the company for the benefit of its members. However, this subjective approach does not justify a director breaching the 'no-profit' or 'no-conflict' rule because he thinks that this is in the best interests of the company.[1]

[1]   *Re Southern Counties Foods* [2008] EWHC 2810 (Ch) at [53].

Have regard to (amongst other matters)

3.20 However, CA 2006, s 172(1) sets out six matters to which a director must have regard in deciding whether a particular decision will promote the success of the company.[1] To the extent that a director 'must act in the way he considers in good faith', taking into consideration the matters set out in s 172(1)(a)–(f), they impose an objective requirement on the exercise of his duties. This list is not exhaustive, it is 'amongst other matters'. It is far from clear what falls within other matters. Two possible examples are charitable or political contributions[2] in so far as they contribute to the 'success' of the company. The enumeration of the six matters does not introduce independent, free-standing duties, there is one primary duty to promote the success of the company in the interests of the members and these six matters have to be taken into consideration when directors are discharging this primary duty. However, the directors must 'have regard' to these matters in reaching a decision, and this obligation is unqualified. It is not intended that the directors should indulge in a box ticking exercise, each matter has to be independently considered.[3] In many situations certain of the six matters will have limited relevance to a particular company. For example, a company may carry on a business that has little to no impact on the environment and this will impact on the extent of the director's duty to have regard to the duty set out in s 172(1)(d). Have regard to does not guide directors as to the *weight* that should be attached to any of the six matters, this will be a matter of directorial discretion. Also, there may well be a conflict between the various matters which directors have to have regard to. For example, a company may for cost reasons outsource its production to another jurisdiction and the directors can plausibly claim that these cost savings will be in the long-term interests of the members by promoting the success of the company. However, such relocation is obviously not in the interests of the company's employees or the community in which the company currently operates. But if the directors in good faith decide that it will promote the success of the company, the decision is compliant with their s 172 duty. Also the directors will have to give consideration to the 'matters' even if they take effect outside the jurisdiction. This is not giving extra-jurisdictional effect to the legislation as what is involved is the 'success' of the company, something which obviously relates to the UK jurisdiction, but which can be impacted upon by a company's extra-jurisdictional activities. There will inevitably be conflict as to how the matters in s 172(1)(a)–(f) are to be balanced and this is a matter for the good faith judgment of the directors in promoting the success of the company.

[1]   CA 2006, s 172(1)(b) (interests of employees) is the only duty recognised in the pre-2006 legislation: see the CA 1985, s 309.
[2]   See the CA 2006, Pt 14.
[3]   House of Lords, Report (First Day), cl 852.

Business Review

3.21 The directors' report must contain a business review unless the company is subject to the small companies' regime.[1] Section 172(2) provides that the 'purpose of the business review is to inform members of the company and help them assess how the directors have performed their duty under section 172 (duty to promote the success of the company)'.

[1] Section 417. Quoted companies have enhanced disclosure obligations: section 417(5), see generally para 6.17.

Charitable and social purpose companies

3.22 Companies are often formed for charitable or social purposes where, although profit making, it is not intended that any profit should be distributed to members but rather used for the benefit of the purposes for which the company was formed.[1] It is obvious that 'the benefit of members' is not a purpose of such a company. To deal with this CA 2006, s 172(2) provides:

'(2) Where or to the extent that the purposes of the company consist of or include purposes other than the benefit of its members, subsection (1) has effect as if the reference to promoting the success of the company for the benefit of its members were to achieving those purposes.'

Thus achieving the 'purposes' of the company is substituted for 'benefit of its members' when determining whether the directors are compliant with their s 172 duty. What are the 'purposes' of the company will be a function of the company's constitution[2] and any relevant law which has a bearing on the legality of the particular purpose, for example, charity law.

[1] See the Companies (Audit, Investigations and Community Enterprise) Act 2004.
[2] The company will need to have objects.

Creditors of the company

3.23 In certain circumstances the interests of the company are the interests of the creditors. Where, for example, the company is insolvent, the creditor's interests prevail as the shareholders no longer have any interest.[1] Creditor interests also probably intrude where the company, although not insolvent, cannot avoid insolvency.[2] CA 2006, s 172(3) deals with this issue and provides:

'(3) The duty imposed by this section has effect subject to any enactment or rule of law requiring directors, in certain circumstances, to consider or act in the interests of creditors of the company.'

Thus this covers both the common law duty to creditors ('rule of law') and the wrongful trading provisions of the Insolvency Act 1986 ('enactment').[3] Where these are applicable the interests of the company are the interests of the creditors, and thus, for example, in determining whether directors have exercised their duty of care, skill and diligence,[4] it is the interests of creditors that have to be considered. Also, where creditors' interests intrude there can be no ratification of a breach of directors' duties by the shareholders as they no longer have an interest in the matter.

1   *West Mercia Safetywear Ltd v Dodd* [1988] BCLC 250; *Colin Guyer & Associates Ltd v London Wharf Limehourse Ltd* [2003] 2 BCLC 153. However, even in the case of an insolvent company a shareholder could argue that the directors should have taken certain steps which would have promoted the success of the company and this could constitute the basis for a derivative action for negligence.
2   See the Insolvency Act 1986, s 214 (no reasonable prospect that a company could avoid insolvent liquidation).
3   See the Insolvency Act 1986, s 214.
4   See para 3.28.

DUTY TO EXERCISE INDEPENDENT JUDGMENT

3.24 At common law, a director, as a fiduciary, has a duty to exercise his judgment in the interests of the company and may not abdicate this responsibility by acting on the instructions of another director[1] or a third party.[2] The common law rule does not preclude a director from acting on the advice of others[3] (for example, directors acting on the advice of the finance director) but, even though taking into consideration the advice, the director must exercise his own independent judgment. If a director could not rely on the advice of others it would 'render anything like an intelligent devolution of management impossible'.[4] The duties also apply to 'nominee directors',[5] once appointed they must exercise independent judgment and to act unquestionably on the instructions of their nominator would be a breach of duty.[6] A nominee's primary loyalty is to the company but '[H]e is entitled to have regard to the interests or requirements of his appointor to the extent that those interests or requirements are not incompatible with his duty to act in the best interests of the company'.[7] Boards of directors will inevitably enter into contracts on behalf of a company which constrain the future acts of the company and, as a consequence, also constrain the manner in which they may exercise their powers. For example, directors may agree to a corporate restructuring that involves the company issuing shares to a designated party and thus requires the directors agreeing to exercise their powers of allotment in a particular manner. However, provided they act in good faith in the interests of the company, this would not constitute an improper fettering of their discretion.[8]

1   *Re Landhurst Leasing plc, Secretary of State for Trade and Industry v Ball* [1999] 1 BCLC 286 (a case decided under the CDDA 1986).
2   *Fulham Football Club Ltd v Cabra Estates plc* [1994] 1 BCLC 363.
3   *Dovey v Cory* [1901] AC 477.
4   *Dovey v Cory* [1901] AC 477 at 495 (per Lord Halsbury).
5   This is a commercial characterisation and not a legal one.
6   *Selangor United Rubber Estates Ltd v Cradock* [1967] 2 All ER 1255.
7   *Re Neath Rugby Club* [2008] 1 BCLC 527 at 27.
8   *Thorny v Goldberg* (1964) 112 CLR 597 (Aust. HC), cited with approval in *Fulham Football Club Ltd v Cabra Estates plc* [1994] 1 BCLC 363.

3.25 Section 173(1) of the CA 2006 provides that: 'A director of a company must exercise independent judgment'. This replicates the common law.[1] It is not intended to alter the position that directors can still rely on others. It does not preclude the appointment of a 'nominee' director. However, in both situations directors will still have to exercise their own independent judgment.

¹   678 HL Official Report GC (5th series) cols GC281–282 (6 February 2006).

3.26 There still remains the issue of directors entering into an agreement on behalf of a company which constrains the future exercise of the powers of the board. This is dealt with in CA 2006, s 173(2) which provides:

'(2)   This duty [ie the duty imposed by section 173(1)] is not infringed by his acting—
(a)   in accordance with an agreement duly entered into by the company that restricts the future exercise of discretion by its directors, or
(b)   in a way authorised by the company's constitution.'

The agreement covered by 173(2)(a) is one which restricts 'the future exercise of discretion by its directors.' This would be the directors acting as a board. It is important to note that it is only an 'agreement duly entered into by the company'¹ that falls within s 173(2)(a). Anything short of an agreement, for example, an understanding or arrangement, does not fall within the provision. Also, the agreement must be 'duly' entered into, that is, there must be compliance with the company's constitution. It follows from this that an agreement not duly entered into, even though binding on the third party and the company, would not give protection to a director in an action for breach of duty. No statutory provision is made for ratification of an agreement that has not been 'duly' entered into but as a matter of general law the shareholders would have authority to ratify such a transaction.² Where a transaction does fall within s 173(2), it will still be necessary for the directors to satisfy any other relevant general duties, for example, the general duty in s 172 (promote the success of the company): the contract must have been 'duly' entered into.

¹   Normally the company would act through its directors.
²   It is not made specifically ratifiable ('approval') by s 180. But the general power of shareholders to ratify a breach of duty would be applicable: see s 239.

3.27 CA 2006, s 173(2)(b) makes provision for the company's constitution to restrict the duty of directors to exercise independent judgment. In the parliamentary debates the Solicitor General stated that this subsection¹ 'will allow the status of nominee director to be enshrined in the company's constitution so that the nominee is able to follow the instructions of the person who appointed him without breaching that duty' (that is the duty to exercise independent judgment). However this merely removes from the nominee director the duty to exercise 'independent' judgment. The nominee director remains subject to his other duties, for example, the duty of care and skill and the duty to promote the interests of the company.² It would be no defence to a nominee director to an action for breach of these duties that he was acting on the instructions of a person authorised by the company's constitution to issue instructions to him. If a director refused to act on instructions of his nominator which breached, for example, his duty of care and skill he would not incur any liability to his nominator by refusing to follow the instructions as the nominator cannot order a breach of duty other than the duty to exercise independent judgment.[]

1. HC Official Report, SC D (Company Law Reform Bill) 11 July 2006, col 601 (the Solicitor General). Section 173 was clause 159 of the Bill.
2. HC Official Report, SC D (Company Law Reform Bill) 11 July 2006, col 601 (the Solicitor General). Section 173 was clause 159 of the Bill.

DUTY TO EXERCISE REASONABLE CARE, SKILL AND DILIGENCE

3.28 CA 2006, s 174 provides:

'(1) A director of a company must exercise reasonable care, skill and diligence.
(2) This means the care, skill and diligence that would be exercised by a reasonably diligent person with—
    (a) the general knowledge, skill and experience that may be reasonably expected of a person carrying out the functions carried out by the director in relation to the company,
    (b) the general knowledge, skill and experience that the director has.'

This section is modelled on s 214 of the Insolvency Act 1986 and also reflects the common law.[1] Section 174(1) requires a director to exercise 'reasonable care, skill and diligence'. At common law the duty of care did not require a continuous carrying out of his duties by a director, and in appropriate circumstances his duties may be discharged intermittently.[2] However, under s 174(1) a director must exercise 'diligence' and this will have an impact on the way in which a director should discharge his duties. The standard in s 174(2)(a) is objective in that the directors must display the requisite competence of a person carrying out similar functions. It is unclear to what extent this will allow a tailoring of the duties to reflect the functions being performed by a director, for example, executive as opposed to non-executive directors. While the language would permit some differentiation ('the *subjective* standard'), the starting point is that all directors are subject to the same *objective* standard of care and thus the objective standard will apply across the board and set the minimum standard. However, even with respect to the objective standard, cases decided under the Company Directors Disqualification Act 1986 fine tune the director's duty to the role he performs in managing the company.[3]

1. *Re d'Jan of London Ltd* [1994] 1 BCLC 561; 678 HL Official Report (5th series) cols GC285–286 (9 February 2006).
2. See *Re Produce Marketing Consortium Ltd* [1989] BCLC 513 (dealing with liability under s 214); *Re City Equitable Fire Insurance co Ltd* [1925] Ch 407 at 429 ('A director is not bound to give continuous attention to the affairs of his company. His duties are of an intermittent nature to be performed at periodical board meetings ...'). Section 174 does not contain a provision equivalent to s 214(5) (failure to discharge a duty can be wrongful trading). However, a failure to carry out a specific function would constitute a breach of the diligence standard.
3. *Re Barings plc, Secretary of State for Trade and Industry v Baker (No 5)* [1999] 1 BCLC 433 at 489 (upheld on appeal [2000] 1 BCLC 523).

3.29 The standard in s 174(2)(b) is subjective and requires the court to take into consideration the special skills of a particular director, for example, the director may be an accountant. This duty establishes an upper limit in that it operates to enhance the duty in s 174(2)(a) and does not operate to lower it.[1] Obviously it will be a standard that applies to a director individually.

[1] In *Re DKG Contracts Ltd* [1990] BCC 903 at 912 the court stated in connection with s 214: 'Patently [the directors] own knowledge, skill and experience were hopelessly inadequate for the task they undertook. That is not sufficient to protect them.'

3.30 Where an action is brought against more than one director, liability is probably several and not joint and several.[1] It is unclear whether s 174 applies to shadow directors. Section 214(7) of the Insolvency Act 1986 specifically applies s 214 to shadow directors. There has been no common law decision on whether the duties of care and skill apply to shadow directors but it is difficult to see why they should not.

[1] See liability under s 214 where this is the case: *Re Continental Assurance Co of London Ltd* [2001] BPIR 733 at 382–396.

3.31 CA 2006, s 178(2) dealing with remedies provides that the duty to exercise reasonable care, skill and diligence, does not fall within the subsection which[1] makes the general duties enforceable in the same way as any other fiduciary duty,[2] the s 174 duty is not a fiduciary duty.[3]

[1] See para 3.37.
[2] A derivative action could be bought with respect to breach of s 174, see paras 5.22 ff.
[3] Not all duties owed by a fiduciary are fiduciary duties: see *Bristol & West Building Society v Mothew (t/a Stapley & Co)* [1998] Ch 1.

CONSENT, APPROVAL OR AUTHORISATION BY MEMBERS

3.32 The consent, approval or authorisation by members of a company with respect to breach of duty by a director play a central role at common law in providing a safe harbour for a director who has breached his duty. Not all breaches of duty are ratifiable[1] but many are and the safe harbour for the directors required shareholder approval. How these common law principles interact with general duties is dealt with in s 180.

[1] See, eg, *Cook v Deeks* [1916] 1 AC 554.

3.33 As discussed at para 4.4, s 175 provides that directors can authorise a transaction involving a conflict of interest by a fellow director,[1] and a duty to declare an interest in a proposed transaction is satisfied by disclosure to the board.[2] This does mark a departure from the common law which would, with respect to these transactions, at the minimum require disclosure to the shareholders in order to provide directors with protection unless the articles of association provided otherwise as did Art 85 of Table A. Section 180 provides that in a case where ss 175 and 177 apply:

> '(1) ... the transaction or arrangement is not liable to be set aside by virtue of any common law rule or equitable principle requiring the consent or approval of the members of the company.
> This is without prejudice to any enactment, or provision of the company's constitution, requiring such consent of approval.'

This effectively disapplies any common law or equitable principle requiring members' consent or approval to transactions involving conflicts of interest (s 175) or interests in proposed transactions (s 177). Thus in a situation like that in *Regal (Hastings) Ltd v Gulliver*,[3] involving a transaction which would have fallen within s 175, where the House of Lords held that the breach could have been either prospectively or retrospectively approved by the shareholders, such approval ('authorisation') can now also be given by the board. However, to the extent that any enactment, or more importantly any provision in the company's constitution requires shareholder consent, these remain applicable.[4] This will require a careful examination of the articles of association of pre-2006 companies to determine if, and to what extent, they require shareholder approval of transactions falling within ss 175 and 177.

[1]   CA 2006, s 175(4).
[2]   CA 2006, s 177. See paras 4.12 ff.
[3]   [1967] 2 AC 134n.
[4]   CA 2006, s 180(1).

Other qualifications to the operation of the general duties

3.34 CA 2006, s 180 also deals with other aspects of the interaction of the general duties with (a) other enactments, (b) a rule of law, and (c) the company's constitution.

(a) Other enactments

Section 180(2) deals with the relationship between Chap 4 of the Act (transactions requiring approval of members) and the general duties. Transactions within Chap 4 and the general duties can overlap. Section 180(2) provides:

> '(2) The application of the general duties is not affected by the fact that the case also falls within Chapter 4 (transactions requiring approval members), except that where that Chapter applies and—
> (a)   approval is given under that Chapter, or
> (b)   the matter is one as to which it is provided that approval is not needed,
> it is not necessary also to comply with section 175 (duty to avoid conflicts of interest) or section 176 (duty not to accept benefits from third parties).'

Thus compliance with Chap 4, and it is important to note that this includes matters for which Chap 4 provides that approval is not needed, exempts the directors from having to comply with ss 175 or 176. The converse is not the case, s 180(3) provides that compliance with the general duties does not remove the need to seek approval of the shareholders under Chapter 4. Even though there has been compliance with s 177 or s 175, the other general duties remain applicable.[1]

Another example of an enactment which qualifies the general duties is s 247 which empowers directors to make payment to a company's employees in connection with the cessation of a company's business. Section 247(2) provides that these powers can be exercised notwithstanding the general duty in s 172 (duty to promote the success of the company).

(b) Rule of Law

The general duties are also made subject to rules of law. Section 180(4)(a) provides that the general duties:

> '(a) have effect subject to any rule of law enabling the company to give authority, specifically or generally, for anything to be done (or omitted) by the directors, or any of them, that would otherwise be a breach of duty.'

This preserves the common law power of shareholders to ratify or authorise a transaction which is in breach of the general duties.[2]

(c) Company's Constitution

Section 180(4)(b) deals with the relationship between the company's constitution and the general duties. It provides that:

> '(b) where the company's articles contain provisions for dealing with conflicts of interest, [the general duties] are not infringed by anything done (or omitted) by the directors, or any of them, in accordance with those provisions.'

On one interpretation of s 180(4)(b) compliance with a company's constitutional provisions relating to conflict of interest results in all of the general duties not being infringed and not just s 175 (conflicts of interest). Such an interpretation could release a director from the duty to promote the success of the company (s 172) and this cannot have been intended. Section 180(4)(b) must be restricted to the specific duty that it refers to, namely, the duty in s 175.

(d) Enactment or Rule of Law

Section 180(5) provides that 'otherwise the general duties have effect (except as otherwise provided for or the context otherwise requires) notwithstanding any enactment or rule of law'.

1   CA 2006, ss 171–174 and 177.
2   See also s 239.

Duties cumulative

3.35 CA 2006, s 179 provides that 'Except as otherwise provided, more than one of the general duties may apply in any given case'. Thus, if a director takes a bribe this would constitute breach of his duty not to accept benefits from a third party (s 176) and, depending on the circumstances, could constitute a failure to promote the success of the company (s 172), or evidence a failure to exercise independent judgment (s 173). However, as regards a duty to avoid conflicts of interest (s 175), this duty, as we have already seen,[1] does not arise in connection with a transaction or arrangement with the company. Such transactions would be caught by s 177 (declaration of interest in proposed transaction)[2] or s 182 (declaration of interest in existing transaction or arrangement).

[1]   Paragraph 4.1, s 176(3).
[2]   Paragraph 4.14.

CIVIL CONSEQUENCES OF BREACH OF GENERAL DUTIES

3.36 CA 2006, s 178 deals with (a) the consequences of breach of the general duties, and (b) the enforceability of the general duties.

Consequences of breach

3.37 CA 2006, s 178(1) provides:

'(1)   The consequences of breach (or threatened breach) of sections 171 to 177 are the same as would apply if the corresponding common law rule or equitable principle applied.'

Central to the effect of this subsection is s 170(3) as this subsection links the 'general duties' to their 'common law rules or equitable principles' equivalents on which the general duties are based. Where the general duties replicate the common law, the consequences of breach will be those of the common law. This will not only cover issues of substantive remedy (eg rescission, accounting for profits etc) but also issues such as causation and foreseeability as they apply to breach of fiduciary duties. Also, it is clear that not all breaches of duty by a fiduciary constitute a breach of fiduciary duty; this distinction will remain relevant.[1]

CA 2006, s 178(2) provides for enforcement:

'The duties in those situations (with the exception of section 174, duty to exercise reasonable care, skill and diligence) are, accordingly enforceable in the same way as any other fiduciary duty owed to a company by its directors.'

This recognises that there are 'other' fiduciary duties to which a director may be subject and that ss 171–177 do not exhaustively state the duties to which directors are subject.

[1]   *Bristol and West Building Society v Mothew (t/a Stapley & Co)* [1998] Ch 1.

Chapter 4

DIRECTORS AND CONFLICTS OF INTEREST

Brenda Hannigan

DUTY TO AVOID CONFLICTS OF INTEREST

4.1 The Companies Act 2006 ('CA 2006'), s 175(1) provides that:

'(1) A director of a company must avoid a situation in which he has, or can have, a direct or indirect interest that conflicts, or possibly may conflict, with the interests of the company.'

This section imposes a positive duty to avoid conflicts of interest and departs from the common law which merely imposed a 'disability' in a situation of conflict[1] but did not impose a duty to avoid conflict. Also, the no conflict rule subsumes the no profit rule (set out in s 175(2)), which is not identified as a separate duty. Section 175(1) is extremely broad.[2] It covers 'a direct or *indirect* interest' that conflicts, or *'possibly* may conflict' with the company's interests. Thus it would cover being a director of another company which carries on an activity which is similar to the business of a company of which he is also a director.[3] The prohibition also applies to situations where the director *'can* have' an interest which 'possibly may conflict'. Thus potential conflicts as well as actual conflicts are covered. This obviously creates difficulties in the case of a director who is intending to take on an additional appointment as a director or who already holds multiple directorships. Where the possibility of conflict is clear,[4] the director must disclose the conflict and seek authorisation,[5] which can be given by disinterested directors under s 175(4)(b). Where the conflict is speculative in the sense that the test that 'the reasonable man looking at the relevant facts and circumstances of the particular case would think that there was a real sensible possibility of conflict'[6] is not satisfied, a director can rely on s 175(4)(a). The prohibition extends to 'indirect' interests and while not linked to, nor limited by, the definition of connected persons in s 252, that section offers some indication of how indirect interests might arise.

The GC100 group, which represents general counsel and company secretaries of the FTSE 100 companies has issued guidance on the application of the provision, see GC100, *Companies Act 2006 – Directors' Conflicts of Interest*, 18 January 2008 (hereafter the GC100 Guidance), available at http:// www.practicallaw.com/6-378-7923.

1 *Movitex v Bulfield* [1988] BCLC 104.
2 The liability under s 175 is subject to s 180 ('Consent, approval or authorisation by members'), see paras 4.22 ff.
3 The conflict would exist with respect to both companies.
4 HC Official Report SC D (Company Law Reform Bill) 11 July 2006, col 613.
5 HC Official Report SC D (Company Law Reform Bill) 11 July 2006, col 614. As to the obligation on a director to disclose information of relevance or concern to the company, see *Bhullar v Bhullar* [2003] 2 BCLC 241 at 255–256; *Item Software Ltd v Fassihi* [2005] 2 BCLC 91.
6 *Boardman v Phipps* [1967] 2 AC 46 at 124.

4.2 CA 2006, s 175(2) extends the reach of s 175(1) by providing that the no conflict prohibition 'applies in particular to the exploitation of any property, information or opportunity (and it is immaterial whether the company could take advantage of the property, information or opportunity)'. This reflects the common law: whether the company could or would have taken the opportunity is not to the point.[1] It was a breach of duty for directors to take up for their own benefit an opportunity falling within the company's line of business which the company did not have the resources to exploit,[2] or where the third party with whom the opportunity was associated did not wish to deal with the company.[3] However, it is important to keep in mind that the exploitation of the property, information or opportunity must be such as to give rise to a conflict and accordingly the exploitation of the type of opportunity which a director has no duty to pass on to the company could not constitute a breach of duty by the director. The scope of the section is further extended by s 175(7) which provides that any 'reference in this section [ie 175] to a conflict of interest includes a conflict of interest and duty and a conflict of duties', this, however, replicates the common law.

Section 175 only applies to transactions involving a third party; s 175(3) excludes a 'conflict of interest arising in relation to a transaction or arrangement with the company.' Transactions with the company are dealt with by other provisions (ss 177 and 182, see paras 4.14 and 4.29) and where the transaction is approved by the shareholders or exempt from approval under Part 10, Chapter 4, there is no need to comply with s 175 (s 180(2)).

1 *Bhullar v Bhullar* [2003] 2 BCLC 241 at 256.
2 *Regal (Hastings) Ltd v Gulliver* [1967] 2 AC 134n.
3 *Industrial Development Consultants Ltd v Cooley* [1972] 2 All ER 162.

4.3 The no conflict duty is not infringed 'if the situation cannot reasonably be regarded as likely to give rise to a conflict of interest' (s 175(4)(a)). This replicates the common law that a fiduciary, hence a director, will not be liable for breach of duty where there is no real sensible possibility of conflict.[1] This also provides protection to a director who, for example, holds multiple directorships where there is a possibility that he 'can have' a direct or indirect conflicting interest but on the facts the 'situation cannot reasonably be regarded as likely to give rise to a conflict of interest'.

[1]   *Boardman v Phipps* [1967] 2 AC 46.

Authorisation

4.4 The duty under CA 2006, s 175 is not infringed if the matter has been 'authorised by the directors' (s 175(4)(b)). Section 175(5) sets out how such authorisation must be given: (i) s 175(5)(a) deals with authorisation as regards private companies, and (ii) s 175(5)(b) deals with public companies. Authorisation with respect to both types of company only deals with the issue of conflict, directors (including the director seeking authorisation) are still subject to the general duty in s 172 to promote the success of the company, and the duties in s 171 (duty to act within powers) and s 174 (duty of care and skill) may also be relevant.

Authorisation may be by independent directors (s 175(4)(b)) and provision may also be made in the articles for conflicts to the extent permitted by s 232(4). The uncertain effect of s 232(4) ('such provision as has previously been lawful') means that authorisation by independent directors, if that is possible, will be the preferred route to deal with conflicts.

Private companies

4.5 As regards private companies, CA 2006, s 175(5)(a) provides that authorisation may be given by directors:

> '(a) where the company is a private company and nothing in the company's constitution invalidates such authorisation, by the matter being proposed to and authorised by the directors ...'

Thus the default position for private companies is that the directors can give authorisation unless the company's constitution actually *invalidates* the authorisation. A provision which is facultative, that is, to enable a board to specifically authorise a transaction would not be an invalidating provision, it would be a provision relating to the manner of the exercise of the board's powers but not a constraint on the scope of those powers. Failure to comply with such a facultative provision may constitute breach of duty by directors but it would not fall within s 175(5)(a) as an invalidating provision. The provision in the company's constitution must actually invalidate the authorisation, that is, expressly prohibit it or, for example, provide that the authorisation by the board shall have no effect or that the authorisation has to be given by the shareholders.[1]

Private companies formed under the CA 2006 (ie from 1 October 2009) are able automatically to rely on s 175(5)(a). Private companies incorporated under the Companies Act 1985 ('CA 1985') must pass an ordinary resolution (which must be filed with the registrar of companies) permitting authorisation to be given by the directors in accordance with s 175(5)(a).[2]

There is no provision for the disclosure of authorisations granted (other than the record in the board minutes, s 248) and this lack of transparency may be a problem in smaller companies.

[1] CA 2006, s 180(1).
[2] See the Companies Act 2006 (Commencement No 5, Transitional Provisions and Savings) Order 2007, SI 2007/3495, Art 9, Sch 4, para 47.

Public companies

4.6 As regards public companies, s 175(5)(b) provides that authorisation may be given by the directors:

> '(5) where the company is a public company and its constitution includes provision enabling the directors to authorise the matter, by the matter being proposed to and authorised by them in accordance with the constitution.'

As regards public companies, the default position is that such transactions are prohibited unless the company's constitution contains a provision whereby the directors can authorise the matter (the ability of the shareholders to authorise a conflict is preserved by s 180(4)(a)). If an authorisation provision is included, authorisation must be given in accordance with the provision and failure to so comply would result in the authorisation being ineffective. Where there has been a failure to so comply and therefore a breach of duty, the shareholders could *ex post* ratify the transaction, in that shareholders can ratify what they could have authorised, subject to the common law limits to that power to ratify (s 239(7)) and the voting constraints in s 239(3), (4).[1]

Public companies formed under the CA 1985 need to amend their articles to adopt an authorisation provision. Practice may develop that the inclusion of an article providing for authorisation becomes standard for public companies formed under the CA 2006 (from 1 October 2009) though the model articles for public companies limited by shares do not contain a model provision.[2]

The expectation is that shareholders in public companies are unlikely to raise objections to the exercise of these authorisation powers provided the company has a sound governance structure, effective procedures for exercising the powers and confirms compliance with such procedure.[3]

[1] See para 4.50.
[2] See The Companies (Model Articles) Regulations 2008, SI 2008/3229.
[3] See GC100 Guidance on Conflicts of Interests, para 1.8, see para 4.1 above.

Limits to authorisation

4.7 There is no express limitation on the power to authorise a particular transaction but the directors authorising the transaction must act in accordance with their obligations, especially their duty under s 172 to act to promote the success of the company, see para 3.17 and under s 174 to exercise care and skill in carrying out their functions, see para 3.28. There is no provision for disclosure of authorisations to shareholders, but for larger companies the GC100 Guidance suggests that boards might provide an explanation of how these authorisation powers have been exercised in the company's corporate governance report.[1]

Authorisation must be of 'the matter' and, if circumstances change, a further authorisation may be required and authorisation may be conditional on such further authorisation being sought. Authorisation once given may be varied or terminated.

[1]   See GC100 Guidance on Conflicts of Interest, para 4.12, see para 4.1 above.

Independent directors

4.8 CA 2006, s 175(6) also requires (both in the case of private and public companies) that the authorisation be independent. The requirements of independence apply with respect to quorum requirements and voting at a directors' meeting authorising the matter. As regards the quorum, s 175(6)(a) provides that the 'authorisation is effective' only if 'any requirement as to the quorum at the meeting at which the matter is considered is met without counting the director in question or any other interested director'. 'Interested' is not defined. It probably refers to the director having a financial or commercial interest in the transaction or in some way benefiting from it. Thus, for example, the spouse of a director, who is also a director, would not be an interested director.[1] There is no requirement that the disqualifying interest of a director be identical to that of 'any other interested director'. For example, one director may be acquiring a property from the company and another director may have been retained before the acquisition takes place to give professional advice as to its development after the acquisition, obviously the interests of the directors are different but they would both be caught by s 175. There is no de minimis exception. As regards voting, s 175(6)(b) provides that the authorisation is effective if 'the matter was agreed to without their [ie the director or any other interested director] voting or would have been agreed to if their votes had not been counted'. Interested directors are disenfranchised and do not count towards the quorum but they are not prevented from taking part in the directors' meeting where the matter is raised. Thus, the vote of an interested director will simply be ignored but the fact that it is cast does not invalidate the authorisation provided the plurality of the directors voting in favour is disinterested.

[1]   If it had been intended to have such an extended definition of interested director reference could have been made to the definition of connected person in the CA 2006: see s 252. See also *Newgate Stud Co v Penfold* [2008] 1 BCLC 46. On the other hand, a spouse in that situation has to be mindful of his/her own duties, especially the duty to promote the success of the company (s 172), and may be in a position of conflict, not with respect to the transaction, but the authorisation of the transaction.

4.9 It is important to note that authorisation is effective '*only* if' the quorum and voting provisions in s 175 are complied with. These are the minimum statutory mandatory requirements for authorisation but a company's constitution may stipulate other requirements.[1] The section does not permit a general disclosure in advance,[2] nor can authorisation be retrospective. There are differing views as to whether authorisation can be by committee, but it would seem not.[3] While the articles confer powers to manage the business on the directors, which powers may be delegated to a committee,[4] this power to authorise conflicts is a statutory power relaxing a legal rule conferred on 'the directors' and as such must be exercised by the board. The GC100 Guidance recommends the use of a committee to regularly review conflict authorisations, but actual authorisation should be a matter for the board.[5]

There will be many situations where a board, particularly in the case of a private company, cannot satisfy the independence requirements of s 175(6). In these situations the directors could proceed with the transaction and rely on s 239 (ratification of acts of directors), assuming the necessary votes can be mustered. Authorisation under s 175 prevents a breach from occurring, ratification under s 239 presumes that there has been a breach but that it is being condoned. However, the power of ratification is restricted by s 239(7) which provides that s 239 does 'not affect any other enactment or rule of law imposing additional requirements for valid ratification or any rule of law as to acts that are incapable of being ratified by the company'. Thus the law on what is a ratifiable breach or what are or are not ratifiable wrongs remains applicable, see paras 5.48–5.56, all that s 239 does is lay down the requirements for what constitutes effective ratification. Section 239(6)(a) preserves the unanimous consent rules even where the directors are ratifying their own breach of duty.[6] Also, directors could obtain authorisation from the shareholders under s 180(4)(a) subject to the common law limits to that power, see paras 5.48–5.56.

---

[1] See CA 2006, s 180(1); 678 HL Official Report (5th series) cols GC325–326 (9 February 2006).

[2] 678 HL Official Report (5th series) col GC328 (9 February 2006).

[3] In *Guinness plc v Saunders* [1988] BCLC 607 at 611–612 (appealed on other grounds) there is support for the view that a statutory requirement for disclosure 'at a meeting of the directors' means disclosure to a duly convened meeting of the full board, not a meeting of a committee of the board. CA 2006, s 175(6)(a) refers to the matter being considered at a meeting which likewise should be construed as meaning a duly convened meeting of the full board of directors.

[4] See the Companies (Model Articles) Regulations 2008, SI 2008/3229, reg 2, Sch 1, arts 3, 5 (Ltd); reg 4, Sch 1, arts 3, 5 (plc).

[5] See GC100 Guidance, para 4.10, see 4.1 above.

[6] Though even unanimous consent cannot authorise *ultra vires* or illegal acts or acts which are a fraud on the creditors: see *Rolled Steel Products (Holdings) Ltd v British Steel Corp* [1984] BCLC 466 at 508.

DUTY NOT TO ACCEPT BENEFITS FROM THIRD PARTIES

4.10 CA 2006, s 176(1) provides that:

'(1) A director of a company must not accept a benefit from a third party conferred by reason of—
(a) his being a director, or
(b) his doing (or not doing) anything as director.'

4.11 The section only proscribes benefits received from a third party and for the purpose of the section 'third party' means 'a person other than the company, an associated body corporate or a person acting on behalf of the company or an associated body corporate.'[1] The prohibition applies also to a former director who may not accept benefits from third parties conferred by reason of things done or omitted by the director before he ceased to be a director (s 170(2)(b)).

Obviously benefit will include a pecuniary benefit but it extends to any type of benefit, for example, free holidays. Benefit could extend to an indemnity granted to a director in connection with his office as director or the appointment to the position as a non-executive director of another company[2] where that is conferred because of his directorship. In *Cronins v Grierson*[3] dealing with the meaning of benefit in s 2(3) of the Betting, Gaming and Lotteries Act 1964, Lord Upjohn stated that 'Benefit is a word of wide import, it means in this context no more than advantage. I cannot construe it as being limited to a tangible, corporeal advantage ...'.[4] In the Parliamentary proceedings, this case was cited by the Solicitor-General as being appropriate in interpreting the meaning of benefit in s 176 and thus, although ultimately what constitutes benefit within the terms of s 176 is a matter of statutory interpretation for the courts, benefit is clearly intended to include non-financial benefits.[5]

1   CA 2006, s 176(2).
2   678 HL Official Report (5th series) col GC330 (9 February 2006).
3   [1968] AC 895.
4   [1968] AC 895 at 909.
5   HC Official Report SC D (Company Law Reform Bill) 11 July 2006, col 622.

4.12 There are certain exclusions to liability under s 176. The most important of which is s 176(4) which provides that the duty under the section is 'not infringed if the acceptance of the benefit cannot reasonably be regarded as likely to give rise to a conflict of interest'. This would obviously cover de minimis benefits. The benefit must be 'likely' to give rise to a conflict of interest and this would exclude fanciful possibilities of conflict, see para 4.1. A director might seek reassurance in the form of a board minute that a benefit offered is not likely to give rise to a conflict so allowing for his acceptance of it. The articles might also be used, it would seem, to identify permissible benefits (s 180(4)(b)), subject to the constraints of s 232. A conflict of interest includes a conflict of interest and duty and a conflict of duties.[1] Also excluded are situations where the director's services are provided to a company by another person and that other person provides benefits to the director. In this case such benefits are not within s 176.[2] The type of situation covered by this is where a director provides his services through his own company which in turn remunerates him.[3] A director is not required to comply with s 176 if the transaction in respect of which the benefit arises is approved or is exempt from approval in accordance with Part 10, Chapter 4 (transactions requiring members' approval) (s 180(2)).

1   CA 2006, s 176(5).
2   CA 2006, s 176(3).
3   678 HL Official Report (5th series) col GC330 (9 February 2006).

Overlap of duties

4.13 There could be an overlap between CA 2006, ss 175 and 176. Section 179 provides that 'Except as otherwise provided, more than one of the general duties may apply in any given case'. A significant distinction between these sections is that s 175 permits authorisation by the directors[1] whereas s 176 does not permit authorisation by the directors with respect to a departure from its terms. No special provision is made to deal with any overlap between ss 175 and 176, though other overlaps are expressly addressed (as in s 175(3) with respect to the overlap with s 177, and in s 180(2) with respect to the overlap between ss 175, 176 and Part 10, Ch 4). Given the structure of ss 175 and 176, presumably the specific provision in s 176 dealing with benefits from third parties (which encompasses bribes) precludes authorisation of such benefits under s 175(4)(b), though the position would have been clearer had there been an express exclusion. While there can be no question of directors' authorising bribes, it is difficult to see why directors can authorise conduct which would otherwise be a breach of s 175(1) or (2), but cannot authorise the acceptance of benefits (short of a bribe) which give rise to a conflict of interest. Of course, there is a difficult issue as to the point when a benefit turns into a bribe. As noted at para 4.12, it also seems that the articles may make some provision for the acceptance of benefits, but to what extent is unclear, given the constraint of s 232(4). Shareholders may also authorise or ratify the acceptance of benefits in breach of s 176[2], but not bribes.

[1]   See paras 4.4 ff.
[2]   See CA 2006, ss 180(4)(a) and 239(7).

DUTY TO DECLARE INTEREST IN PROPOSED TRANSACTION WITH COMPANY

4.14 CA 2006, s 177 deals with declarations of interest in proposed transactions between a director and a company. This previously was dealt with in a company's articles of association, as in CA 1985, Table A, Art 85.

CA 2006, s 177(1) provides:

> '(1)   If a director of a company is in any way, directly or indirectly, interested in a proposed transaction or arrangement with the company, he must declare the nature and extent of that interest to the other directors.'

The proposed transaction must be with the company and not with a subsidiary or holding company – transactions with those companies may fall within s 175. The disclosure must be of any 'direct or indirect' interest. The director does not have to be a party to the transaction or arrangement as the director may have an interest in a transaction entered into by another person with the company and this would make his interest indirect.[1] It is in any 'proposed' transaction or arrangement with respect to which disclosure has to be made, a point which is spelt out by sub-s (4) which provides that 'Any declaration required by this section must be made *before* (emphasis added) the company enters into the transaction or arrangement'. Declarations with respect to existing transactions are caught by s 182, see para 4.31. The section applies to, *inter alia*, 'arrangements'. As has been stated with respect to 'arrangement' in another context[2] which is equally applicable to s 175, arrangement is 'apt to include an agreement or understanding between parties, whether formal or informal, oral or in writing'.[3] Disclosure has to be made to the 'other directors' (so no disclosure is required where a private company only has one director) and disclosure to the members would not suffice.[4]

1   DTI Explanatory Notes to the CA 2006, para 347.
2   Insolvency Act 1986, ss 423 and 426.
3   *Feakins v Department for Environment, Food and Rural Affairs* [2007] BCC 54, at 76.
4   See, however, the CA 2006, s 180(4)(a), para 4.24.

Form of declaration

4.15 CA 2006, s 177(2) makes provision for the form of declaration. It provides that:

'(2)   The declaration may (but need not) be made—
    (a)   at a meeting of the directors, or
    (b)   by notice to the directors in accordance with—
        (i)   section 184 (notice in writing), or
        (ii)   section 185 (general notice).'

It is important to note that this provision does not dictate the manner of the declaration. Thus, it seems, an oral communication to each director individually would suffice and such declaration would not have to be made on the same date or at the same time or place. There may be evidential difficulties subsequently with an oral communication, however, so it is not an advisable way of proceeding. It is notable that the methods specified in s 177(2) result in inclusion in the board minutes (see below) so there is a record of the disclosure.

Whatever the form of communication, all directors need to be informed, and each director must receive the same declaration of 'the nature and extent of that interest'. Section 184 deals specifically with the form of a declaration by notice in writing, a provision which is new. Such notice may be in hard copy or if the recipient has agreed in electronic form.[1] It may be sent by hand or by post or, if the recipient has agreed, in electronic form.[2] Where such a notice is given it forms part of the proceedings of the next meeting of directors and thus forms part of the minutes of that meeting.[3] Section 185 permits a general notice to be given that a director is interested in another body corporate or firm or is connected with another person.[4] The director must state the nature and extent of the interest in the other body corporate or firm, for example he is a sole shareholder of the company, or the nature and extent of his connection with the person, for example, a spouse.[5]

Whether a director, having made a declaration, is able to participate in the meeting which considers the proposed transaction is a matter for the articles. The model articles provide that the director is excluded from the quorum and voting, subject to:

(a)   a decision of the company by ordinary resolution to allow him to participate for quorum and voting purposes; or

(b)   where the director's interest cannot reasonably be regarded as likely to give rise to a conflict of interest (which is somewhat pointless since the section does not apply in that case, s 177(6)(a)); or

(c)   where the conflict arises from a narrow range of permitted causes.[6]

1   CA 2006, s 184(3).
2   CA 2006, s 184(4).
3   CA 2006, s 184(5).
4   CA 2006, s 185(2).
5   CA 2006, s 185(3).
6   See The Companies (Model Articles) Regulations 2008, SI 2008/3229, reg 2, Sch 1, Art 14 (Ltd); reg 4, Sch 3, Art 16 (plc). 'Permitted causes' are defined (Art 14(4); Art 16(4)) respectively as: (a) guarantees given, or to be given, by or to a director in respect of an obligation incurred by or on behalf of the company or any of its subsidiaries; (b) subscription, or an agreement to subscribe, for shares or other securities of the company or any of its subsidiaries, or to underwrite, sub-underwrite, or guarantee subscription for any such shares or securities; and (c) arrangements pursuant to which benefits are made available to employees and directors or former employees and directors of the company or any of its subsidiaries which do not provide special benefits for directors or former directors.

Exemptions from need for declaration

4.16 CA 2006, s 177(5)–(6) exempt a director in a number of situations from having to make a declaration. These are situations where (a) the director is unaware of his interest or of the transaction in which he has an interest, (b) the interest cannot reasonably be regarded as likely to give rise to a conflict of interest, (c) the other directors know of his interest, and (d) service contracts.

(i) Interest or transaction or arrangement unknown

4.17 CA 2006, s 177(5) provides that:

'(5)   This section does not require a declaration of an interest of which the director is not aware or where the director is not aware of the transaction or arrangement in question.
        For this purpose a director is treated as being aware of matters of which he ought reasonably to be aware.'

This covers the situation where (i) a director is not aware of his *interest* or (ii) is not aware of the *transaction* or *arrangement*. The position in (i) would arguably be rare if the director is aware of the transaction, although the fact that indirect interests are covered does raise the possibility of it occurring. But the position in (ii) is more possible particularly in the case of complex groups of companies. Ignorance as defined for the purpose of (i) or (ii) is not an absolute defence as a director will be deemed to be aware of matters of which 'he ought reasonably to be aware'. The test of what is reasonable must be objective as to give it a subjective interpretation would afford protection to the wilfully or incompetently ignorant director. The test is different from that in s 174 ('Duty to exercise reasonable care, skill and diligence') which contains a subjective component in determining reasonableness with respect to director's duty of care, see para 3.28.[1] The sections of course deal with different issues: (a) s 174 deals with the duty of care that a director needs to display when going about the company's business, whereas (b) s 177 deals with the situation where a director ought to be aware of his own interests in a transaction involving the company.[2]

[1]   CA 2006, s 174(2)(b).
[2]   678 HL Official Report (5th series) col GC334 (9 February 2006).

(ii) No conflict

4.18 Disclosure is not required where there is no reasonable possibility of conflict.[1] CA 2006, s 177(6)(a) provides that a director need not declare an interest:

> '(a) if it cannot reasonably be regarded as likely to give rise to a conflict of interest.'

This would cover de minimis interests and also probably *de minimis* transactions. It would be possible for a director to have a substantial interest in a *de minimis* transaction, but because of the minimal nature of the transaction, this would not be considered to have the potential to distort the director's independent judgment by giving rise to a conflict of interest. For something to be 'reasonably regarded' as giving rise to a conflict of interest there probably needs to be a real sensible possibility of a conflict, see para 4.1.

[1]   A bare trusteeship, without duties, does not place a director in a position of conflict, see *Cowan de Groot v Eagle Trust* [1991] BCLC 1045 at 1115.

(iii) Other directors know

4.19 Disclosure is not needed where the other directors know of the interest. CA 2006, s 177(6)(b) provides that a director need not declare an interest:

> '(b) if, or to the extent that, the other directors are already aware of it (and for this purpose the other directors are treated as aware of anything of which they ought reasonably to be aware),'

The awareness has to be of the 'interest' and not of the 'transaction'. In determining whether the directors ought to have been aware, it is a reasonableness standard. What is reasonable will turn very much on the facts obviously, but the more significant the interest, the greater the likelihood that the directors, as reasonable directors, ought to have been aware of the interest. Where a director invokes the actual or deemed awareness of his fellow directors as a defence, the onus will probably be on the director to satisfy it, he who asserts must prove. Other than in clear-cut situations (where the interest is evident to all) it may be unwise to rely on this defence.

(iv) Service contracts

4.20 Obviously a service contract between a director and a company will give rise to a conflict of interest but also obviously the board that entered into the contract will be aware of its existence.[1] This issue is dealt with in CA 2006, s 177(6)(c) which provides that a director need not declare an interest,

> '(c) if, or to the extent that, it concerns terms of his service contract that have been or are to be considered—
> (i) by a meeting of the directors, or
> (ii) by a committee of the directors appointed for the purpose under the company's constitution.'

For this provision to apply, the 'terms' of the contract must have been or are to be considered. This would require disclosure of all of the terms. The past tense ('have been') would cover a situation where terms have been resolved on by the board of directors and then an approach is made to a person to become a director on the already agreed terms. The requirement for a committee 'appointed for the purpose' is restrictive and limited, it would seem, to a committee tasked with considering the terms of directors' service contracts such as a nomination, remuneration or appointments committee.

[1] See *Runciman v Walter Runciman plc* [1992] BCLC 1084.

Erroneous declaration

4.21 It may be that a declaration of interest is revealed to be, or becomes, inaccurate or incomplete. This is dealt with by CA 2006, s 177(3) which provides:

> '(3) If a declaration under this section proves to be, or becomes, inaccurate or incomplete, a further declaration must be made.'

This subsection deals with the situation where the declaration (a) 'proves' to be inaccurate or incomplete, or (b) 'becomes' inaccurate or incomplete. Both of these requirements are, of course, subject to s 177(5), ignorance by the director of either his interest or the transaction (see para 4.17). This will be particularly important with respect to (b), which covers a change of circumstances. In many situations involving complex corporate groups, it may be difficult for a director to know or appreciate how a change of circumstances has triggered an obligation to declare. A declaration that 'proves' to be inaccurate involves a situation where at the time it is made facts exist which as subsequently revealed disprove its accuracy.

There are a number of permutations:

- the director makes a declaration which proves to be or becomes inaccurate or incomplete and makes a further declaration before the transaction is entered into, so complying fully with s 177;
- the director makes a declaration that proves to be or becomes inaccurate or incomplete and he is unable to correct the declaration in time under s 177 (because of s 177(4) – declaration must be before the

transaction is entered into). In such circumstances, he is not in breach of s 177 (he could only be so if the facts which render the declaration incomplete or inaccurate were known to him or ought to have been known to him, s 177(5), so that in effect he made a false declaration). A declaration is required, however, under s 182(1), to the extent that the interest has not been declared already under s 177.

- the director fails to make a declaration as required or makes a false declaration. In either case he is in breach of s 177 and liable for breach of duty, even if he subsequently makes a declaration under s 182 (so avoiding a fine under that provision).

CONSENT, APPROVAL OR AUTHORISATION BY MEMBERS

4.22 The consent, approval or authorisation by members of a company with respect to breach of duty by a director plays a central role at common law in providing a safe harbour for a director who has breached his duty. Not all breaches of duty are ratifiable[1] but many are and the safe harbour for the directors required shareholder approval. The interaction between the common law principles and the general duties is dealt with in s 180 which addresses the relationship between the general duties and (i) CA 2006, Part 10, Ch 4, (ii) authorisation by the shareholders, (iii) the company's constitution and (iv) any enactment or rule of law.

[1]   See, eg, *Cook v Deeks* [1916] 1 AC 554, and paras 5.48–5.56.

4.23 As we have seen, s 175 provides that directors can authorise a transaction involving a conflict of interest by a fellow director,[1] and a duty to declare an interest in a proposed transaction is satisfied by disclosure to the board.[2] This does mark a departure from the common law which would, with respect to these transactions, at the minimum require disclosure to the shareholders in order to provide directors with protection unless the articles of association provided otherwise (as did Art 85 of Table A). Section 180 provides that in a case where ss 175 and 177 apply:

> '(1) ... the transaction or arrangement is not liable to be set aside by virtue of any common law rule or equitable principle requiring the consent or approval of the members of the company.
> This is without prejudice to any enactment, or provision of the company's constitution, requiring such consent of approval.'

This effectively disapplies any common law or equitable principle requiring members' consent or approval to transactions involving conflicts of interest (s 175) or interests in proposed transactions (s 177). Thus in a situation like that in *Regal (Hastings) Ltd v Gulliver*,[3] involving a transaction which would have fallen within s 175, where the House of Lords held that the breach could have been either prospectively or retrospectively approved by the shareholders, such approval ('authorisation') can now be given by the board. However, to the extent that any enactment, or more importantly any provision in the company's constitution requires shareholder consent, these remain applicable (s 180(1)). This will require a careful examination of the articles of association of pre-2006 companies to determine if, and to what extent, they require shareholder approval of transactions falling within ss 175 and 177. Equally, some companies, especially private companies, may find it appropriate to require shareholder approval rather than permit directors to authorise conflicts of interest; likewise in some group structures shareholder approval may be desirable rather than allowing boards of subsidiary companies to approve conflicts.

1   CA 2006, s 175(4). See para 4.4.
2   CA 2006, s 177. See paras 4.14 ff.
3   [1967] 2 AC 134n.

(i) Part 10, Chapter 4

4.24 Section 180(2) deals with the relationship between Chap 4 of the Act (transactions requiring approval of members) and the general duties. Transactions within Chap 4 and the general duties can overlap. Section 180(2) provides:

> '(2) The application of the general duties is not affected by the fact that the case also falls within Chapter 4 (transactions requiring approval members), except that where that Chapter applies and—
> (a)   approval is given under that Chapter, or
> (b)   the matter is one as to which it is provided that approval is not needed,
> it is not necessary also to comply with section 175 (duty to avoid conflicts of interest) or section 176 (duty not to accept benefits from third parties).'

Thus compliance with Chap 4, and it is important to note that this includes matters for which Chap 4 provides that approval is not needed, exempts the directors from having to comply with ss 175 or 176. The converse is not the case, s 180(3) provides that compliance with the general duties does not remove the need to seek approval of the shareholders under Chapter 4.

(ii) Authorisation

4.25 The general duties are also made subject to rules of law. Section 180(4)(a) provides that the general duties:

> '(a) have effect subject to any rule of law enabling the company to give authority, specifically or generally, for anything to be done (or omitted) by the directors, or any of them, that would otherwise be a breach of duty.'

This preserves the common law power of shareholders to authorise a transaction which is in breach of the general duties, see paras 5.48–5.56.

(iii) The Company's Constitution

4.26 Section 180(4)(b) deals with the relationship between the company's constitution and the general duties. It provides that:

'(b) where the company's articles contain provisions for dealing with conflicts of interest, [the general duties] are not infringed by anything done (or omitted) by the directors, or any of them, in accordance with those provisions.'

On one interpretation of s 180(4)(b) compliance with a company's constitutional provisions relating to conflict of interest results in all of the general duties not being infringed and not just the duties dealing with conflicts of interest (ss 175–177). Such an interpretation could release a director from the duty to promote the success of the company (s 172) and this cannot have been intended. Section 180(4)(b) must be restricted to the duties that it refers to, namely, the duties dealing with conflicts of interest (ie ss 175–177). The extent to which the articles may make provision is governed by s 232(4). It may be that public companies will limit themselves to providing for authorisation under s 175(4)(b) and for the holding of other offices and positions (so as to deal with multiple directorships) and otherwise deal with procedural matters arising such as the obligations of the conflicted director with regard to confidential information of the company (and of the other business or businesses) and his need to absent himself from meetings dealing with particular matters etc.[1]

[1]   See GC100 Guidance on Conflicts of Interest, see para 4.1.

(iv) Any Enactment or Rule of Law

4.27 Section 180(5) provides that 'otherwise, the general duties have effect (except as otherwise provided for or the context otherwise requires) notwithstanding any enactment or rule of law'.

An example of an enactment which qualifies the general duties is s 247 which empowers directors to make payment to a company's employees in connection with the cessation of a company's business. Section 247(2) provides that these powers can be exercised notwithstanding the general duty in s 172 (duty to promote the success of the company).

DUTIES ARE CUMULATIVE

4.28 CA 2006, s 179 provides that 'Except as otherwise provided, more than one of the general duties may apply in any given case'. Thus, if a director takes a bribe this would constitute breach of his duty not to accept benefits from a third party (s 176) and, depending on the circumstances, could constitute a failure to promote the success of the company (s 172), or evidence a failure to exercise independent judgment (s 173). However, as regards a duty to avoid conflicts of interest (s 175), this duty, as we have already seen,[1] does not arise in connection with a transaction or arrangement with the company. Such transactions would be caught by s 177 (declaration of interest in proposed transaction)[2] or s 182 (declaration of interest in existing transaction or arrangement). Within an evolving business relationship, it is easy to see that a director might from time to time be within s 175, s 177 or s 182.

DECLARATION OF INTEREST IN EXISTING TRANSACTIONS OR ARRANGEMENTS

4.29 CA 2006, s 177, duty to declare interests in proposed transactions or arrangements is supplemented by Pt 10, Chap 3, which deals with a duty to declare interests in existing transactions or arrangements.

4.30 CA 2006, s 187 applies the provisions of Chap 3 to shadow directors with some minor modifications reflecting the fact that shadow directors will not be members of the board of directors.

4.31 CA 2006, s 182 requires a director to disclose to the other directors an interest in an existing transaction and replaces s 317 of the CA 1985. Section 182 does not apply 'if or to the extent that the interest has been declared under s 177 (duty to declare interest in proposed transaction or arrangement)'.[1] The requirements of s 182 mirror those of s 177:[2]

(a)   A director must declare to the other directors the nature and extent of any direct or indirect interest he has in a transaction or arrangement with the company.[3] As with s 177, a director does not need to be a party to the transaction for a declaration to be required and where a director's spouse enters into a transaction this may create an indirect interest requiring the director to make a declaration of interest.[4]

(b)   there is no obligation to make a declaration where (i) the interest cannot reasonably be regarded as likely to give rise to a conflict of interest, (ii) the other directors know of it or as reasonable directors should have been aware of it, or (iii) it concerns the terms of the director's service contract that has been or is to be considered by the board or a committee of the board.[5] A declaration is also not required if the director is not aware of the transaction or his interest in it.[6]

(c)   the declaration must be made[7] (i) at a meeting of the directors, (ii) by notice in writing (in accordance with the requirements of s 184), or (iii) by general notice (in accordance with the requirements of s 185). The declaration must be made as soon as reasonably practicable but even if it is not made when it should have been it still must be made.[8] If any declaration proves to be or becomes inaccurate or incomplete, a further declaration must be made.[9]

1   CA 2006, s 182(1).
2   See commentary on s 177, para 4.14.
3   CA 2006, s 182(1).
4   See *Newgate Stud Co v Penfold* [2008] 1 BCLC 46.
5   CA 2006, s 182(6).
6   CA 2006, s 182(5).
7   CA 2006, s 182(2).
8   CA 2006, s 182(4).
9   CA 2006, s 182(3). See para 4.21 dealing with the same phrase in s 177(3).

4.32 Failure to comply with s 182 is a criminal offence punishable by way of a fine.[1] As with s 317 of the CA 1985, the consequences of breach of s 182 are purely criminal and its breach has no civil consequences.[2]

[1] CA 2006, s 183.
[2] See *Hely-Hutchinson v Brayhead Ltd* [1968] 1 QB 549; *Guinness plc v Saunders* [1990] 2 AC 663.

4.33 Where s 186 requires a declaration to be made by a 'sole director of a company that is required to have more than one director,'[1] the declaration must be recorded in writing. The making of the notice is deemed to form part of the next meeting of the directors after the notice is given[2] and s 248 (minutes of the meetings of directors) applies as if the declaration had been made at that meeting.[3] In the case of a company which is only required to have one director, no declaration is needed as there are no other directors to whom a declaration can be made.

[1] CA 2006, s 186(1)(a). This would apply to a public company or a private company the constitution of which requires more than one director (s 154).
[2] CA 2006, s 186(1)(b).
[3] CA 2006, s 186(1)(c).

4.34 CA 2006, s 186 does not affect anything in s 231. Section 231 applies where a company enters into a contract with its sole member who is also a director, or a shadow director, and the contract is not entered into in the ordinary course of the company's business. If the contract is not in writing it must be set out in a written memorandum or recorded in the minutes of the directors' meeting after the contract is entered into. The company is no longer subject to a fine but the officer of the company who is in default is so liable. The section applies to public as well as to private companies, which reflects the fact that it is now possible to incorporate a public company with one member (see s 7). The directors involved remain subject to their general duties (see s 231(7)).

CA 2006, PART 10, CHAPTER 4: SPECIFIC CONFLICTS OF INTEREST

Introduction

4.35 CA 2006, Pt 10, Chap 4, regulates certain types of transactions where the conflict of interests may be particularly acute, namely directors' service contracts, substantial property transactions, loan and similar financial transactions, and payments for loss of office.

The provisions apply to directors including shadow directors (s 223(1)). In many instances, the provisions extend also to transactions with connected persons, a category defined at length in CA 2006, ss 252–256. Essentially, the key categories of persons connected with a director are members of his family;[1] any body corporate with which he is connected;[2] trustees of any trust under which the director or his family or companies with which he is connected are beneficiaries; and any partner of the director or a partner of any person who by virtue of any of the other categories is connected with that director.

To a large extent, the provisions of Chap 4 reflect the long-established position on these transactions previously set out in the CA 1985, Pt X. However, the opportunity was taken in the CA 2006 to make a number of mainly technical changes to the provisions and to align them more closely (especially the civil remedies available for breach) to give greater consistency of approach. The criminal penalties previously imposed by the CA 1985, Pt X have been removed as the Government considered that the civil consequences of breach are sufficient.[3]

Such changes as have been made are a result, primarily, of a Law Commission review[4] of the CA 1985, Pt X. That review made a wide range of recommendations, many (but not all) of which were adopted by the Company Law Review and endorsed in general terms by the White Papers, *Modernising Company Law* and *Company Law Reform*.[5] The emphasis below is on highlighting the changes made by the CA 2006.

[1]   Defined in the CA 2006, s 253 and extended to include a director's parents, his children or step-children of whatever age (previously, the category was limited to minor children); any cohabiting partner and minor children of the cohabitant if they live with the director.

[2]   Defined in the CA 2006, s 254. Essentially, a director is connected with a body corporate if the director and persons connected with him together are interested in at least 20 per cent of the equity share capital of that company or are entitled to exercise or control the exercise of more than 20 per cent of the voting power at any general meeting. See also s 255.

[3]   See 678 HL Official Report (5th series) col GC359 (9 February 2006).

[4]   See Law Commission, *Company Directors: Regulating Conflicts of Interests and Formulating a Statement of Duties* (1999) Law Com No 261, especially Part 8 (hereinafter 'Law Commission Report'); also Law Commission, *Company Directors: Regulating Conflicts of Interests and Formulating a Statement of Duties: A Joint Consultation Paper* (1998) No 153.

[5]   See *Modernising Company Law* (2002) Cm 5553–I, paras 3.19–3.20; *Company Law Reform* (2005) Cm 6456, para 3.3. See also Company Law Review, *Developing the Framework* (2000), paras 3.86–3.89 and Annex C where these provisions are considered in detail. There is further limited discussion of these matters in *Completing the Structure* (2000), paras 4.8–4.21; and the *Final Report* (2001), paras 6.8–6.14.

Overview

4.36 The overall scheme adopted in the CA 2006, Pt 10, Ch 4 is that, for each class of conflicted transaction (ie directors' service contracts, substantial property transactions, loan and similar financial transactions, and payments for loss of office), shareholder approval is required by an ordinary resolution unless the articles specify a higher majority.[1] The directors involved remain subject to their general duties, but where the transaction is approved or exempt from approval under Pt 10, Ch 4, there is no need to comply with ss 175 (see para 4.1) and 176 (see para 4.10) (s 180(2)).

Shareholder approval is not required in respect of these transactions where the company is not a UK-registered company[2] or where the company is a wholly-owned subsidiary of another body corporate.[3]

Where approval is by way of a written resolution, a memorandum setting out particulars of the proposed transaction/payments etc must be circulated to the members eligible to vote on the resolution at or before the time at which the proposed resolution is sent to the members.[4] An accidental failure to send a memorandum to one or more members is disregarded for the purposes of determining whether this requirement has been met, subject to any provision to the contrary effect in the company's articles.[5] The one exception to this requirement for a memorandum is in respect of substantial property transactions, though such transactions would appear to be exactly the type of transactions where shareholders would value additional transparency.

Where approval is by way of a resolution at a meeting, a like memorandum must be made available for inspection by the members for not less than 15 days before the meeting and at the meeting itself.[6]

Where a transaction which falls within more than one provision (for example a director may obtain a loan from the company and enter into a substantial property transaction at the same time), the requirements of each applicable provision must be met. This should not prove a problem in practice since the provisions are relatively uniform in their approach and it is not necessary to pass a separate resolution for the purposes of each provision.[7]

[1]   References to a resolution (as in the CA 2006, s 188, payments for loss of office, for example) are to an ordinary resolution: s 281(3). The ability to approve these transactions by ordinary resolution is restricted for charitable companies, see s 226, also 686 HL Official Report (5th series) col 440 (2 November 2006).

[2]   Defined s 1158; the effect is to exclude companies not formed and registered under the CA 2006 or its predecessors.

[3]   CA 2006, ss 188(6), 190(4), 197(5), 200(6), 201(6), 217(4), 218(4), 219(6).

[4]   CA 2006, ss 188(5), 197(3), 198(4), 200(4), 203(3), 217(3), 218(3), 219(3).

[5]   CA 2006, s 224; this provision was added for the avoidance of doubt on this matter, but it does seem generously worded. 681 HL Official Report (5th series) col 872, (9 May 2006).

[6]   CA 2006, ss 188(5)(b), 197(3)(b), 198(4)(b), 200(4)(b), 203(3)(b), 217(3)(b), 218(3)(b), 219(3)(b).

[7]   CA 2006, s 225. 678 HL Official Report (5th series) col GC360 (9 February 2006).

DIRECTORS' LONG-TERM SERVICE CONTRACTS: CA 2006, SS 188–189

4.37 The length of directors' service contracts, particularly in public companies, has been controversial because of the level of compensation payable in the event of termination of the contract.

CA 2006, s 188 requires shareholder approval[1] of any provision under which the guaranteed term of a director's employment[2] with the company, or where he is a director of a holding company, within the group consisting of that company and its subsidiaries, is, or may be, longer than two years (reduced from five years under the CA 1985).[3] The Law Commission and the Company Law Review had recommended that the period of five years be reduced.[4]

The guaranteed term of employment, for these purposes, is the period during which the director is employed and the contract cannot be determined by the company by notice or it can be so terminated only in specified circumstances (s 188(3)). A provision included without the approval of the members is void and the contract is deemed to contain a term entitling the company to terminate the contract at any time by the giving of reasonable notice (s 189).

Directors' service contracts are defined in s 227 as including contracts of service, contracts for services *and,* for the first time, letters of appointment as directors (commonly used for non-executive appointments).[5]

'**CA 2006, s 227 Directors' service contracts**
(1) For the purposes of this Part a director's "service contract", in relation to a company, means a contract under which—
    (a) a director of the company undertakes personally to perform services (as director or otherwise) for the company, or for a subsidiary of the company, or
    (b) services (as director or otherwise) that a director of the company undertakes personally to perform are made available by a third party to the company, or to a subsidiary of the company.
(2) The provisions of this Part relating to directors' service contracts apply to the terms of a person's appointment as a director of a company.
  They are not restricted to contracts for the performance of services outside the scope of the ordinary duties of a director.'

The scope of the section was explained by Lord Sainsbury in the Parliamentary debates in the following terms:[6]

'Subsection (1)(a) covers contracts of service such as any employment contract that the director may hold with a company or a subsidiary of the company of which he is director, for example, as executive director, or any contract for services that he personally undertakes to perform as such.

Subsection (1)(b) covers the case where those services are made available to the company through a third party such as a personal services company. In either case, the contract must require the director personally to perform the service or services in question.

Subsection (2) brings within the definition of a service contract letters of appointment to the office of director. Many directors will have no contract of service or for services with the company. The second sentence of subsection (2) ensures that the definition of "service contracts" includes arrangements under which the director performs duties within the scope of the ordinary duties of the director, as well as contracts to perform duties outside the scope of the ordinary duties of the director. Without that, the term "service contract" might be interpreted as applying only to the latter type of contract.'

Details of service contracts (as now defined in s 227) must be available for inspection by any member at the company's registered office or other specified place.[7]

---

[1] Informal unanimous consent also suffices: *Wright v Atlas Wright (Europe) Ltd* [1999] 2 BCLC 301, CA.

[2] 'Employment' is defined as including any employment under a director's service contract which is then broadly defined in s 227.

[3] CA 2006, s 188(1); the reduction from five years to two years was on the initiative of the Opposition, see 678 HL Official Report (5th series) col GC344 (9 February 2006); 681 HL Official Report (5th series), col 869 (9 May 2006). The aggregation of periods in certain circumstances is provided for so that the provision cannot be avoided by a string of

contracts: s 188(4). The Law Commission's recommendation that the provision be extended to include rolling contracts because they are used as a device to circumvent the statutory policy was not accepted by the Government: see Law Commission Report, paras 9.31–9.33. For listed companies, the Combined Code on Corporate Governance recommends that notice or contract periods should be set at one year or less (Code Provisions, B.1.6).

4   See Company Law Review, *Developing the Framework* (2000), Annex C, para 24. As before, rolling contracts, where the contract is novated daily so that on any day there is always a two-year period of notice to run, remain an option. The Company Law Review took the position that such rolling contracts are consistent with the policy objective of limiting the maximum period of notice in respect of which the director can receive compensation on termination: see Company Law Review, *Developing the Framework* (2000), paras 3.86–3.89 and Annex C.

5   For the first time the definition covers the terms under which the director is appointed to that office alone, see 678 HL Official Report (5th series) cols GC361–362 (9 February 2006); and Law Commission Report, paras 9.9–9.11.

6   678 HL Official Report (5th series) cols GC361–362 (9 February 2006).

7   CA 2006, s 228; see The Companies (Company Records) Regulations 2008, SI 2008/3006; members have rights to inspect and to take copies of any service contract: s 229; these disclosure requirements extend to shadow directors: s 230. The previous exclusions from disclosure for contracts of directors working outside the UK (CA 1985, s 318(5)) and for contracts with less than 12 months to run (CA 1985, s 318(11)) have been repealed.

PAYMENTS FOR LOSS OF OFFICE: CA 2006, SS 215–221

4.38 A company may not make a payment for loss of office (or on retirement) to a director of the company or to a director of its holding company unless the payment has been approved by a resolution of the members of the company and, if necessary, of the holding company (s 217).[1]

Similar provisions apply: (i) where a payment is made in connection with the transfer of the whole or any part of the undertaking or property of the company (s 218); and (ii) where a payment is made in connection with a transfer of shares in the company, or in a subsidiary of the company, resulting from a takeover bid (s 219).

The scope of these provisions has been expanded considerably from that in the CA 1985, ss 312–316 with an emphasis on anti-avoidance provisions. The starting point is that the definition of 'payments for loss of office' has been expanded.

'CA 2006, s 215 **Payments for loss of office**
(1)   In this Chapter a "payment for loss of office" means a payment made to a director or past director of a company—
　　(a)   by way of compensation for loss of office as director of the company,
　　(b)   by way of compensation for loss, while director of the company or in connection with his ceasing to be a director of it, of—
　　　　(i)   any other office or employment in connection with the management of the affairs of the company, or
　　　　(ii)   any office (as director or otherwise) or employment in connection with the management of the affairs of any subsidiary undertaking of the company,
　　(c)   as consideration for or in connection with his retirement from his office as director of the company, or

      (d)   as consideration for or in connection with his retirement, while director of the company or in connection with his ceasing to be a director of it, from—

         (i)   any other office or employment in connection with the management of the affairs of the company, or

        (ii)   any office (as director or otherwise) or employment in connection with the management of the affairs of any subsidiary undertaking of the company.

(2)   The references to compensation and consideration include benefits otherwise than in cash and references in this Chapter to payment have a corresponding meaning.

(3)   For the purposes of sections 217 to 221 (payments requiring members' approval)—

      (a)   payment to a person connected with a director, or

      (b)   payment to any person at the direction of, or for the benefit of, a director or a person connected with him, is treated as payment to the director.

(4)   References in those sections to payment by a person include payment by another person at the direction of, or on behalf of, the person referred to.'

---

[1]   The director does not have to be a director at the time of the payment, he may well have left office by the time of the payment, the focus is the reason for payment: 678 HL Official Report (5th series) col GC356 (9 February 2006).

Definitions

4.39 The definition of 'payment for loss of office' now includes:

- payments for loss of any office in connection with the management of the company's affairs, rather than merely loss of the office of director as such; the Law Commission had particularly recommended this change in order to close this gap in the previous provision which had been identified by the Privy Council in *Taupo Totara Timber Co Ltd v Rowe*[1] (interpreting the equivalent New Zealand section);
- payments and benefits in cash and in kind (s 215(2));
- payments by persons at the direction of the company (s 215(3));
- payments to connected persons and to other persons at the direction of the director or connected person (s 215(3)); the Law Commission took the view that the provision should not be extended to connected persons, but the Company Law Review disagreed on the basis that other provisions of this Part of the CA 2006 apply to connected persons and therefore this loophole should also be closed;[2]
- payments to directors of holding companies; the Law Commission had recommended this change to reflect the reality that many companies are today organised in groups and to prevent avoidance.[3]

CA 2006, s 219 is a modified version of requirements previously set out in the CA 1985, ss 314, 315. Section 219 provides that no payment for loss of office (as defined in s 215, above) may be made by any person to a director of a company in connection with a transfer of shares in the company, or in a subsidiary of the company, resulting from a takeover bid unless the payment has been approved by a resolution of the holders of the shares to which the bid relates and any holders of shares of the same class as any of those shares.[4] Given that shareholder approval of any payment is now required by s 219, the

CA 2006 does not retain the requirement under the CA 1985, s 314, for a director to take all reasonable steps to secure that details of the proposed payments be sent to shareholders. Giving effect to a recommendation of the Law Commission, neither the person making the offer, nor any associate of his (as defined in s 988), is entitled to vote on the resolution (s 219(4)).[5] There is a presumption in s 219(7) (carried over from the CA 1985) that a payment made in pursuance of an arrangement: (a) entered into as part of the agreement for the transfer in question, or within one year before or two years after that agreement, and (b) to which the company whose shares are the subject of the bid, or any person to whom the transfer is made, is privy, is presumed, except in so far as the contrary is shown, to be a payment to which s 219 applies.

[1]   [1978] AC 537, [1977] 3 All ER 123. See Law Commission Report, paras 7.38–7.48.
[2]   See the Company Law Review, *Developing the Framework* (2000), Annex C, para 5.
[3]   See Law Commission Report, paras 7.68–7.71.
[4]   The purpose of the provision is to avoid the risk that directors may obtain advantageous payments from persons launching a takeover bid which should in fact go to the members in return for their shares: see comments by Lord Sainsbury, 678 HL Official Report (5th series) col GC358 (9 February 2006).
[5]   See Law Commission Report, paras 7.60–7.65.

Exceptions

4.40   There are a number of exceptions set out in s 220 when approval is not required:

'CA 2006, s 220 Exception for payments in discharge of legal obligations etc
(1)   Approval is not required under section 217, 218 or 219 (payments requiring members' approval) for a payment made in good faith—
   (a)   in discharge of an existing legal obligation (as defined below),
   (b)   by way of damages for breach of such an obligation,
   (c)   by way of settlement or compromise of any claim arising in connection with the termination of a person's office or employment, or
   (d)   by way of pension in respect of past services.
(2)   In relation to a payment within section 217 (payment by company) an existing legal obligation means an obligation of the company, or any body corporate associated with it, that was not entered into in connection with, or in consequence of, the event giving rise to the payment for loss of office.
(3)   In relation to a payment within section 218 or 219 (payment in connection with transfer of undertaking, property or shares) an existing legal obligation means an obligation of the person making the payment that was not entered into for the purposes of, in connection with or in consequence of, the transfer in question.
(4)   In the case of a payment within both section 217 and section 218, or within both section 217 and section 219, subsection (2) above applies and not subsection (3).
(5)   A payment part of which falls within subsection (1) above and part of which does not is treated as if the parts were separate payments.'[1]

The exemption in s 220(1)(a) (new in the CA 2006) gives statutory effect to the interpretation of the previous provision adopted by the Privy Council in *Taupo Totara Timber Co Ltd v Rowe*[2] (interpreting the equivalent New Zealand provision). The Law Commission had recommended that, as that decision was likely to be followed, the statutory provision should be amended to make the position clear.[3] This exemption has also been expanded to allow payments to be made by associated companies (see sub-s (2) above) so a subsidiary may make a payment to a director in respect of a legal obligation of its holding company.[4] That subsection also clarifies that the 'existing legal obligation' must arise independently (for example, from a contract of employment) of the event giving rise to the payment for loss of office. It will not suffice if as part of the event giving rise to the loss of office, a legal obligation is entered into to pay compensation.

[1]   There is also an irrelevant exception for small payments which do not exceed £200 in CA 2006, s 221.
[2]   [1978] AC 537, [1977] 3 All ER 123.
[3]   Law Commission Report, paras 7.6–7.16.
[4]   See 678 HL Official Report (5th series) col GC350 (9 February 2006).

Civil consequences

4.41 The civil consequences of breach of these provisions is clarified so that if a payment is made in contravention of the requirement for member approval, the payment is held by the recipient on trust for the company making the payment and any director who authorised the payment is jointly and severally liable to indemnify the company that made the payment for any loss resulting from it.[1]

[1]   CA 2006, s 222(1); s 222(2)–(5) set out the permutations where more than one requirement is breached. In particular, the claims of the offeree shareholders under s 219 have priority over those of the company under s 217.

SUBSTANTIAL PROPERTY TRANSACTIONS: CA 2006, SS 190–196

4.42 Substantial property transactions are governed by the CA 2006, s 190 which provides that, subject to certain exceptions, a company may not enter into an arrangement under which:

'(a) a director of the company or its holding company, or a person connected with such a director,[1] acquires or is to acquire from the company (directly or indirectly) a substantial non-cash asset; or

(b) the company acquires or is to acquire a substantial non-cash asset (directly or indirectly) from such a director or a person so connected;

   unless the arrangement has been approved by a resolution of the members of the company or is conditional on such approval being obtained.'

[1]   Defined in the CA 2006, s 252.

Shareholder approval

4.43 The possibility of entering into conditional arrangements is new and follows a Law Commission recommendation that companies should have the commercial freedom and flexibility to enter into such arrangements.[1] If the transaction is conditional on approval which is not secured, the company is not subject to any liability by reason of the failure to obtain the approval required by this provision (s 190(3)).

For the avoidance of doubt, s 190(6) makes clear that approval is not required in respect of a transaction so far as it relates to anything to which a director of the company is entitled under his service contract (as defined in s 227, see para 4.37 above) or to payments for loss of office (as defined in s 215, see para 4.38 above).[2]

The consequences of contravening s 190 are set out in detail in s 195 and there are no substantive changes from the position under the CA 1985, s 322.

Approval is required only if the value of the non-cash asset[3] at the time the arrangement is entered into exceeds 10 per cent of the company's net asset value and is more than £5,000 (previously £2,000: CA 1985), or exceeds £100,000 (s 191).

If approval is not obtained, it is still possible for the shareholders of the company (and if necessary of the holding company) to affirm the arrangement within a reasonable period (s 196). Informal unanimous assent also suffices.[4]

1   See the Law Commission Report, paras 10.8–10.10.
2   See the Law Commission Report, paras 10.11–10.13.
3   'Non-cash asset' is defined in the CA 2006, s 1163 (unchanged from the CA 1985, s 739). A new anti-avoidance provision requires assets and transactions to be aggregated: see CA 2006, s 190(5).
4   See *NBH Ltd v Hoare* [2006] 2 BCLC 649.

Approval not required

4.44 Approval is not required for a transaction between a company and a person in his character as a member of the company (s 192(a)), whether the acquisition is by or from a member. This is a change from the position under the CA 1985, s 321(3), when the exemption only applied where a member acquired an asset *from* the company.

Approval is not required in the case of transactions between a holding company and its wholly-owned subsidiary, or between two wholly-owned subsidiaries of the same holding company (s 192(b)). There is also an exemption for transactions on a recognised investment exchange (s 194).

Approval is not required for an arrangement entered into by a company which is being wound up (unless it is a members' voluntary winding up) or is in administration as s 193 makes clear:[1]

> '(1) This section applies to a company—
>> (a) that is being wound up (unless the winding up is a members' voluntary winding up), or
>> (b) that is in administration within the meaning of Schedule B1 to the Insolvency Act 1986 (c. 45) or the Insolvency (Northern Ireland) Order 1989 (S.I. 1989/2405 (N.I. 19)).

(2) Approval is not required under section 190 (requirement of members' approval for substantial property transactions)—
  (a) on the part of the members of a company to which this section applies, or
  (b) for an arrangement entered into by a company to which this section applies.'

The first limb of the provision (s 193(2)(a)) means that the approval of members of a holding company which is being wound up or is in administration is not needed with respect to transactions between a company and a director of the holding company. Secondly, the provision clarifies that a liquidator or administrator is not required by s 190 to obtain the approval of the members when the company enters into such an arrangement with a director etc. The intention being to ensure that the liquidator or administrator is not hampered in the execution of his duties when the directors may be the only purchasers of the assets. This flexibility has facilitated the use of pre-pack administrations whereby a pre-packaged sale of the business is agreed immediately before the company enters administration and the sale is then executed immediately on the company going into administration.

[1]   See 681 HL Official Report (5th series), col 870 (9 May 2006). The exemption was not extended to receivers or administrative receivers apparently for fear of abuse of the provision. See HC Official Report, SC D (Company Law Reform Bill), 11 July 2006, col 632.

LOANS, QUASI-LOANS AND CREDIT TRANSACTIONS: CA 2006, SS 197–214

4.45 Loans to directors are governed by the CA 2006, s 197 which provides that:

'(1) A company may not—
  (a) make a loan to a director of the company or of its holding company, or
  (b) give a guarantee or provide security in connection with a loan made by any person to such a director, unless the transaction has been approved by a resolution of the members of the company.'[1]

This section significantly alters the position from that which applied under the CA 1985. A major change is that the criminal penalties which attached to breaches by public companies or companies associated with public companies under the CA 1985 have been abolished. The civil consequences of contravening these loan etc provisions are set out in detail in s 213 and there is no substantive change from the position under the CA 1985.

[1]   Director includes shadow directors: s 222(1)(c). Loans to directors of subsidiary companies are not affected provided that the director is not also a director of the holding company.

Shareholder approval

4.46 The Companies Act 1985 prohibited loans to directors and to connected persons. Now loans are permissible with the approval of the members (sometimes the approval of members of the holding company is also required).

This change may have a significant impact (and some potential for abuse) in private companies where the members and the directors are the same people, but directors remain subject to the fiduciary duties set out in the CA 2006, Pt 10, Chap 2.

Another significant change is that if approval is not obtained, it is still possible for the shareholders of the company (and if necessary of the holding company) to affirm the arrangement within a reasonable period (s 214), but that merely means that the transaction cannot be avoided, and affirmation has no effect on the liability of those involved to account for any gain made and to indemnify the company against any loss, see s 213(3).

For public companies and companies associated with a public company (associated company is a new term[1] defined in s 256), the requirement for shareholder approval extends to quasi-loans (defined in s 199(1)) and credit transactions (defined in s 202) and guarantees and the provision of security for a director of a company or a director of its holding company or a person connected with such a director. This is a major change from the position under the CA 1985 which prohibited such transactions.

As before, and in order to reduce the possibility of transactions being constructed in a way which circumvents the requirements for approval, a variety of anti-avoidance provisions are included dealing with back-to-back transactions and the assignment and assumption by the company of rights and obligations which if entered into directly by the company would require shareholder approval. Such arrangements are no longer prohibited but are subject to a requirement of shareholder approval (s 203(1)).

[1]   The term 'associated company' (defined CA 2006, s 256(b)) is a substitute for the more complex definition of a relevant company in CA 1985, s 331. A holding company is associated with all its subsidiaries and a subsidiary is associated with its holding company and all the other subsidiary companies of its holding company: see Explanatory Notes to s 256.

Exemptions

4.47   There are a variety of exemptions when approval by the members is not required and generally the CA 2006 has relaxed the exemptions and in some cases modified their application so, for example, to extend them to directors of holding companies and to connected persons.

(i)   *Expenditure incurred on company business*
Approval is not required for anything done by a company to provide a director of the company and (now extended to) a director of the company's holding company or a person connected with any such director[1] with funds to meet expenditure incurred or to be incurred by him for the purposes of the company or for the purpose of enabling him properly to perform his duties as an officer of the company, or to enable any such person to avoid incurring such expenditure (s 204). In this case, the aggregate value of the transactions must not exceed £50,000 (previously £20,000). This exemption has been significantly modified

and is now much more generous than was the case under the CA 1985. There is no requirement for prior approval of the shareholders, no requirement for the disclosure of details of the funding, the threshold has been significantly raised and the provision has been extended to directors of the holding company and to connected persons.

(ii) *Expenditure on defending proceedings or regulatory action or investigation*

Approval is not required for anything done by a company to provide a director of the company or of its holding company with funds to meet expenditure incurred or to be incurred by him in defending any criminal or civil proceedings in connection with any alleged negligence, default, breach of duty or breach of trust by him in relation to the company or an associated company (defined s 256(b)) or in connection with an application for relief or to enable any director to avoid incurring such expenditure. This exemption has been narrowed from the equivalent provision in the CA 1985, s 337A which applied to expenditure incurred in defending 'any criminal or civil proceedings'. The terms of the loan must provide for the loan to be repaid, or any liability of the company incurred in connection with any such loan to be discharged, in the event that the director is convicted in the proceedings or judgment is given against him (s 205(2)).

A new provision, added for the avoidance of doubt,[2] is an exception from the need for approval for anything done by the company for a director to meet expenditure incurred, or to be incurred, in defending himself in an investigation by a regulatory authority, or against action proposed be taken by a regulatory authority, in relation to any breach of duty by him in relation to the company or an associated company (defined s 256(b)) or to enable any director to avoid incurring such expenditure (s 206). In this instance, there is no requirement that the loan be repaid.

(iii) *Small amounts*

A company may make a loan or quasi-loan to or give a guarantee or provide security (whether to/for a director of the company or of a holding company or even a connected person) provided the aggregate of the relevant amounts does not exceed £10,000, previously £5,000 (s 207(1)). Approval is not required for credit transactions where the aggregate value does not exceed £15,000, previously £10,000 (s 207(2)). There is also an exemption for credit transactions if the company enters into the transaction in the ordinary course of its business and the value of the transaction is not greater and the terms are no more favourable than those which it is reasonable to expect the company to have offered to a person of the same financial standing but who is unconnected with the company (s 207(3)).

(iv) *Loans to associated companies*

Approval is not required for loans or quasi-loans to, or credit transactions for, an associated body corporate (defined s 256(a)) or the giving of a guarantee or provision of security in connection with a loan or quasi-loan to an associated body corporate (s 208). The definition of

associated body corporate means that this exemption has been extended in scope to allow in essence for any transactions within a group.
(v)   *Moneylending companies*
A company which is a moneylending company may make a loan or quasi-loan to any person provided the loan is made in the ordinary course of the company's business and the amount of the loan is not greater than, and the terms are not more favourable than that or those which it is reasonable to expect the company to have offered to a person of the same financial standing but unconnected with the company (s 209). There is no monetary limit (previously £100,000).

A moneylending company may also make a loan to a director or a director of its holding company or any of its employees[3] to enable such a person to purchase their only or main residence, to improve their dwelling house, or in substitution for a loan provided by a third party for any of those purposes, provided that loans of that type are ordinarily made by the company to its employees on terms no less favourable (s 208(3), (4)).

[1]   While the statute has been modified to permit funding to a connected person, it may be difficult in practice to justify such funding.
[2]   In the Government's opinion such expenditure is included within the exemption for defence expenditure in the CA 2006, s 205, but this provision was included for the avoidance of doubt: 678 HL Official Report (5th series) cols GC351–352,(9 February 2006); 681 HL Official Report (5th series) col 871 (9 May 2006).
[3]   Employees were added to this exemption to allow directors to take advantage of an employee home loan scheme operated by moneylending companies and to ensure that connected persons are able to take advantage of such schemes as long as they are employees of the company making the loan: see 678 HL Official Report (5th series) col GC353 (9 February 2006).

DIRECTORS' LIABILITY, INSURANCE AND INDEMNITY PROVISIONS

4.48   Section 232 restates the position on indemnity and insurance provision with limited modifications.

'**CA 2006, s 232   Provisions protecting directors from liability**
(1)   Any provision that purports to exempt a director of a company (to any extent) from any liability that would otherwise attach to him in connection with any negligence, default, breach of duty or breach of trust in relation to the company is void.
(2)   Any provision by which a company directly or indirectly provides an indemnity (to any extent) for a director of the company, or of an associated company, against any liability attaching to him in connection with any negligence, default, breach of duty or breach of trust in relation to the company of which he is a director is void, except as permitted by—
     (a)   section 233 (provision of insurance),
     (b)   section 234 (qualifying third party indemnity provision), or
     (c)   section 235 (qualifying pension scheme indemnity provision).
(3)   This section applies to any provision, whether contained in a company's articles or in any contract with the company or otherwise.
(4)   Nothing in this section prevents a company's articles from making such provision as has previously been lawful for dealing with conflicts of interest.'

The main change in the CA 2006 is to include provision for qualifying pension scheme indemnity provisions within the exceptions in sub-s (2). Otherwise no changes are made to the provisions relating to qualifying third party indemnity provisions which were introduced by the Companies (Audit, Investigations and Community Enterprise) Act 2004. That Act provided for four main possible exceptions to indemnification: criminal penalties; penalties imposed by regulatory bodies; costs incurred by a director in defending criminal proceedings in which he is convicted; and costs incurred by a director in defending civil proceedings brought by the company in which final judgement is given against him.

The extension in s 235 to allow for pension scheme indemnities was justified on the basis that there were concerns that directors were inhibited from acting as trustees of occupational pension schemes because they were beyond the scope of the previous law. Given that such directors perform a vital role, as the Government acknowledged,[1] it is appropriate to allow for pension scheme indemnities. All qualifying indemnity provisions must be disclosed in the directors' report and a copy must be available for inspection.[2] A broadly worded indemnity provision is included in the model articles.[3]

[1]   See HC Official Report, SC D (Company Law Reform Bill), 11 July 2006, col 636.
[2]   CA 2006, ss 236–237; the Companies (Company Records) Regulations 2008, SI 2008/3006.
[3]   See the Companies (Model Articles) Regulations 2008, SI 2008/3229, reg 2, Sch 1, Art 52 (Ltd); reg 4, Sch 3, Art 85 (Plc).

RATIFICATION OF ACTS OF DIRECTORS

4.49 An important provision to note is s 239 which makes significant changes to the ratification of conduct of a director amounting to negligence, default, breach of duty or breach of trust in relation to the company.

'CA 2006, s 239 **Ratification of acts of directors**
(1)   This section applies to the ratification by a company of conduct by a director amounting to negligence, default, breach of duty or breach of trust in relation to the company.
(2)   The decision of the company to ratify such conduct must be made by resolution of the members of the company.
(3)   Where the resolution is proposed as a written resolution neither the director (if a member of the company) nor any member connected with him is an eligible member.
(4)   Where the resolution is proposed at a meeting, it is passed only if the necessary majority is obtained disregarding votes in favour of the resolution by the director (if a member of the company) and any member connected with him.
   This does not prevent the director or any such member from attending, being counted towards the quorum and taking part in the proceedings at any meeting at which the decision is considered.

(5)   For the purposes of this section—
   (a)   "conduct" includes acts and omissions;
   (b)   "director" includes a former director;
   (c)   a shadow director is treated as a director; and

(d)   in section 252 (meaning of "connected person"), subsection (3) does not apply (exclusion of person who is himself a director).

(6)   Nothing in this section affects—

(a)   the validity of a decision taken by unanimous consent of the members of the company, or

(b)   any power of the directors to agree not to sue, or to settle or release a claim made by them on behalf of the company.

(7)   This section does not affect any other enactment or rule of law imposing additional requirements for valid ratification or any rule of law as to acts that are incapable of being ratified by the company.'

The major change is in sub-ss (2) and (3) which for the first time limit the ability of a director, if a member of the company, to vote to ratify his own wrongdoing.[1] The director may attend any meeting and take part in the proceedings and count towards the quorum, but his votes and the votes of any member connected with him (defined in s 252, subject to s 239(5)(d) above)) must be disregarded. In earlier versions of the Bill, the intention was to exclude the votes of all members with a direct or indirect interest but, following concerns that this would be difficult to apply, the provision was restated and limited to the director and any member connected with him. The definition of connected persons in s 252 should operate to identify those votes which must be disregarded in any given situation.

The restriction here applies only to ratification of the director's breach of duty (ie to a resolution condoning his conduct, see s 239(2)), it does not apply to a resolution (also sometimes called ratification) affirming or authorising the transaction which has been rendered voidable or void by the breach of duty so there is no restriction on the director and connected persons as shareholders voting on such a resolution.

It is important to note that subsection 6 preserves the *Duomatic* principle[2] (so a director and a member connected with him may be counted in the voting for those purposes) and also the ability of the board to abandon or compromise a claim,[3] subject always to the obligations of the directors to observe the general duties as set out in the CA 2006, Pt 10, Chap 2.

Subsection 7 preserves the common law on ratification; the changes effected by the section are limited to restricting in some circumstances the voting rights of a member who is a director.

[1]   A line of authorities from *North West Transportation Co Ltd v Beatty* (1887) 12 App Cas 589 onwards has established that a shareholder is free to vote as he chooses.

[2]   *Re Duomatic Ltd* [1969] 2 Ch 365.

[3]   See *Smith v Croft (No 2)* [1987] 3 All ER 909.

Chapter 5

THE DERIVATIVE CLAIM – AN INVITATION TO LITIGATE?

Brenda Hannigan

INTRODUCTION

5.1 The Companies Act 2006 ('CA 2006'), Pt 11, sets out the procedure for a derivative claim, ie a claim by a member in respect of a cause of action vested in the company where the member seeks relief on behalf of the company.[1] Part 11 came into effect on 1 October 2007.[2]

[1] The Parliamentary Debates on the CA 2006, Pt 11 can be found at: 679 HL Official Report (5th series) cols GC1–34 (27 February 2006); 681 HL Official Report (5th series) cols 883–891 (9 May 2006); HC Official Report, SC D (Company Law Reform Bill), 13 July 2006, cols 653–681.

[2] See the Companies Act 2006 (Commencement No 3, Consequential Amendments, Transitional Provisions and Savings) Order 2007, SI 2007/2194, Art 2(e); note the transitional arrangements in Art 9, Sch 3, para 20; if or to the extent that, the claim arises from acts or omissions that occurred before 1 October 2007, the court must exercise its powers so as to secure that the claim is allowed to proceed as a derivative claim only if, or to the extent that, it would have been allowed to proceed as a derivative claim under the law in force immediately before that date: Sch 3, para 20(3). This provision is included because the statutory procedure allows for a claim based on negligence, though such a claim could not have been brought at common law. A director is protected therefore against a claim under the new procedure in respect of alleged negligence before 1 October 2007.

5.2 At common law shareholders' remedies are dominated by the rule in *Foss v Harbottle*[1] which has two elements: first, the proper plaintiff in respect of a wrong allegedly done to a company is prima facie the company; second, where the alleged wrong is a transaction which might be made binding on the company by a simple majority of the members, no individual member of the company is allowed to maintain an action in respect of that matter.[2]

[1] (1843) 2 Hare 461.

2   *Prudential Assurance Co Ltd v Newman Industries Ltd (No 2)* [1982] 1 All ER 354, CA;
     and see *Edwards v Halliwell* [1950] 2 All ER 1064 at 1066, per Jenkins LJ. The rule in
     Foss v Harbottle does not preclude a shareholder bringing a personal action to remedy
     wrongs to a member's substantive rights, see *Pender v Lushington* (1877) 6 Ch D 70; or to
     restrain proposed *ultra vires* or illegal acts: *Smith v Croft (No 2)* [1987] 3 All ER 909 at
     914.

5.3 Where the wrong is committed by those in control of the company,
however, it is inappropriate that the (first element of) the rule should prevent
the company bringing an action in respect of that wrongdoing. Hence the
development of an exception to the rule whereby, in limited circumstances
(consistent with respect for the second element of the rule), a shareholder
might sue derivatively, ie on behalf of the company, in respect of that wrong
and in order to obtain redress for the company. The development of the
derivative claim was explained as follows in *Burland v Earle*:[1]

> '... [it] is mere matter of procedure in order to give a remedy for a wrong which
> would otherwise escape redress, and it is obvious that in such an action the
> plaintiffs cannot have a larger right to relief than the company itself would have
> if it were plaintiff, and cannot complain of acts which are valid if done with the
> approval of the majority of the shareholders, or are capable of being confirmed
> by the majority. The cases in which the minority can maintain such an action
> are, therefore, confined to those in which the acts complained of are of a
> fraudulent character or beyond the powers of the company. A familiar example
> is where the majority are endeavouring directly or indirectly to appropriate to
> themselves money, property, or advantages which belong to the company, or in
> which the other shareholders are entitled to participate, as was alleged in the
> case of *Menier v Hooper's Telegraph Works*.[2] It should be added that no mere
> informality or irregularity which can be remedied by the majority will entitle
> the minority to sue, if the act when done regularly would be within the powers
> of the company and the intention of the majority of the shareholders is clear.
> This may be illustrated by the judgment of Mellish L.J. in *MacDougall v
> Gardiner*.[3]'

1   [1902] AC 83 at 93–94, per Lord Davey.
2   (1874) 9 Ch App 350.
3   (1875) 1 Ch D 13.

5.4 As a preliminary matter, the court required the claimant in a derivative
claim to establish a prima facie case that the company was entitled to the relief
claimed and that the action fell within the proper boundaries of the exception
to the rule in *Foss v Harbottle* as identified above, namely:

(1)   that the wrong was an unratifiable wrong not capable of 'cure' by the
      majority; and
(2)   that wrongdoer control of the company prevented the company itself
      bringing an action in its own name.[1] Even when a prima facie case
      existed, the court would not permit a derivative action to proceed
      where the majority of the shareholders who were independent of the
      wrongdoers, for disinterested reasons, did not wish the proceedings to
      continue.[2]

Unsurprisingly, derivative claims were rare.

1   *Prudential Assurance Co Ltd v Newman Industries Ltd (No 2)* [1982] 1 All ER 354 at 366; *Smith v Croft (No 2)* [1987] 3 All ER 909 at 945.
2   *Smith v Croft (No 2)* [1987] 3 All ER 909.

THE BACKGROUND TO PART 11

5.5 The derivative claim provided in the CA 2006, Pt 11, originated from a review of shareholders' remedies carried out by the Law Commission in 1997 which recommended replacing the common law action with a statutory derivative procedure with more modern, flexible and accessible criteria for determining whether a shareholder may bring a claim.[1] In the Commission's view, a statutory procedure would give greater transparency to the requirements for a claim; would alert interested parties to the availability of a derivative claim; and would ensure that the Companies Act constituted a more complete code (with the unfairly prejudicial remedy) with regard to shareholders' remedies.[2] The Law Commission also thought that, in an age of international business, it was important to set out the rules in the statute in keeping with other jurisdictions[3] such as Canada,[4] New Zealand,[5] and Australia.[6]

1   Law Commission, *Shareholder Remedies*, Cm 3769, Law Com No 246, 1997 (hereafter 'Law Commission Report'), paras 6.4, 6.15. The Report was preceded by a Consultation Paper of the same name, Con Paper No 142 (1996). For comments on the Law Commission's proposals, see Boyle, *Minority Shareholders' Remedies* (2002), Chapter 3; Poole and Roberts, 'Shareholder Remedies – Corporate Wrongs and the Derivative Action' [1999] JBL 99.
2   Law Commission Report, paras 6.16–6.18.
3   Law Commission Report, para 6.9.
4   Canadian Business Corporations Act 1975, s 239; see Kaplan and Elwood, 'The Derivative Action: A Shareholders' "Bleak House" ' (2003) 36 UBCL Rev 443; Cheffins, 'Reforming the Derivative Action: The Canadian Experience and British Prospects' [1997] Company, Financial and Insolvency Law Review 227.
5   New Zealand Companies Act 1993, ss 165–168; see Watson, 'A Matter of Balance: The Statutory Derivative Action in New Zealand' (1998) 19 Co Law 236.
6   Australian Corporations Act 2001, Part 2F.1A, ss 236–242; see Ramsay and Saunders, 'Litigation by Shareholders and Directors: An Empirical Study of the Australian Statutory Derivative Action' [2006] 6 JCLS 397.

5.6 The Law Commission's recommendations were endorsed by the Company Law Review without much further deliberation[1] and the provisions contained in the CA 2006, Pt 11 largely reflect the Law Commission's proposals.

1   See Company Law Review, *Modern Company Law for a Competitive Economy: Developing the Framework*, (March 2000), paras 4.112–4.139 ('*Developing the Framework*') for the main discussion of the issues; there are limited references to derivative claims in Company Law Review, *Modern Company Law for a Competitive Economy: Completing the Structure* (November 2000), paras 5.82–5.89; and Company Law Review, *Final Report* (2001), paras 7.46 –7.51.

5.7 Despite this long gestation, the possibility of a statutory derivative procedure gave rise to concerns as to its scope and its practical application. A particular concern was that the proposals put forward by the Law Commission in 1997 were drawn up as part of a review of shareholders' remedies, but

5.7 The Derivative Claim – an Invitation to Litigate?

Pt 11 operates within the framework of a Companies Act which for the first time contains (in Part 10) a statutory statement of directors' duties. This statutory statement introduces requirements which are perceived (at least) to expand the obligations and therefore potential liabilities of directors.[1]

[1]   The combination of CA 2006, Pts 10 and 11 was described in Parliament as '… a double whammy. In Pt 10, directors' duties are widened, while Pt 11 makes it easier for shareholders to commence actions against directors' (Lord Hodgson); see 679 HL Official Report (5th series) col GC2 (27 February 2006); 681 HL Official Report (5th series) col 886 (9 May 2006).

5.8 A key provision in this context is CA 2006, s 172 which imposes on directors a duty to promote the success of the company and requires them to have regard to a wide variety of factors when so acting, see para 3.17. The concern is that shareholder activists might use the combination of the new derivative procedure and the expansion of s 172 to challenge business decisions of directors on the basis of an alleged failure to have regard to the factors set out in that section. For example, shareholders with an interest in environmental issues might try to challenge a board decision to open a new mine on the grounds that the directors did not have regard to 'the impact of the company's operations on the community and the environment' as required by s 172(1)(d). A derivative claim, it is argued, could be used to seek judicial review, in effect, of a commercial decision of management.

5.9 Meanwhile, the restrictive thresholds of fraud on the minority and wrongdoer control (noted at para 5.4) have been replaced and derivative claims are possible in respect of a breach of any duty owed by a director to the company including, for the first time, in respect of alleged negligence by a director (s 260(3)). In addition, the rules on ratification have been altered to preclude directors, as shareholders, voting to ratify their own wrongdoing (s 239), see para 4.49, though such ratification would have been permissible at common law. As the critics would see it, the result is that there are more grounds for a derivative claim, but less possibility of ratification.

5.10 At a practical level, the concern was that there is more scope for speculative or vexatious litigation now for a variety of reasons: the availability of conditional fee agreements;[1] the rise of activist shareholders ranging from those representing a particular 'lobby' (such as environmentalists) to hedge funds with deep pockets and a concern to maximise the return on their investments; and the increased presence of US shareholders and lawyers in London who may be more attuned to vindicating investor rights through the courts rather than a discreet market exit and for whom derivative actions are merely another mechanism for holding underperforming directors to account.

[1]   There is some debate as to whether conditional fee agreements are possible with respect to derivative claims, see the differing views of Payne, 'Sections 459–461 Companies Act 1985 in Flux: The Future of Shareholder Protection' (2005) CLJ 647 at 665; Reisberg, 'Funding Derivative Actions: A re-examination of costs and fees as incentives to commence litigation' (2004) 4 JCLS 345 at 380; and on the deficiencies of conditional fee agreements in this context, if they are permissible, see Reisberg, 'Derivative Actions and the Funding Problem: The Way Forward' [2006] JBL 445.

5.11 This combination of factors (expanded duties; the expanded availability of a derivative claim; and activist shareholders) creates, it was argued, an increasing threat of litigation which will deter people from taking up directorships of public companies.

5.12 Throughout the Parliamentary debates, the Government emphasised that Pt 11 does not introduce any major change of principle and there is no reason to expect any significant increase in the number of derivative actions.[1] The intention behind Pt 11 is to strike a balance between protecting directors from vexatious and frivolous claims[2] so allowing them to take business decisions in good faith while protecting the rights of shareholders to bring meritorious claims.[3] The derivative action is a well-established mechanism which has certain inherent characteristics which limit the potential for speculative litigation.[4] In particular, a claim can only be brought on behalf of the company with any sums recovered going to the company and not to the claimant who runs the risk of incurring substantial costs.[5] Derivative claims are subject to strict judicial control (the need for which had been emphasised by the Law Commission[6]) and the Government expects the judiciary to continue to respect the commercial judgments of directors and the tradition of non-interference in matters of internal management.[7]

1 For the Government's position, see 679 HL Official Report (5th series) cols GC4–5 (27 February 2006); 681 HL Official Report (5th series) col 883 (9 May 2006); HC Official Report, SC D (Company Law Reform Bill), 13 July 2006, cols 664–666. The Law Commission pointed to the experience in Canada when it introduced a statutory derivative action, see Law Commission Report, para 6.14; and see Cheffins, 'Reforming the Derivative Action: The Canadian Experience and British Prospects' [1997] Company, Financial and Insolvency Law Review 227, who concluded that the statutory derivative action in Canada, on balance, had not made the impact on Canadian corporate law which might have been expected with most of the cases involving closely held firms rather than publicly held corporations.
2 679 HL Official Report (5th series) col GC6 (27 February 2006). As was noted in the debates, it is important to avoid 'opening a Pandora's box to every disenchanted individual in the country' (Lord Sharman): 681 HL Official Report (5th series) col 885 (9 May 2006).
3 See 681 HL Official Report (5th series) col 883 (9 May 2006).
4 See 679 HL Official Report (5th series) col GC4 (27 February 2006); HC Official Report, SC D (Company Law Reform Bill) col 665, 13 July 2006.
5 See 679 HL Official Report (5th series) cols GC4–5 (27 February 2006); HC Official Report, SC D (Company Law Reform Bill), 13 July 2006, col 665. The mechanism is not akin to class actions in the United States (where members of the class sue for their own benefit) and in respect of which directors are well protected by the indemnities permitted by CA 2006, ss 234–238.
6 Law Commission Report, para 6.6; also 679 HL Official Report (5th series) cols GC5, GC15 (27 February 2006); see Reisberg, 'Judicial Control of Derivative Actions' (2005) ICCLR 335 on the positive value of such judicial controls; also *Portfolios of Distinction Ltd v Laird* [2004] EWHC 2071 (Ch), [2004] 2 BCLC 741.
7 See 679 HL Official Report (5th series) col GC5 (27 February 2006).

5.13 Recognising the concerns raised about the potential for speculative litigation, however, and anxious that this should not act as a deterrent to holding directorships, especially in publicly traded companies, the Government brought forward amendments to Pt 11 at the Report Stage in the House of Lords.[1] These amendments were designed to enhance the protection for directors in two related ways:

(1)   by strengthening judicial control of a derivative claim by setting a two stage threshold (discussed below) which must be crossed before a claim can proceed; and

(2)   by restating the duty of directors to act to promote the interests of the company (in CA 2006, s 172(1)) to emphasise that the overriding obligation of directors remains to promote the success of the company for the benefit of its members as a whole. In this way, it is hoped to curb the scope for allegations of a breach of duty arising from a supposed failure to have regard to one or more of the factors set out in that section. See the discussion of s 172 at para 3.17.

[1]   See 681 HL Official Report (5th series) cols 883–884 (9 May 2006).

BRINGING A DERIVATIVE CLAIM

5.14

'**CA, 2006, s 260   Derivative claims**
(1)   This Chapter applies to proceedings in England and Wales or Northern Ireland by a member of a company—
   (a)   in respect of a cause of action vested in the company,[1] and
   (b)   seeking relief on behalf of the company.
   This is referred to in this Chapter as a "derivative claim".

(2)   A derivative claim may only be brought—
   (a)   under this Chapter, or
   (b)   in pursuance of an order of the court in proceedings under section 994 (proceedings for protection of members against unfair prejudice).'

[1]   'Company' is defined in CA 2006, s 1 essentially as companies formed and registered under the CA 2006 and previous Companies Acts so excluding overseas companies.

5.15   On the recommendation of the Law Commission,[1] the statutory derivative claim supersedes the common law derivative action in order to allow for the development of a coherent body of law based on Pt 11 alone.[2]

Any possibility of a derivative claim being brought by a shareholder of a parent company on behalf of a subsidiary company (so-called multiple derivative claims) is excluded (as the claim must be by a member of a company in respect of a cause of action vested in that company).[3]

It is worth emphasising that the rule in *Foss v Harbottle*[4] has not been swept aside by the CA 2006, Pt 11. As noted in para 5.2 above, there are two elements to the rule: the proper plaintiff element and the majority rule element; and the derivative claim developed as a procedural mechanism in order to give a remedy for a wrong which would otherwise escape redress.

[1]   Law Commission Report, paras 6.51–6.55.
[2]   Though the CA 2006, s 260(2), set out in para 5.14, states that a derivative claim can 'only' proceed under Pt 11 or s 994, derivative claims in respect of improper political donations are possible under ss 370–373.
[3]   See Law Commission Report, para 6.109; Boyle, *Minority Shareholders' Remedies* (2002), p 85. See *Waddington Ltd v Chan Chun Ho Thomas* [2008] HKEC 1498, a decision of the Final Court of Appeal of Hong Kong where the court accepted that, though the Hong

Kong company statute made no provision for a multiple derivative claim, such a claim was possible under the common law, see note Reisberg & Prentice [2009] LQR 209. The difference in this jurisdiction being that the common law is expressly superseded by CA 2006, Part 11 (see s 260(2)).

4 (1843) 2 Hare 461.

5.16 As regards the proper plaintiff aspect, the position remains that the proper plaintiff in respect of a wrong allegedly done to a company is prima facie the company. The majority rule element has been modified in that, at common law, a derivative action did not lie in respect of an act which was capable of being confirmed by the majority.[1] Under Pt 11, actual authorisation or ratification is required to bar a claim (s 263(2)(b), (c)). Otherwise, the possibility of authorisation or ratification is a matter to be taken into account by the court when deciding whether to give permission for a claim to proceed (s 263(3)(c) and (d)). In practice, the courts are likely to adjourn proceedings to allow the majority the opportunity to authorise or ratify the conduct complained of[2] and so bar the claim. Apart from that procedural distinction, the law on authorisation or ratification has not been altered by Pt 11 and the common law is retained by ss 180(4) and 239(7) respectively, see the discussion at paras 5.48–5.56 below.

1 *MacDougall v Gardiner* (1875) 1 Ch D 13 at 25, CA; *Burland v Earle* [1902] AC 83 at 93–94.
2 The common law on ratification is preserved by the CA 2006, s 239(7), subject to the new constraints on voting set out in s 239(3), (4) – the text of s 239 is set out at para 4.49; the common law on authorisation is preserved by s 180(4)(a).

5.17 What has altered is that the derivative action (ie the procedural mechanism) invented by the courts as an exception to the rule in *Foss v Harbottle* (based on wrongdoer control and unratifiable wrongs, see para 5.4 above) is replaced by the statutory mechanism and thresholds laid down in Pt 11. Derivative claims, though facilitated by the new procedural mechanism of Pt 11, remain subject to the general principle of majority rule.

5.18 The option of pursuing a derivative claim via a court order in proceedings under CA 2006, s 994 (proceedings for unfairly prejudicial conduct) is preserved by s 260(2)(b). In practice, it would be exceptional for a successful petitioner under s 994 to seek such an order under s 996(2)(c) given that he will be entitled to a personal remedy (typically an order under s 996(2)(e) requiring the respondents to purchase his shares).[1]

1 The Government resisted Opposition attempts to remove this option (see 679 HL Official Report (5th series) col GC6 (27 February 2006)), accepting the view of the Law Commission (see Law Commission Report, para 6.55) that it is preferable to maintain these two routes by which a derivative claim can be brought, but it is difficult to envisage the circumstances in which any shareholder would wish to use s 996(2)(c). Section 996(1) allows the court to make such order as it thinks fit and see Reisberg & Prentice [2009] LQR 209 at 212–213 who suggest that this wide jurisdiction might allow the court to authorise a multiple derivative claim, see note 3 to para 5.15 above.

5.19 There are three possible ways in which a derivative claim can be brought under CA 2006, Part 11:

5.19 *The Derivative Claim – an Invitation to Litigate?*

(1) Section 261(1) – a derivative claim may be initiated by a member who then requires the permission of the court to continue with it.

Later member

The claimant must be a member[1] at the time of the proceedings and it is immaterial whether the cause of action arose before or after the would-be claimant became a member of the company (s 260(4)), reflecting the current law that a member is entitled to pursue any existing cause of action, regardless of when he became a shareholder.[2] No minimum shareholding is required[3] and while, in theory, this means that litigious parties could purchase one share with a view to bringing a case against the directors, whether the court would permit such a claimant to proceed (see below) is another matter. There is little advantage to a person acquiring a single share with a view to bringing a derivative claim since any recovery is for the benefit of the company and the claimant runs the risk that he will be penalised in costs.

(2) Section 262(1), (2) – a company claim may be continued as a derivative claim. Where a company has brought a claim, and the cause of action on which the claim is based could be pursued as a derivative claim, a member of the company may apply to the court for permission to continue the claim as a derivative claim.[4]

(3) Section 264(1), (2) – an existing derivative claim may be continued as a derivative claim. Where a member of a company has brought a derivative claim (ie under s 261), or has continued as a derivative claim a claim brought by the company (ie under s 262), or has continued a derivative claim brought by another member (ie under s 264), a member of the company may apply to the court for permission to continue the claim as a derivative claim.

[1] References to a member of a company include a person who is not a member but to whom shares in the company have been transferred or transmitted by operation of law: CA 2006, s 260(5)(c).

[2] See Law Commission Report, para 6.98; 679 HL Official Report (5th series) col GC15 (27 February 2006); *Seaton v Grant* (1867) 2 Ch App 459.

[3] As Lord Cairns explained in *Seaton v Grant* (1867) 2 Ch App 459 at 465, the quantum of the claimant's interest is irrelevant, if the claim is one which should otherwise be brought, for the aggregate interest of all the shareholders is amply sufficient to sustain the claim.

[4] The Act does not make provision for the possibility that a company might want to take over a claim commenced by a member. There is no need for such provision as the company can at any time commence action in its own name – it is the company's claim: 679 HL Official Report (5th series) col GC34 (27 February 2006).

5.20 In claims under CA 2006, ss 262 or 264 (continuing claims commenced by the company or by another member) the member seeking to continue the claim may apply to the court to do so on the ground that: (a) the manner in which the proceedings have been commenced or continued by the company/ other member amounts to an abuse of the process of the court; (b) the company/other member has failed to prosecute the claim diligently; and (c) it is appropriate for the member applying to the court to continue the company's claim as a derivative claim or to continue a derivative claim already commenced by another member. It may be that the company's intention in commencing proceedings is to frustrate a shareholder and prevent a successful claim being brought[1] and so it is useful that a member can apply to the court to take over the claim. The question for the court will be whether a reasonable amount of diligence has been shown and whether the company is willing to bring the claim.[2]

1   Law Commission Report, para 6.63.
2   HC Official Report, SC D (Company Law Reform Bill), 13 July 2006, col 674.

5.21 Where a member applies to continue a claim commenced by the company or by another member, the application to the court is treated in the same way as if the member was applying to continue a derivative claim under s 261. The applicant member will not be allowed to proceed if (at the first stage) it appears to the court that the application does not disclose a prima facie case for giving permission (ss 262(3), 264(3), to the same effect as s 261(2)). At the hearing of the permission application (the second stage) the factors in s 263 which govern the exercise of the court's discretion to grant permission (discussed below) apply where the application is to take over a claim commenced by the company, but they do not apply where the application (under s 264) is to take over a derivative claim already commenced by another member (s 263(1)). In the latter case, those matters will already have been taken into account by the court in allowing the derivative claim to have been brought or continued in the first place. The issue for the court under s 264 is to decide whether to give permission to another member to continue a derivative claim previously begun by a member. On that issue, the court has an open-ended discretion to consider whatever factors appear to it to be relevant to the application.

Claims against directors and other persons

5.22 A derivative claim may be brought against a director or another person or both: s 260(3). Former directors are included[1] by s 260(5)(a) and claims against such directors might arise, for example, where directors have resigned in order to exploit an opportunity which came to their attention while they were directors (s 170(2)(a)) or where they receive benefits from third parties in respect of things done or omitted before they ceased to be directors (s 170(2)(b)).[2]

1   Their inclusion avoids the problem that they would otherwise be classed as third parties whom the current board would be expected to sue (or not) on behalf of the company: see Ford's *Principles of Corporations Law* (11th edn, 2003), para 11.250.
2   Reflecting what was the position at common law, the CA 2006, s 170(2) provides that a person who ceases to be a director continues to be subject to the duty to avoid conflicts of interests in s 175 as regards the exploitation of any property, information or opportunity of which he became aware at the time he was a director; and continues to be subject to the duty in s 176 (duty not to accept benefits from third parties) as regards things done or omitted by him before he ceased to be a director.

5.23 Shadow directors are included by s 260(5)(b), but this extension of derivative claims to them is of uncertain significance, given that it is not clear that shadow directors owe fiduciary duties to the company (an issue which the CA 2006 fails to resolve, see s 170(5) and para 3.14).[1] The Law Commission recommended their inclusion on the basis that it should be possible to base a claim against a shadow director on the grounds of 'default'; for example, for non-compliance with the CA 2006, Pt 10, Chap 4, where many of the provisions expressly apply to shadow directors. The initial obstacle to bringing a claim against a shadow director, of course, is establishing that the

Shadow Director

person is a shadow director.[3] This combination of uncertainty as to the nature of the duties owed by a shadow director and the evidential difficulties in establishing that someone is a shadow director would suggest that derivative actions against shadow directors are unlikely.

[1]   See *Ultraframe Ltd v Fielding* [2005] EWHC 1638 (Ch), [2005] All ER (D) 397 (Jul), paras 1279–1291 where Lewison J reviews the small number of authorities on this issue before concluding that, in his view, the 'indirect influence exerted by a paradigm shadow director who does not directly deal with or claim the right to deal directly with the company's assets will not usually … be enough to impose fiduciary duties upon him; although he will, of course, be subject to those statutory duties and disabilities which the Companies Act creates' (at para 1289); but for criticism of his approach, see Prentice and Payne [2006] 122 LQR 558.

[2]   See Law Commission Report, para 6.36.

[3]   See *Secretary of State for Trade and Industry v Deverell* [2000] 2 BCLC 133.

3d party

5.24   As regards derivative claims against 'another person', the intention is to allow a claim to be made against a person who has assisted a director in a breach of duty or who is a recipient of corporate assets in circumstances where he knows the director is acting in breach of his duties.[1] It is not possible for a claim to be brought where the breach of duty etc is solely that of the third-party, such as a negligent auditor. As the Law Commission noted, the decision whether to sue a third-party (ie someone who is not a director and where the claim is not closely connected with the breach of duty by a director) is one for the board.[2] A derivative claim could lie, however, where the board's decision not to pursue a claim against a third party is itself a breach of duty by the directors.[3]

[1]   See Law Commission Report, paras 6.35, 6.36; 679 HL Official Report (5th series) cols GC9–10 (27 February 2006); HC Official Report, SC D (Company Law Reform Bill), 13 July 2006, col 666: it is efficient to allow the claim to be made against the director and the third party to ensure recovery for the company which is the purpose of the derivative claim.

[2]   See Law Commission Report, paras 6.34, 6.35.

[3]   There would be difficulties of causation and quantification, however, in such circumstances: see Law Commission Report, para 6.32.

scope

THE BASIS OF A DERIVATIVE CLAIM

Any breach of the dir.

5.25

'CA 2006, s 260   Derivative claims

(3)   A derivative claim under this Chapter may be brought only in respect of a cause of action arising from an actual or proposed act or omission involving negligence, default, breach of duty or breach of trust by a director of the company.

The cause of action may be against the director or another person (or both).'

The significant change here is that a claim may be brought in respect of any breach of duty by a director. At common law the conduct complained of had to amount to an unratifiable wrong not capable of 'cure' by the majority, ie acts of a fraudulent character or beyond the powers of the company which typically involved the misappropriation of money, property, or advantages belonging to the company, and which were generally described as a fraud on the minority.[1] All other breaches of duty, being ratifiable, could not be the subject of a derivative action at common law, even if the breaches had not actually been ratified.[2] Now the restrictive concept of 'fraud on the minority' no longer applies and breach of any duty is potentially actionable. Directors' duties are now stated in CA 2006, Pt 10 and potentially widened by provisions such as s 172 (duty to promote the success of the company, see para 3.17); s 176 (statutory expression for the first time of a duty not to accept benefits from third parties, see para 4.10); and s 177 (restating the conflict rule as a duty, see para 4.14).[3]

[1] *Burland v Earle* [1902] AC 83 at 93–94, per Lord Davey; and see *Cook v Deeks* [1916] 1 AC 554; *Daniels v Daniels* [1978] 2 All ER 89, see para 5.3.
[2] *MacDougall v Gardiner* (1875) 1 Ch D 13 at 25; *Burland v Earle* [1902] AC 83 at 93–94.
[3] So ending the 'duty versus disability' debate generated by *Movitex Ltd v Bulfield* [1988] BCLC 104.

5.26 The extension of the derivative action to negligence was recommended by the Law Commission which noted that, while investors take the risk that those who manage companies may make mistakes, they do not have to accept that directors will fail to comply with their duties.[1] This view was endorsed by the Company Law Review which considered that 'the developments in the law in relation to directors' duties of skill and care should have their counterpart in policing procedures'.[2] It is no longer necessary therefore to show that the negligence is of the self-serving variety seen in *Daniels v Daniels*[3] where the board sold an asset at a gross undervalue to one of the directors. Of course, while negligence will found a derivative claim, the courts will continue to distinguish between commercial misjudgements and negligent conduct (and negligence is ratifable).

[1] See Law Commission Report, para 6.41.
[2] *Developing the Framework*, para 4.127.
[3] [1978] 2 All ER 89. At common law, mere negligence from which the director did not benefit personally could not found a derivative claim: *Pavlides v Jensen* [1956] 2 All ER 518.

5.27 'Default' enables claims to be brought in respect of breaches of statutory obligations imposed by the companies legislation[1] (particularly relevant here may be breaches of the CA 2006, Chap 10, Pt 4 in respect of transactions with directors requiring members' approval).

[1] *Customs and Excise Comrs v Hedon Alpha Ltd* [1981] 2 All ER 697.

5.28 To sum up, a derivative claim may be brought:

- by any member (however few shares he holds and however recently acquired);
- against any director (including former and shadow directors) and other persons implicated in the breach;
- in respect of negligence, default, breach of duty and breach of trust by a director of the company.

5.29 It may seem, therefore, as if Pt 11 is indeed an invitation to litigate, but the scope of the mechanism is only part of the picture. It is possible to commence a derivative claim in a much wider category of case than at common law, but the claim may not proceed very far for the claimant must navigate a two-stage process and obtain the permission of the court to continue the claim.

5.30 At the first stage, a prima facie case must be made; at the second stage, a variety of factors must be considered, some of which oblige the court to dismiss the application. In particular, actual authorisation or ratification by the majority bars a claim (s 263(2)(b), (c)) and the possibility of authorisation or ratification may mean that the proceedings will be adjourned to allow majority rule to prevail (assuming the act is capable of authorisation or ratification).

5.31 In effect, therefore, the claim will only proceed if, as before, the wrong is not capable of authorisation or ratification or, where the wrong may be authorised or ratified, the majority choose not to do so. The common law on authorisation is retained by s 180(4)(a) while the common law on acts that are incapable of ratification is retained by s 239(7). The scenario where the wrong may be authorised or ratified but the majority choose not to do so is unlikely since, in such a case, it might be expected that the majority would deal with the wrongdoing director without the need for the minority to bring a derivative action.

5.32 In practice, there may be little difference between, at common law, being allowed to proceed only in limited circumstances (an unratifiable wrong) and, under Pt 11, being allowed to commence a claim on broad grounds only for permission to proceed to be refused on the grounds of authorisation or ratification.

JUDICIAL CONTROL OF A DERIVATIVE CLAIM

5.33

> '**CA 2006, s 261   Application for permission to continue derivative claim**
> (1) A member of a company who brings a derivative claim under this Chapter must apply to the court for permission (in Northern Ireland, leave) to continue it.
>   ...'

The explanation for this section with its reference to continuing a derivative claim rather than to bringing a derivative claim lies in the Civil Procedure Rules ('CPR').[1] A derivative claim is commenced by the issue of a claim form which must be served within four months after it has been issued (CPR 7.5(1); 19.9(2)). The company must be named as a defendant (CPR 19.9(3)). Once the claim form has been issued, the claimant must not take any further step in the proceedings without the permission of the court other than notifying the company (by sending a copy of the claim form, the application notice, the written evidence filed in support of the application for permission and the notice set out in the Practice Direction on derivative claims) or making an urgent application for interim relief.[2] Notification to the company must be as soon as reasonably practicable after the issue of the claim form (CPR 19.9A(4)), subject to any order of the court to contrary effect (CPR 19.9A(7)). Part 11 assumes therefore that the claimant may commence the claim without any court intervention, but must then seek permission to continue.[3]

[1] See 679 HL Official Report (5th series) cols GC14, GC19 (27 February 2006).

[2] See CPR 19.9(4), 19.9A(4) and Practice Direction 19C – Derivative Claims; see Reed 'Derivative Claims: The Application for Permission to Continue' (2000) 21 Co Law 156 who is critical of the paucity of the 'written evidence' required and of the willingness of the courts, acting on such inadequate evidence, to permit a derivative claim to continue. He suggests that the courts are nervous about stifling a claim, especially where there are obvious disputes of fact. But see *Portfolios of Distinction Ltd v Laird* [2004] 2 BCLC 741 where the court emphasised the need for judicial control of all stages of a derivative action and that the requirement for permission is not a mere technicality.

[3] At this permission stage, the claimant may also ask the court to order the company to indemnify the claimant against any liability in respect of costs incurred in the claim: see CPR 19.9E(1).

5.34 The Law Commission had recommended that a shareholder wishing to bring a derivative action be required to serve a notice on the company at least 28 days *before* the commencement of the proceedings, specifying the grounds of the proposed derivative action,[1] but that recommendation was not taken up.[2] In a similar vein, the Opposition proposed an amendment to the Bill which would have permitted a derivative claim to be brought only if the directors had declined a request by a member for the company to bring a claim.[3] The Government's position was that it did not wish, through such requirements, to reintroduce an element of the 'wrongdoer control' test.[4] As Lord Goldsmith explained, the issue of whether there is wrongdoer control can become a protracted debate spun out by directors in order to buy time;[5] and a wrongdoer control requirement may make it impossible for a derivative claim to be brought successfully by a member of a widely held company (which would include almost all major traded companies).[6] The Government's view was that these issues are better dealt with by the court in the exercise of its discretion under s 263(3) which requires the court to have regard to a wide variety of matters, one of which is whether the company has decided not to pursue the claim (see s 263(3)(e)).

[1] Law Commission Report, paras 6.58–6.59. In part, this 28-day period would allow the company time to take remedial action so rendering the proceedings unnecessary: see Law Commission Consultation Paper No 142 (1996), paras 16.15–16.17.

[2] Notice to the company 28 days before the proceedings is a requirement with respect to a derivative action to recover unauthorised political donations: see CA 2006, s 371.

[3] See 679 HL Official Report (5th series) cols GC6–7, GC29 (27 February 2006); HC Official Report, SC D (Company Law Reform Bill), 13 July 2006, cols 660, 672.

[4] 679 HL Official Report (5th series) cols GC7–8 (27 February 2006). For example, there could be disputes about whether the request had been made to the board; whether the directors had sufficient information on which to reach a decision; and whether they had reached a decision on the matter or were giving it further consideration.

[5] 679 HL Official Report (5th series) col GC8 (27 February 2006).

[6] 681 HL Official Report (5th series) col 883 (9 May 2006).

5.35 The position then is that a claim form may be issued without any prior notice or any request to the company, but no further steps in the proceedings, other than notifying the company or making an urgent application for interim relief, can be taken without the permission of the court.

THE NEED FOR A PRIMA FACIE CASE

5.36

'CA 2006, s 261   Application for permission to continue derivative claim

...

(2)   If it appears to the court that the application and the evidence filed by the applicant in support of it do not disclose a prima facie case for giving permission (or leave), the court—

(a)   must dismiss the application, and

(b)   may make any consequential order it considers appropriate.'

5.37 The Government was initially reluctant to set any particular threshold requirements, preferring to let the matter progress to a hearing for permission to continue the claim under the CPR (as noted above) when the court would consider the factors set out in s 263(3). The intention was to avoid turning the preliminary stages of a claim into an expensive and time-consuming mini-trial and to allow the court over a period of time to develop appropriate thresholds for these claims.[1]

[1]   See 679 HL Official Report (5th series) col GC22 (27 February 2006); Law Commission Report, paras 6.4, 6.71.

5.38 Following criticisms that there were inadequate filters to prevent vexatious litigation, however, the Government was persuaded that the court should have a specific power to dismiss unmeritorious cases at an early stage without involving the company,[1] and so the statute includes this *prima facie* threshold.[2] The court's power to dismiss the application at this stage is reinforced by s 261(2)(b) which enables the court to penalize an applicant with costs orders or deter a nuisance applicant with a civil restraint order (restraining a person from making any application to a civil court without the consent of a judge).[3]

[1]   681 HL Official Report (5th series) col 883 (9 May 2006). This power to dismiss the claim is in addition to the ability of a defendant to apply to have the claim struck out under CPR 3.4, PD3 – the difference being that that application requires active steps by the company, whereas the CA 2006, s 261(2) requires the court to dismiss the application without hearing from the company.

[2]   The provision was added at Report Stage in the House of Lords: see 681 HL Official Report (5th series) cols 883–884 (9 May 2006). The court considers the matter initially 'on the papers' alone, but if permission is refused, the claimant may ask for the decision to be reconsidered at an oral hearing and that request must be made within seven days of being served with notice of the decision to refuse permission – see CPR 19.9A(10). The intention is to minimise the company's involvement (and therefore expense) at these initial stages so Practice Directive 19C – Directive Claims provides that the decision whether the claimant's evidence discloses a prima facie case is normally made without submissions from or (in the case of an oral hearing to reconsider such a decision reached pursuant to rule 19.9A(10)) attendance by the company. If without invitation from the court the company volunteers a

submission or attendance, the company will not normally be allowed any costs of that submission or attendance (see PD 19C, para 5).

3   See 681 HL Official Report (5th series) col 883 (9 May 2006).

5.39 It remains to be seen whether this *prima facie* requirement will present much of a challenge to the would-be claimant. Faced with a new procedure designed to make derivative actions more accessible to shareholders, the courts may be reluctant to throw out a remotely plausible case at the first threshold.[1] There may be some judicial willingness to allow shareholder claimants the opportunity at least for a second stage consideration of their concerns, bearing in mind that it is still possible for the court to stop the proceedings at that stage.[2]

1   See 679 HL Official Report (5th series) col GC14 (27 February 2006).
2   See Cheffins, 'Reforming the Derivative Action: The Canadian Experience and British Prospects' [1997] Company, Financial and Insolvency Law Review 227 at 244, who noted that the Canadian courts, while not granting leave as a matter of course, were unwilling to impose particularly onerous thresholds at the equivalent stage in a statutory derivative claim. Instead they were content to restrict their enquiry to whether the complainant had raised fair questions which should properly be considered in an action.

5.40 Part 11 does not expressly address the situation where a company is in (or about to go into) liquidation or administration. At common law, the court would not allow a derivative claim to be brought where the company was in liquidation or was to be put into liquidation on the basis that, in those circumstances, the liquidator (as an independent office holder) is the proper person to determine whether a claim should be brought in the company's name,[1] subject to any challenge by a member to the liquidator's decision under the Insolvency Act 1986 ('IA 1986'), ss 112(1) or 168(5). Likewise, in an administration, the administrator has power to bring or defend any action or other legal proceedings in the name and on behalf of the company.[2] In neither scenario is it necessary therefore for a derivative claim to be brought to remedy a wrong done to the company so it is unlikely that the courts will entertain a claim under Pt 11 in either situation.

1   *Barrett v Duckett* [1995] 1 BCLC 243; *Fargro Ltd v Godfroy* [1986] 3 All ER 279; see too *Ferguson v Wallbridge* [1935] 3 DLR 66 at 83.
2   IA 1986, s 8, Sch B1, para 60, Sch 1, para 5.

5.41 If the case is not dismissed at this *prima facie* threshold, the court may give directions as to the evidence to be provided by the company, and may adjourn the proceedings to enable the evidence to be obtained: s 262(4). An adjournment at this stage also allows the company to seek authorisation or ratification of the conduct in question which then acts as a complete bar to the claim proceeding (see s 263(2)(b), (c)).

PERMISSION TO CONTINUE THE CLAIM

5.42 At this stage the court can:

- give permission to the claimant to continue the claim on such terms as it thinks fit;[1] or

- refuse permission and dismiss the claim (and in some circumstances the court must refuse permission); or
- adjourn the proceedings on the application and give such directions as it thinks fit. Proceedings might be adjourned, for example, to see if the parties can reach an accommodation on dropping the claim or the company continuing it or indeed on the shareholder being bought out.

As the court may give permission on such terms as it thinks fit, there would seem to be no reason why the court might not impose a condition, as appropriate, requiring the parties to return to court in the event of a change of circumstances making it no longer appropriate for the derivative claim to proceed, where the conditions for permission to continue the claim are no longer met.[2] Once permission has been given to continue a derivative claim, the court may order that the claim cannot be discontinued, settled or compromised without the permission of the court (CPR 19.9F); court approval is also required before settling a derivative claim in respect of political donations: see CA 2006, s 371(5).

[1]   The court could give permission for the claim to continue, but then immediately adjourn the proceedings before revisiting the permission at a later stage (see 681 HL Official Report (5th series) cols 883–891 (9 May 2006)).
[2]   See *Re Wishart* [2009] CSOH 20, 12 February 2009, para 40.

ABSOLUTE BARS TO PROCEEDING

5.43

'CA 2006, s 263   **Whether permission to be given**

...

(2)   Permission (or leave) must be refused if the court is satisfied—
  (a)   that a person acting in accordance with section 172 (duty to promote the success of the company) would not seek to continue the claim, or
  (b)   where the cause of action arises from an act or omission that is yet to occur, that the act or omission has been authorised by the company, or
  (c)   where the cause of action arises from an act or omission that has already occurred, that the act or omission—
      (i)   was authorised by the company before it occurred, or
      (ii)   has been ratified by the company since it occurred.'

The hypothetical director

5.44   The Government was invited to draft the requirement in s 263(2)(a) in terms merely of a director acting in good faith in the interests of the company, but this was rejected on the basis that consistency with the rest of the CA 2006 requires that the clause be stated in the terms of Pt 10.[1]

[1]   679 HL Official Report (5th series) cols GC23–24 (27 February 2006).

5.45   This section requires the court to ask whether a director, acting in the way he considers in good faith would be most likely to promote the success of the company for the benefit of the members as a whole, would not seek to continue the claim. The director in so acting must have regard to the factors identified in s 172, such as the likely consequences of any decision in the long term, the interests of the company's employees, etc;[1] and the court stepping into his shoes must do likewise.

1   See paras 3.17 and 3.20 above for a discussion of the balancing act required by CA 2006, s 172.

5.46 The court will also have to take a commercial perspective on the matter, bearing in mind factors which would influence a director in that position, such as the size of the claim; the likelihood of success and of recovery; the time and costs involved including the distraction/diversion of management from core activities; the impact on relationships within the company; and the risk to reputation of pursuing/not pursuing the claim. The issue is not what conclusion the court would come to nor what a reasonable director would conclude: the question is whether a director acting in the way he considers most likely to promote the success of the company would not seek to continue the claim.[1]

1   See *Regentcrest plc v Cohen* [2001] 2 BCLC 80; HC Official Report, SC D (Company Law Reform Bill), 13 July 2006, col 678. As the Law Commission noted, 'this does not mean that the court is bound to accept the views of the director – the existence of a conflict of interest may affect the weight to be given to those views and the court would give no weight to views which no reasonable director could hold': see Law Commission Report, para 6.79, note 110.

5.47 As a director's obligations under s 172 have been written in quite expansive (and novel) terms, the court may be reluctant to conclude under s 236(2)(a) that a director, faced with a prima facie case of a breach of duty (which there must be for the application to have reached this stage), and given his obligation to have regard to the factors listed, would not seek to continue the claim.[1] In that case, the focus of attention shifts to s 236(2)(b) and (c) which require evidence of actual authorisation or ratification. Looking at evidence of such tangible matters may be more palatable to the court than attempting to decide what a hypothetical director might have concluded in the circumstances.

1   See *Franbar Holdings Ltd v Patel* [2009] 1 BCLC 1 at 10–11.

Authorisation/ratification

5.48 Authorisation or ratification provides a complete defence to a derivative claim. Authorisation ensures that there is no breach of duty while ratification cures any breach that previously existed. The scope for a derivative claim will be determined therefore by the ability (and willingness) of the members to authorise the conduct complained of or to ratify breaches of duty.

5.49 Actual authorisation or ratification is required for a complete bar to the claim[1] and it is open to the court to adjourn proceedings (under s 261(3), (4)) to allow for the matter to be authorised or ratified. In a widely held company, of course, authorisation or ratification may not be a realistic option, either in terms of the time and costs involved in holding shareholder meetings, or indeed in terms of the wider dissemination of information on the matter which would then occur.

1   This is a change from the common law where a derivative action did not lie in respect of an act which was capable of being confirmed by the majority: *Burland v Earle* [1902] AC 83 at 93–94, PC; *MacDougall v Gardiner* (1875) 1 Ch D 13, CA.

5.50 Whether effective authorisation or ratification has taken place requires consideration of what has occurred within the company (an evidential matter), but mere evidence of a majority resolution authorising or ratifying the matter is insufficient. It is also necessary to consider whether the conduct complained of was capable of being authorised or ratified and, with respect to ratification, whether the requirements as to voting (in s 239) were observed.

5.51 The ability of shareholders to authorise or ratify acts of the directors is limited by common law restrictions which are preserved by s 180(4)(a) (authorisation) and s 239(7) (ratification). Shareholders cannot authorise or ratify acts which are of a fraudulent character or beyond the powers of the company.[1] More specifically, shareholders cannot authorise or ratify acts in breach of the company's constitution where the matter complained of amounts to more than a mere matter of internal management and is a breach of a shareholder's substantive rights,[2] nor can they authorise or ratify acts which amount to the misappropriation of 'money, property or advantages which belong to the company or in which the other shareholders are entitled to participate'.[3] On the other hand, bona fide misuse of powers[4] or incidental profit making is ratifiable[5] as is mere negligence, even when it causes significant loss to the company.[6]

1   *Burland v Earle* [1902] AC 83 at 93–94, per Lord Davey, see above at para 5.2. In particular, shareholders cannot authorise or ratify transactions which constitute a return of capital to shareholders other than with the sanction of the court or in accordance with a statutory scheme – such transactions are ultra vires, incapable of ratification and void: *Trevor v Whitworth* (1887) 12 App Cas 409; *Ridge Securities Ltd v IRC* [1964] 1 All ER 275; *Re Halt Garage (1964) Ltd* [1982] 3 All ER 1016; *Aveling Barford Ltd v Perion Ltd* [1989] BCLC 626. See also *Barclays Bank plc v British and Commonwealth Holdings plc* [1996] 1 BCLC 1 at 7. Such transactions can be described as a fraud on the creditors and cannot be authorised or ratified by the shareholders even unanimously: see *Rolled Steel Products (Holdings) Ltd v British Steel Corpn* [1985] 3 All ER 52 at 86, per Slade LJ.
2   See *Pender v Lushington* (1877) 6 Ch D 70; *MacDougall v Gardiner* (1875) 1 Ch D 13 at 25, CA.
3   *Burland v Earle* [1902] AC 83 at 93, per Lord Davey; *Cook v Deeks* [1916] 1 AC 554; *Daniels v Daniels* [1978] 2 All ER 89.
4   *Bamford v Bamford* [1969] 1 All ER 969.
5   *Regal (Hastings) Ltd v Gulliver* [1967] 2 AC 134n, [1942] 1 All ER 378.
6   *Pavlides v Jensen* [1956] 2 All ER 518.

5.52 The CA 2006 does add two glosses to the common law position – one on authorisation and one on ratification. On authorisation, the CA 2006 allows disinterested directors to authorise a director to exploit property, information or opportunity, though there is a conflict between the director's interests and the interests of the company (s 175). The significance of this change is that such exploitation of property, information, opportunity etc by a director where he has a conflict of interest is precisely the type of conduct which at common law was unratifiable 'fraud on the minority' conduct[1] which justified bringing a derivative claim. The result is that, though such conduct still cannot be ratified (the common law on ratification having been preserved by s 239(7)), it can be authorised in advance by the directors under s 175(4)(b), see discussion at para 4.4. This change of position, assuming a director can secure authorisation, significantly reduces any risk to directors arising from the apparently expansive statutory jurisdiction to bring a derivative claim for any breach of any duty.

[1]   See *Cook v Deeks* [1916] 1 AC 554; *Atwool v Merryweather* (1867) LR 5 Eq 464n; *Menier v Hooper's Telegraph Works* (1874) 9 Ch App 350.

5.53 At a practical level, it may be difficult for a would-be claimant to determine whether shareholder authorisation has been given, particularly where there is reliance on informal unanimous assent[1] given before he became a member. In the absence of general meetings in private companies, a member will need to exercise his inspection rights under CA 2006, s 358 to determine whether authorisation (or ratification, where ratification is possible) has occurred. Crucially, there is no requirement for board authorisation of conflicts of interest under s 175(4)(b) to be disclosed to the shareholders.

[1]   Applying *Re Duomatic Ltd* [1969] 1 All ER 161.

5.54 As regards ratification, as noted above the common law limits on ratification are relatively well settled (even if the case law is not always easily reconcilable) and the focus may be, not on whether the breach of duty is capable of ratification, but whether it has been effectively ratified. The change made by the CA 2006 is that, on any resolution to ratify a breach of duty, the votes of the interested director (if a member of the company) and any member connected with him (as defined in ss 252–255) must be disregarded (see s 239(3), (4)) – the text of s 239 is set out at para 4.49.[1] Determining whose votes must be disregarded may not be straightforward, given the breadth of the definition of a connected person, and the issue of whether there has been effective ratification may itself occupy considerable court time.

[1]   As before, other shareholders are entitled to exercise their votes as they please: *North-West Transportation Co Ltd v Beatty* (1887) 12 App Cas 589.

5.55 Even if a director cannot muster sufficient votes for ratification, it does not necessarily follow that a derivative claim can be brought. Effective ratification is an absolute bar to a claim, but its absence merely means that the court has a discretion as to whether the claim can proceed which it must exercise in the light of the factors set out in s 263(3).

5.56 Looking at the absolute bars in s 263(2), it is clear that there is the potential for this to be a lengthier and costlier stage than is desirable. Equally, practice may evolve such that little use is made of this power in s 263(2) to dismiss a claim. For the reasons discussed above at para 5.47, the courts may be reluctant to decide under s 263(2)(a) that a director would not continue the case and to dismiss the claim on that basis. It is also quite likely that there will be no evidence of authorisation or ratification for, had there been, the shareholder would not have considered bringing a derivative claim (unless he wishes to dispute whether the matter was capable of authorisation or validly ratified). The result may be that, in most instances, there will be no basis on which to dismiss the claim under s 263(2) for, had there been evidence to support dismissal under that provision, the claim would not have progressed to this stage. In so far as the small number of applications under Part 11 to date can be said to be representative of the courts' approach, the general thrust has been a move to consider the discretionary factors rather than to look to dismiss the claim on the basis of the absolute bars in s 263(2).[1]

In practice, successful reliance on s 263(2) will probably only arise where the court has adjourned proceedings under s 261(3) or (4) and the company uses the adjournment to authorise or ratify the breach of duty which allows the court to dismiss the case under s 263(2)(b) or (2)(c).

[1]   See *Mission Capital plc v Sinclair* [2008] EWHC 1534 (Ch), [2008] BCC 866; *Franbar Holdings Ltd v Patel* [2009] 1 BCLC 1.

DISCRETIONARY FACTORS TO BE CONSIDERED BY THE COURT

5.57

'CA 2006, s 263   **Whether permission to be given**

...

(3)   In considering whether to give permission (or leave) the court must take into account, in particular—
   (a)   whether the member is acting in good faith in seeking to continue the claim;
   (b)   the importance that a person acting in accordance with section 172 (duty to promote the success of the company) would attach to continuing it;
   (c)   where the cause of action results from an act or omission that is yet to occur, whether the act or omission could be, and in the circumstances would be likely to be—
      (i)   authorised by the company before it occurs, or
      (ii)   ratified by the company after it occurs;
   (d)   where the cause of action arises from an act or omission that has already occurred, whether the act or omission could be, and in the circumstances would be likely to be, ratified by the company;
   (e)   whether the company has decided not to pursue the claim;
   (f)   whether the act or omission in respect of which the claim is brought gives rise to a cause of action that the member could pursue in his own right rather than on behalf of the company.
(4)   In considering whether to give permission (or leave) the court shall have particular regard to any evidence before it as to the views of members of the company who have no personal interest, direct or indirect, in the matter.'

5.58   The factors listed in s 263(3) are very much those identified by the Law Commission, but the list is not exhaustive[1] and so, while the court must take them into account 'in particular', it can also consider any other matter which it considers to be relevant. It was argued in the Parliamentary debates that the list should include a reference to whether the company has suffered any loss,[2] but the issue of loss would be relevant to s 263(3)(a), (b) and (e). Likewise, the

Government did not wish to make wrongdoer control a specific factor, but it would be relevant to s 263(3)(c), (d) and (e). The court is expected to take into account all of the factors together, in no particular order, and how important each is in any case is for the court to determine having regard to all the circumstances.[3] Given the width of the factors, there is a risk that consideration of these matters could be a lengthy process.[4] In weighing up the merits of the application, the court is likely to be guided by the purpose of a derivative claim, namely to give a remedy for a wrong which would otherwise escape redress.[5]

[1]   The Secretary of State may by regulations amend this provision to alter or add to the matters the court is required to take into account in considering whether to give permission: CA 2006, s 263(5)–(7); see 679 HL Official Report (5th series) cols GC31–32 (27 February 2006).

[2]   See 679 HL Official Report (5th series) col GC30–31 (27 February 2006).

[3]   See 679 HL Official Report (5th series) col GC26 (27 February 2006). Boyle, *Minority Shareholders' Remedies* (2002) suggests that the factors are ill-suited to the circumstances likely to arise in public listed companies.

[4]   The experience in Australia has been that the courts have not expended much time at this stage with most applications for leave being dealt with in one to two days, see Ramsay and Saunders, 'Litigation by Shareholders and Directors: An Empirical Study of the Australian Statutory Derivative Action' [2006] 6 JCLS 397 at 427, 442–443.

[5]   See *Burland v Earle* [1902] AC 83 at 93–94; *Prudential Assurance Co Ltd v Newman Industries Ltd (No 2)* [1982] 1 All ER 354 at 357–358; *Smith v Croft (No 2)* [1987] 3 All ER 909 at 945.

Section 263(3)(a): member acting in good faith

5.59 The motives of the claimant will be an important filter used by the courts to deal particularly with the type of speculative litigation which it is alleged Pt 11 will attract and the vulture hedge fund and the opportunistic shareholder may have difficulty in meeting this good faith requirement. An interest in the commercial benefits to be gained from the litigation, however, would not necessarily rule out a claim if the court otherwise thinks it is in the company's interests.[1]

The Australian authorities, applying a similar statutory derivative procedure which requires an applicant to act in good faith, consider that good faith in this context involves two interrelated factors: whether the applicant honestly believes that a good cause of action exists and has a reasonable prospect of success; and whether the applicant is seeking to bring the derivative action for such a collateral purpose as would amount to an abuse of process.[2] The Australian approach was considered in *Re Wishart*[3] where Lord Glennie accepted that this approach identifies the sort of considerations which the court will wish to take into account. He went on to say, however, that:

'In a case where the court is satisfied that a prima facie case is made out, it will be difficult to show that the applicant for leave does not honestly believe that the company has a cause of action and that that cause of action has a reasonable prospect of success ... If there is a *prima facie* case of a director having committed an act or omission of the type covered by the definition of derivative proceedings in the Act, why should an applicant be prevented from bringing the action simply because it may be asserted against him that he has other less creditable motives than a desire to see the company put back into funds? It seems to me that it will be a rare case, requiring precise averments and cogent evidence, where an application for leave is refused on the grounds that the petitioner is not acting in good faith.'[4]

1   See Law Commission Report, para 6.76.
2   See *Swansson v R A Pratt Properties Pty Ltd* (2002) 42 ACSR 313, NSWSC; also *Goozee v Graphic World Holdings Pty Ltd* (2002) 42 ACSR 534, NSWSC. In *Goozee* the claimant was not in good faith when the purpose of the action was to force the majority shareholders to procure the payment of dividends or the purchase of the claimant's shares.
3   [2009] CSOH 20, 12 February 2009, see para 33. The Scottish provisions on derivative claims, set out in Part 11, Chapter 2, are in substance identical to those applicable to the rest of the UK, though the CPR do not apply and therefore there are procedural differences.
4   [2009] CSOH 20, 12 February 2009, see para 33.

5.60 It is for the shareholder seeking permission to establish to the satisfaction of the court that he is a person acting in good faith and should be allowed to sue on behalf of the company.[1] A claimant will not be in good faith if motivated to litigate by personal considerations rather than in the interests of the company.[2] It is clear that while the issues raised in s 263(3)(a) and (b) are separate, there will be considerable overlap between them.[3] A member may be acting in good faith and in the interests of the company; or a member may be acting in good faith, but pursuing the claim may not be in the interests of the company; or the claim may be brought in the interests of the company, but the member is not acting in good faith or is acting partially in good faith, but partially from an ulterior motive. Evidentially it may be difficult to disentangle the various strands and even more difficult to assign a relative weighting to each of them. In circumstances of such mixed motives, the court will be aided in its deliberations by its obligation under s 263(4) to look to any evidence before it as to the views of disinterested shareholders.

1   *Barrett v Duckett* [1995] 1 BCLC 243 at 250.
2   *Barrett v Duckett* [1995] 1 BCLC 243; and see Payne, ' "Clean Hands" in Derivative Actions' (2002) CLJ 76 at 81.
3   See Cheffins, 'Reforming the Derivative Action: The Canadian Experience and British Prospects' [1997] Company, Financial and Insolvency Law Review 227.

5.61 In *Nurcombe v Nurcombe*[1] the Court of Appeal accepted that a defendant in a derivative claim is entitled to raise against the plaintiff any defence which could have been raised had the action been brought by the plaintiff shareholder personally. The court may refuse to allow a claim to proceed, therefore, where the behaviour of the minority shareholder would render it inequitable for a claim brought by him to succeed, as where the claimant has benefited personally from the wrong complained of.[2] It has been argued convincingly[3] that this approach involves the mistaken application of the clean hands doctrine in the context of derivative actions. Instead the authorities in question should more appropriately be seen as cases where, in keeping with the purpose of a derivative action (to do justice to the company), the court has determined that it would be an abuse of jurisdiction in the particular circumstances to allow an action brought by that shareholder to proceed. Whichever analysis is adopted, it is clear that the court will look at the conduct of the particular claimant to a greater degree than might be suggested merely by the good faith requirement in s 263(3)(a).

1   [1984] BCLC 557, CA.
2   *Nurcombe v Nurcombe* [1984] BCLC 557, applying *Towers v African Tug Co* [1904] 1 Ch 558.
3   See Payne, ' "Clean Hands" in Derivative Action' (2002) CLJ 76 at 80 who urges caution in applying the reasoning in *Towers v African Tug Co* [1904] 1 Ch 558 to derivative claims while acknowledging that the mistaken application of this doctrine is likely to continue.

Section 263(3)(b): importance a director would attach to continuing the claim

5.62 Accepting that a director would seek to continue the claim for the purpose of s 263(2)(a) (otherwise the case would not have reached this stage, see para 5.43), the court moves on to assess the importance which a director would attach to continuing it. The court may be as reluctant to reach a firm view on this issue as under s 263(2)(a), see para 5.47. The same type of task is required – the court has to look at the matter from the subjective perspective of the hypothetical director acting to promote the success of the company. The court must assess the commercial considerations (time and costs involved, the distraction of management, damage to reputation, likelihood of success and recovery, size of the loss) which the director would regard as relevant in assessing the importance of continuing the claim.[1] Clearly, it would be influential if independent non-executive directors, whose conduct is not the subject of the claim, were opposed to the claim proceeding.[2]

1   See *Franbar Holdings Ltd v Patel* [2009] 1 BCLC 1 (a hypothetical director might be more inclined to regard pursuit of the derivative claim as less important if the matters could more naturally be formulated as breaches of a shareholders' agreement or acts of unfair prejudice; if a buy out of the minority has been proposed, again a hypothetical director would be less likely to attribute importance to the continuance of the derivative claim).
2   CA 2006, s 263(4) requires the court to have regard to the views of independent members, see para 5.71; s 263(3)(e) requires the court to have regard to the views of the company, see para 5.64; and this provision, s 263(3)(b) provides a mechanism by which the court may have regard to the views of the independent directors. The cumulative effect is to require the court to consider all possible constituencies within the board and the shareholders.

Section 263(3)(c) and (d): curing the breach; authorisation/ratification

5.63 Two issues arise under these provisions. First, whether the breach of duty can be authorised or ratified – the position on authorisation and ratification was discussed in paras 5.48–5.56 – and this involves an assessment not just as to whether the breach is capable of authorisation or ratification, but also whether ratification is possible given the voting constraints set out in s 239(3), (4). Secondly, the question whether an act or omission is likely to be authorised or ratified requires the court to consider the factual position within the individual company, bearing in mind that it is always open to the court to adjourn the proceedings (under s 261(4)(c)) to allow a meeting to be called for the purposes of authorisation or ratification.[1]

1   See 679 HL Official Report (5th series) cols GC27–28 (27 February 2006); HC Official Report, SC D (Company Law Reform Bill), 13 July 2006, col 679. If it is clear that the breach will be ratified, it is pointless to call a meeting, and the court can simply refuse permission to continue the claim: *Smith v Croft (No 2)* [1987] 3 All ER 909 at 957; see also Law Commission Report, para 6.84.

5.64 *The Derivative Claim – an Invitation to Litigate?*

Section 263(3)(e): the company has decided not to pursue the claim

5.64 The decision of the company not to pursue the claim (as opposed to authorising or ratifying the breach) may be taken by the directors or the shareholders.[1] The requirement to serve notice on the company (as discussed above at para 5.33) gives the company an opportunity to form a view on the claim at an early stage.

If the company has not actually considered the matter, the court may use its powers to adjourn proceedings to allow for that consideration.[2] As Knox J explained in *Smith v Croft (No 2)*,[3] the purpose of the adjournment is to obtain for the court a realistic assessment of the practical desirability of the claim going forward made by the organ that has the power and ability to take decisions on behalf of the company.

If the company decides not to pursue the claim that is not conclusive for there may be ulterior reasons for the decision, but it would be influential and the court will not look to undermine or interfere with the commercial decisions of the company properly made.[4]

[1] 79 HL Official Report (5th series) cols GC829–30 (27 February 2006). As was noted in *Prudential Assurance Co Ltd v Newman Industries Ltd (No 2)* [1982] 1 All ER 354 at 365, a board might conclude that to pursue the claim would not be to the company's advantage and to allow a shareholder to do so might result in the company being 'killed by kindness'.
[2] See HC Official Report, SC D (Company Law Reform Bill), 13 July 2006, col 679.
[3] [1987] 3 All ER 909 at 956.
[4] See 679 HL Official Report (5th series) cols GC29–30 (27 February 2006); Law Commission Report, para 6.87.

Section 263(3)(f): a cause of action that a member could pursue in his own right

5.65 The focus of this provision is on whether it is possible for the claimant to bring a personal claim, not whether there is an alternative remedy available to the claimant.[1] The Government declined on two grounds to adopt an Opposition amendment which would have required the court to consider specifically the availability of an alternative remedy, namely (1) that an alternative remedy in the form of an offer to buy the claimant's shares is not an appropriate remedy in the circumstances of a derivative claim, and (2) that this approach might encourage vulture funds to tell companies that they must buy them out or face a possible derivative claim.[2]

[1] At common law, the availability of an alternative remedy was not a bar to a derivative claim. In so far as *Barrett v Duckett* [1995] 1 BCLC 243 at 250 might be so interpreted, Lawrence Collins J in *Konamaneni v Rolls Royce Industrial Power (India) Ltd* [2002] 1 BCLC 336 at 346 suggested that was a mistaken reading of the authorities. In his view, the cases relied upon for that proposition were really cases where there was no wrongdoer control which, at common law, was a bar to a derivative claim: and see *Mumbray v Lapper* [2005] BCC 990.
[2] See 682 HL Official Report (5th series) cols 726–728 (23 May 2006).

5.66 A director's duties are owed to the company so strictly speaking a breach of a director's duty cannot give rise to a cause of action that the member may pursue in his own right. In recent years, however, the courts have been content for minority shareholders to seek redress by way of a petition under s 994 where breaches of directors' duties have resulted in the company's affairs being conducted in an unfairly prejudicial manner.

5.67 The relationship between the statutory derivative claim and s 994 is unclear.[1] In practice, most successful petitioners on an unfairly prejudicial petition rely heavily on breaches of fiduciary duties and, in particular, on misappropriation of corporate assets by the majority shareholders/directors. At common law, such conduct would warrant the bringing of a derivative claim – misappropriation of assets being an unratifiable wrong. The courts have been content to permit such conduct to be the subject of petitions on the grounds of unfairly prejudicial conduct without dwelling on the extent of the overlap between the personal claim and any derivative claim which might also have been brought. One explanation may be that the courts were content to allow these matters to be litigated via what is now s 994 because of a tacit acknowledgment that the matter was very unlikely (given the procedural obstacles) to be the subject of a common law derivative action.

1   See Hannigan, 'Drawing boundaries between derivative claims and unfairly prejudicial petitions' [2009] JBL (July issue); see also Poole and Roberts, 'Shareholder Remedies – Corporate Wrongs and the Derivative Action' [1999] JBL 99; also McIntosh, 'The Oppression remedy: Personal or Derivative?' (1991) 70 Can Bar Rev 29.

5.68 The pattern for the past 20 years, therefore, has been the development of an extensive jurisdiction under s 994 and the shrinking of the derivative jurisdiction to almost a legal footnote. Nothing about the nature of the statutory procedure in Part 11 would suggest any change in that position and the fundamental attraction of s 994 – a personal remedy for the claimant – remains an overwhelming justification for taking that route rather than bringing a derivative claim.

5.69 The issue is how the possibility of pursuing a petition for personal relief under s 994 will be reflected in the court's consideration of s 263(3)(f). It may be that the existence of a statutory derivative procedure will persuade the courts to draw sharper lines now between personal and derivative claims.[1] Where the wrong is a breach of fiduciary duty and, in part, the relief sought is for the benefit of the company[2], the courts may decide that the claim must proceed via Pt 11. Equally, petitioners under s 994 may find themselves faced with the defence that they are pursuing a derivative claim[3] and should be required to cross the thresholds laid down in Pt 11.

Concerns about the expansion of the derivative claim may persuade the courts to take a robust line that, where possible, aggrieved members should proceed with personal claims under s 994 (and run the risk of costs: there is no indemnity for costs[4] under s 994) rather than bring a derivative claim. Such an approach might apply especially where the dispute is a typical shareholder dispute in a family or quasi-partnership business[5] and there is some limited evidence of that type of approach emerging.[6] While a standard direction of would-be derivative claimants to the unfairly prejudicial jurisdiction would render Pt 11 redundant, the courts might usefully impose a clearer demarcation between Part 11 claims and s 994 petitions with quasi-partnership disputes dealt with (as now) under the latter and public company issues dealt with as derivative claims.[7]

1   For an illustration of the overlap, see *Jafari-Fini v Skillglass* [2005] BCC 842, CA (foundation of the claimant's personal action and a proposed derivative claim was the alleged invalidity of a notice of default and demand served on the company by a lender – the court saw no need for a derivative claim if the company was added as a defendant to the personal action so as to be bound by the result). See also *Airey v Cordell* [2007] BCC 785 where the court adjourned an application for permission to proceed with a derivative claim (essentially founded on diversion of corporate assets to another entity) to allow the majority shareholders/directors to put forward a proposal which afforded adequate protection for the *claimant* (as opposed to the company).
2   See, for example, *Clark v Cutland* [2003] 2 BCLC 393.
3   See Cheffins, 'Reforming the Derivative Action: The Canadian Experience and British Prospects' [1997] Company, Financial and Insolvency Law Review 227 at 238, who notes that in Canada claimants under the oppression remedy (the equivalent of the unfairly prejudicial remedy) on occasion were defeated by claims by the defendant that the shareholder petitioner was actually pursuing a derivative claim and should be required to seek the permission of the court to continue the claim.
4   But see *Clark v Cutland* [2003] 2 BCLC 393 at 406 where Arden LJ thought that, to the extent that the relief claimed under s 461 (CA 2006, s 996) by a successful petitioner under s 459 (CA 2006, s 994) is sought for the benefit of the company, the court may make an indemnity order in respect of that relief; see Payne, 'Shareholders' Remedies Reassessed' (2004) 67 MLR 500; Payne, 'Sections 459–461 Companies Act 1985 in Flux: The Future of Shareholder Protection' (2005) CLJ 647.
5   See *Mumbray v Lapper* [2005] BCC 990 where the court refused permission to continue a derivative claim (at common law) describing the situation as essentially a partnership bust-up.
6   In *Mission Capital plc v Sinclair* [2008] BCC 866, one of the reasons for refusing permission to continue a derivative claim under CA 2006, Part 11 was that the court did not consider that the claimants were seeking anything which could not be recovered by means of an unfair prejudice petition; likewise in *Franbar Holdings Ltd v Patel* [2009] 1 BCLC 1, permission was refused when the acts complained of gave rise to claims by the member in his own right for breach of a shareholders' agreement and under CA 2006, s 994 which the court considered should give him all the relief sought.
7   Hannigan, 'Drawing boundaries between derivative claims and unfairly prejudicial petitions' [2009] JBL (July issue).

5.70 Despite the absence of any requirement to consider whether the shareholder is acting unreasonably in pursuing a derivative claim rather than a personal claim which is open to him,[1] that factor would undoubtedly be taken into account by the court when considering s 263(3)(f). It would also be relevant under s 263(3)(a) above as to whether the member is acting in good faith in seeking to continue the claim. Of course, a shareholder may be able to show the court that he wishes to remain a member of the company and so would prefer a corporate remedy rather than a personal remedy under s 996 which would typically see him exit from the company with his shares being purchased by the respondents to the petition.[2]

1   Compare the position under IA 1986, s 125(2) where the court may refuse a winding-up order if a shareholder is acting unreasonably in pursuing an order when an alternative remedy is available.
2   See Law Commission Report, paras 6.10–6.12. In *Airey v Cordell* [2007] BCC 785 the claimant wished to use a derivative claim (essentially founded on a diversion of corporate assets to another entity) to recover those assets for the company (so that he could participate in the long-term gains to be expected from their exploitation) rather than be bought out of the company.

Section 263(4): views of disinterested shareholders

5.71

'CCA 1006, s 263

...

(4) In considering whether to give permission (or leave) the court shall have particular regard to any evidence before it as to the views of members of the company who have no personal interest, direct or indirect, in the matter.'

This obligatory requirement was added to the statute as part of the package of amendments introduced to meet concerns that there were inadequate filters to deter vexatious claims, see para 5.13 above.[1] It is intended to reflect the position adopted by Knox J in *Smith v Croft (No 2)*[2] as to the weight to be given to the influential views of those shareholders who are independent of the wrongdoers.[3] Knox J was unconvinced that a just result is achieved by a single minority shareholder having the right to involve a company in an action for recovery of compensation for the company if all the other minority shareholders are, for disinterested reasons, satisfied that the proceedings will be productive of more harm than good.[4] It was also suggested in debate that this provision allows the opinions of shareholders in a major traded company to be taken into account while acknowledging that it is not practicable or desirable in such companies to ask shareholders formally to approve directors' commercial decisions.[5] Ratification or authorisation may not have taken place, nor be likely to, for the purposes of s 263(3)(c) and (3)(d), see para 5.63; likewise, there may not be an actual decision of the company not to continue the claim for the purposes of s 263(3)(e), see para 5.64, but it may nevertheless be possible to show that the shareholders are content to support the directors in respect of what has occurred.[6]

1   See 681 HL Official Report (5th series) cols 883–884 (9 May 2006). See Chivers and Shaw, *The Law of Majority Shareholder Power* (2008) para 9.59 who consider that the separate status accorded this provision (s 263(4)) reflects the fact that the views of the independent minority – if there is one – are likely to be of greater importance than any of the other factors in s 263(3).
2   [1987] 3 All ER 909 at 957.
3   See 681 HL Official Report (5th series) col 888 (9 May 2006).
4   [1987] 3 All ER 909 at 956.
5   See 681 HL Official Report (5th series) col 884 (9 May 2006); and see Boyle, *Minority Shareholders' Remedies* (2002), pp 8–9, who is critical of the failure of the Law Commission to address the special problems of bringing derivative claims in respect of listed public companies.
6   681 HL Official Report (5th series) col 884 (9 May 2006).

5.72 A practical concern, particularly in widely held companies, is how to identify 'persons who have no personal interest, direct or indirect, in the matter'[1] and how to obtain evidence as to their views on the claim. There must also be a question mark over whether such persons, assuming they can be identified, would be willing to become involved in a claim, even at this level.[2] A scenario may be envisaged where institutional shareholders make known to the court their view that a claim should not continue and the court refuses permission for the claim to continue. If it later emerged that the claim was well founded, the institutions would face criticism for the role they played in preventing the claim from proceeding. Independent shareholders may prefer to remain on the sidelines rather than risk being put in such a position. Where the institutions positively favour a claim being pursued, a derivative claim would probably be unnecessary for the institutions will be able to effect board changes which would ensure that the company pursues the matter.

1   The Law Commission had considered this issue in terms of seeking the opinion of an independent organ (see Law Commission Report, paras 6.88–6.89), a term derived from *Smith v Croft (No 2)* [1987] 3 All ER 909 at 957–960, but it was criticized as being unclear. The formulation in the statute has avoided that problem, but may be difficult to apply in a widely held company.
2   There is nothing to suggest any appetite on the part of institutional shareholders for this type of role, see 'The Responsibilities of Institutional Shareholders and their Agents – Statement of Principles' drawn up by the Institutional Shareholders Committee (June 2007).

COSTS ISSUES

5.73   Part 11 makes no specific provision for costs and the Law Commission's position was that the court's power to make costs indemnity orders in derivative actions should remain unchanged. The position is governed by the Court of Appeal decision in *Wallersteiner v Moir (No 2)*[1] which held that where a shareholder has, in good faith and on reasonable grounds, sued as plaintiff in a minority shareholder's action, the benefit of which if successful will accrue to the company and only indirectly to the plaintiff as a member of the company, and which action it would be reasonable for an independent board of directors to bring in the company name, the court may order the company to pay the plaintiff's costs.[2] Under CPR 19.9E, the court may order the company to indemnify the claimant against liability for costs incurred in the permission application or in the derivative claim or both.

1   [1975] 1 All ER 849.
2   [1975] 1 All ER 849 at 868–869, per Buckley LJ. In *Smith v Croft* [1986] 2 All ER 551, Walton J took a restrictive view of the jurisdiction to make an indemnity order (an approach criticised by Prentice, '*Wallersteiner v Moir*: A Decade Later' 1987 Conv 167; also Reisberg, 'Funding Derivative Actions: A Re-Examination of Costs and Fees as Incentives To Commence Litigation' [2004] 4 JCLS 345 at 360), but this restrictive approach was not followed in *Jaybird v Greenwood Ltd* [1986] BCLC 319. For examples of situations where an indemnity order was refused, see *Halle v Trax BM Ltd* [2000] BCC 1020 (in effect asking company to fund dispute between two partners in a joint venture); *Mumbray v Lapper* [2005] BCC 990 (essentially a partnership break-up); also *Watts v Midland Bank plc* [1986] BCLC 15 (no indemnity order where company hopelessly insolvent). See Quigxiu Bu, 'The Indemnity Order in a Derivative Action' (2006) 27 Co Law 2.

5.74   The ability to secure an indemnity from the company is an important consideration for a shareholder contemplating a derivative action,[1] but concerns that the very possibility of obtaining an indemnity order will encourage vexatious claims are misplaced.[2] Claimants cannot be sure that the court will exercise its discretion and make an indemnity order, so a claimant does have a potential exposure to significant costs and the indemnity does not act as an actual incentive to bring a claim.[3] Of course, for a limited number of claimants, such as hedge funds, the issue of costs may not be a significant deterrent.

1   An application for a *Wallersteiner* order may be included with the application for permission to continue the claim and the order is subject to periodic review by the court. Reisberg, 'Derivative Actions and the Funding Problem: The Way Forward' [2006] JBL 445 argues that, until US-type contingency fee agreements are introduced in this jurisdiction, financing the litigation will remain a major obstacle to use of the derivative claim.

2   See 679 HL Official Report (5th series) col GC13 (27 February 2006).

3   Reisberg, 'Funding Derivative Actions: A Re-Examination of Costs and Fees as Incentives To Commence Litigation' [2004] 4 JCLS 345 argues that the only real incentive for shareholders to bring derivative actions would be if the courts could order some element of personal recovery for them when the claim is successful; see also Reisberg, 'Derivative Actions and the Funding Problem: The Way Forward' [2006] JBL 445 ; and Cheffins, 'Reforming the Derivative Action: The Canadian Experience and British Prospects' [1997] Company, Financial and Insolvency Law Review 227 at 256–260.

5.75 Companies may fund expenditure incurred by a defendant director in defending derivative proceedings, but those costs must be refunded if the director loses the case.[1] In larger companies, directors will also have insurance cover against personal liability (paid for by the company) and they will want to ensure derivative claims and associated legal costs are covered. It is possible that companies may end up funding the claimant (under a *Wallersteiner* order) and the defendant directors (through insurance and by way of loans to meet defence costs) which may make a derivative claim doubly expensive for the company.

1   CA 2006, s 205(1), (2).

CONCLUSIONS

5.76 Initially Pt 11 looks as if it will dramatically alter the landscape of shareholders' remedies, allowing any member (regardless of size of shareholding or length of membership) to bring a derivative claim in respect of any breach of duty (including negligence) or default by any director, but many caveats must be added to that picture of open-ended liability.)

5.77 First, derivative claims, though facilitated by the new mechanism of Pt 11, remain subject to the general principle of majority rule, as discussed above in paras 5.16–5.17. Moreover, the newly available power of directors to authorise conflicts and profit making to the extent permitted by s 175 significantly reduces the potential for 'fraud on the minority' type conduct, see para 4.4, which in the past formed the basis of typical derivative actions.

5.78 Secondly, the threshold tests are sufficient, cumulatively, to deter many would-be claimants, especially when costs issues are factored in, not to mention the informational disadvantages facing a claimant.[1] The judiciary will be anxious not to open the doors here to the sort of speculative litigation sometimes seen in the US and the court rules combine with Pt 11 to ensure strict judicial control. In particular, the courts have power at all stages to adjourn the proceedings to allow for authorisation or ratification. Considerable efforts will be expended also on settling claims before the permission stage turns into a mini-trial. In the Parliamentary debates, there was much emphasis on the expectation that the courts will maintain the long tradition of not second-guessing directors' business judgment and that message may well curb judicial enthusiasm for a liberal approach to the jurisdiction. Overall, few cases are likely to proceed to full blown trials of the issue, and this has been the experience of other jurisdictions which have introduced statutory derivative actions.[2] Two years after the commencement of Part 11 with only a trickle of derivative claims before the courts, there is nothing to suggest that the outcome in this jurisdiction is likely to be any different (unless the current financial difficulties prompt shareholders into action).

[1]   See Kosmin, 'Minority Shareholders' Remedies: A Practitioner's Perspective [1997] Company, Financial and Insolvency Law Review 211.
[2]   The evidence from Canada, New Zealand and Australia is that the statutory derivative procedures in those jurisdictions are used to an insignificant degree and mainly in respect of private companies (not public companies as might have been anticipated): see Ramsay and Saunders, 'Litigation by Shareholders and Directors: An Empirical Study of the Australian Statutory Derivative Action' [2006] 6 JCLS 397 at 420; Cheffins, 'Reforming the Derivative Action: The Canadian Experience and British Prospects' [1997] Company, Financial and Insolvency Law Review 227 at 241.

5.79 Thirdly, the position remains that recovery is for the benefit of the company, not the individual claimant who can only benefit to the extent that benefit to the company is reflected in the value of his shares, so there is no incentive to litigate via a derivative claim. Save where a claimant is determined to remain as a member of the company, it is preferable to petition under CA 2006, s 994 (unfairly prejudicial conduct) without the need for any permission of the court and with the prospect of personal recovery.

5.80 When all these factors are considered, it is difficult to conclude that the mere introduction of the statutory derivative claim dramatically increases the litigation risk to directors, at least to the level that it would deter people from acting as a director of a public company. Occasionally, there may be a high-profile case pursued as much for the publicity as recovery and settled long before trial, but there is unlikely to be any significant increase in the number of claims being brought.

Chapter 6

ACCOUNTS AND AUDIT

Glynis D Morris

INTRODUCTION

Structure

6.1 Part 15 of the Companies Act 2006 ('CA 2006') deals with the preparation, circulation, filing and revision of annual accounts and reports and Pt 16 with requirements relating to auditors. They replace Pt 7 of the Companies Act 1985 ('CA 1985'), and the detailed provisions carried forward from that Act have generally been redrafted and reordered to make them more understandable and accessible. In many cases, there are separate requirements for small companies, other private companies, public companies and quoted companies. Where relevant, the following structure is adopted:

(1) requirements for small companies precede those for other companies;
(2) requirements for private companies precede those for public companies; and
(3) requirements for unquoted companies precede those for quoted companies.

Certain elements of the previous legislation (such as the detailed requirements on the form and content of Companies Act accounts) are not included in the CA 2006, but the Secretary of State is instead empowered to provide for these by regulations (see para 5.7 below). This is intended to allow for greater flexibility in keeping requirements up to date as well as ease of reference.

Small companies

6.2 CA 2006, ss 381–384 establish which companies are subject to the small company regime. The material is based on ss 246, 247 and 249 of the CA

1985 and covers the qualification rules, qualifying conditions, parent companies and small groups, and ineligibility. There are no changes of substance in this area, except in the definition of an ineligible group (the members of such a group are generally excluded from the small companies regime). Under the CA 1985, a group was ineligible if any of its members was a body corporate (other than a company) with the power to offer its shares or debentures to the public, regardless of whether it actually did so in practice. In s 384 of the CA 2006, this element of the definition of an ineligible group is replaced by a reference to a body corporate (other than a company) whose shares are admitted to trading on a regulated market in an EEA State. Consequently, the emphasis is no longer on the ability to offer shares to the public but on whether a company's shares are actually traded on a regulated market in practice. The other minor change is in s 382(5), which sets out the more generalised definition of balance sheet total (the aggregate of the amounts shown as assets in the company's balance sheet) which is currently applied to IAS accounts under the CA 1985. In future, therefore, the same definition of balance sheet total will apply, regardless of the financial framework adopted.

For accounting periods beginning on or after 6 April 2008, the qualifying conditions for small companies and groups set out in ss 382(3) and 383(4) of the CA 2006 are increased to the following by the Companies Act 2006 (Amendment) (Accounts and Reports) Regulations 2008:[1]

	Small company	*Small group*
Turnover of not more than	£6.5m	£6.5m net or £7.8m gross
Balance sheet total of not more than	£3.26m	£3.26m net or £3.9m gross
Number of employees not more than	50	50

The regulations also provide that, where the position in a preceding financial period needs to be considered in determining whether a company or group qualifies as small for an accounting period beginning on or after 6 April 2008, the higher thresholds may also be applied to that earlier year (but only for comparison purposes).

[1] SI 2008/393.

Quoted companies

6.3 CA 2006, s 385 defines a quoted company as a company whose equity share capital:

(1) has been included in the official list in accordance with Pt 6 of the FSMA 2000;
(2) is officially listed in an EEA State; or
(3) is admitted to dealing on the New York Stock Exchange or on Nasdaq.

This retains the definition previously set out in the CA 1985. An unquoted company is one that does not meet the definition of a quoted company. The

Secretary of State is empowered to amend or replace these definitions by regulations and to limit or extend the application of any accounting provisions applying only to quoted companies.

Implementation of accounts and audit requirements

6.4 Under the Companies Act 2006 (Commencement No 5, Transitional Provisions and Savings) Order 2007,[1] most of the CA 2006 provisions relating to accounts and audit were commenced on 6 April 2008 and generally apply for accounting periods beginning on or after that date, although certain provisions on the appointment of auditors and on changes in audit appointments apply in respect of auditors who are appointed or removed, or who resign, on or after 6 April 2008.

However, the following sections were commenced on 1 October 2007 under the Companies Act 2006 (Commencement No 3, Consequential Amendments, Transitional Provisions and Savings) Order 2007:[2]

(1)   section 417 which sets out detailed requirements on the content of the business review to be given in the directors' report (see para 6.17) and applies for accounting periods beginning on or after 1 October 2007;
(2)   sections 485–488 which deal with the appointment of auditors by private companies (see paras 6.39 and 6.40) and which apply in relation to appointments for financial years beginning on or after 1 October 2007.

[1]   SI 2007/3495.
[2]   SI 2007/2194.

PREPARATION OF ACCOUNTS AND THE TRUE AND FAIR VIEW

Accounting records and accounting periods

6.5 CA 2006, ss 386–389[1] deal with the maintenance and retention of accounting records, and ss 390–392 with accounting reference periods and dates. These replace the equivalent provisions in ss 221–225 of the CA 1985. There are no changes of substance, other than a specific requirement for a company to keep 'adequate' accounting records. This is not expected to have significant practical implications, but it achieves a degree of consistency with s 498(1) which requires the auditor to form an opinion on whether adequate accounting records have been kept by the company (rather than 'proper accounting records' as under s 237(1) of the CA 1985).

[1]   Section 388(1) continues to provide that a company's accounting records must at all times be open to inspection by the company's officers but *Oxford Legal Group v Sibbasbridge* [2008] 2 BCLC 381 CA has emphasised that this right is to enable a director to carry out his duties as director and cannot be used for any improper purpose.

True and fair view

6.6 CA 2006, s 393(1) states that the directors must not approve accounts unless they are satisfied that those accounts give a true and fair view of the assets, liabilities, financial position and profit or loss of the company or the group (as appropriate), and s 393(2) requires the auditor to have regard to this duty of the directors when carrying out his functions as auditor. This new section is in addition to the existing requirements on the true and fair view and the true and fair override, which are retained in s 396 in respect of Companies Act individual accounts and in s 404 in respect of Companies Act group accounts.

The requirement for annual accounts to show a true and fair view has been a primary tenet of UK financial reporting for many years. However, the introduction of the option for most companies to adopt international accounting standards for accounting periods beginning on or after 1 January 2005, and the requirement for listed groups to do so, led to concerns over the extent to which this requirement continues to apply under the IAS framework, given that the legislation initially made no reference to the true and fair view in the case of IAS accounts.

In May 2008, the Financial Reporting Council ('FRC') published an Opinion by Martin Moore QC[1] that confirms the continued relevance of the 'true and fair' concept to the preparation and audit of financial statements. The FRC requested this Opinion in view of the significant changes to accounting standards and company law since the original Opinions on this subject were prepared (by Lord Hoffmann and Dame Mary Arden in 1983 and by Dame Mary Arden in 1993), and in particular in the light of the introduction of the IAS framework into UK company law and the implementation of the CA 2006.

The latest Opinion confirms the supremacy of the true and fair requirement and concludes that the requirement under international accounting standards ('IAS') for accounts to 'present fairly' the financial position, financial performance and cash flows of an entity is simply a different articulation of the 'true and fair' concept rather than a different requirement. The Opinion includes specific consideration of the new provision in s 393 of the CA 2006 referred to above, emphasises that this makes no distinction between IAS and Companies Act accounts and notes that the provision was introduced in order to clarify the primacy of the true and fair concept, following concerns that it may have become blurred as a result of the combination of UK and EC law.

The Opinion also emphasises that the preparation of financial statements is not simply a mechanical process under which compliance with relevant accounting standards will automatically achieve a true and fair view or a fair presentation. Professional judgement will invariably be required in applying the requirements of accounting standards, and the relevant decisions and judgements are not made in a vacuum but rather against the requirement for a true and fair view. It also notes that compliance with accounting standards is not an end in itself, but a means to an end – in other words, the achievement of a true and fair view.

The Opinion also includes consideration of the new requirement under the EC Transparency Directive for half-yearly financial reports to show a true and fair view. This initially gave rise to some concern in the UK, as the true and fair concept had previously been reserved for annual accounts, which are inevitably much more detailed than half-yearly statements. The Opinion notes that any set of accounts is of necessity a distillation and summary, and concludes that a half-yearly statement will give a true and fair view if it is prepared in accordance with standards relevant to interim reporting. This confirms the approach taken in the FSA's Disclosure and Transparency Rules (DTR 4.2.10(3) and (4)).

It should also be noted that the provisions on the true and fair override apply only in respect of Companies Act accounts although IAS 1 'Presentation of Financial Statements' requires similar disclosures to be given in IAS accounts when (in rare circumstances) it is considered necessary to depart from strict compliance with a requirement of a standard or related interpretation in order to achieve a fair presentation.

[1] Available at http://www.frc.org.uk/about/trueandfair.cfm.

Individual accounts

6.7 CA 2006, ss 394–397 set out the directors' duty to prepare either Companies Act or IAS individual accounts each year and replace ss 226, 226A and 226B of the CA 1985. The existing IAS framework is retained, with a minor amendment to the detailed wording on when a company preparing IAS accounts may revert to Companies Act accounts. As a result, a company can now revert to the preparation of Companies Act accounts if it ceases to be a subsidiary undertaking.

Section 396 requires Companies Act individual accounts to comply with relevant regulations on the form and content of the balance sheet and profit and loss account and the disclosures to be given in the notes to the accounts. For accounting periods beginning on or after 6 April 2008, the detailed requirements are set out in:

(1)   the Small Companies and Groups (Accounts and Directors' Report) Regulations 2008, SI 2008/409; and
(2)   the Large and Medium-sized Companies and Groups (Accounts and Reports) Regulations 2008, SI 2008/410.

These new regulations generally restate the detailed requirements on the form and content of Companies Act individual accounts previously set out in certain Schedules to the CA 1985 with only minor amendments. The main change is a new requirement for companies that do not qualify as small or medium-sized to disclose details of material related party transactions that have not been concluded under normal market conditions (SI 2008/410, Sch 1, para 72, Sch 2, para 92 and Sch 3, para 90). Adoption of the small companies regime remains voluntary, so that a small company can choose to comply with any corresponding provision of SI 2008/410 if it wishes.

In the case of a small company:

(1)   Schedule 1 to SI 2008/409 restates the requirements on small company accounts that were previously set out in Schedule 8 to the CA 1985;

(2)   Schedule 2 to SI 2008/409 restates the disclosures requirements for a small company in respect of related undertakings that were previously set out in Schedule 5 to the CA 1985;

(3)   Schedule 3 to SI 2008/409 restates the disclosure requirements in respect of directors' remuneration and benefits that were previously set out in Part 1 of Schedule 6 to the CA 1985; and

(4)   Schedule 4 to SI 2008/409 restates the detailed requirements on small company abbreviated accounts that were previously set out in Schedule 8A to the CA 1985.

For the most part, the content of each Schedule to SI 2008/409 referred to above mirrors that in the equivalent Schedule to the CA 1985, except that definitions and other interpretations have been moved into a separate Schedule 8 to SI 2008/409. The regulations also retain the additional disclosure exemptions previously granted to a small company by s 246(3) of the CA 1985.

For other companies:

(1)   Schedule 1 to SI 2008/410 restates the detailed requirements on the form and content of Companies Act individual accounts that were previously set out in Schedule 4 to the CA 1985;

(2)   Schedules 2 and 3 to SI 2008/410 restate the detailed requirements on the accounts of banking and insurance companies that were previously set out in Schedules 9 and 9A to the CA 1985;

(3)   Schedule 4 to SI 2008/410 restates the disclosure requirements in respect of related undertakings that were previously set out in Schedule 5 to CA 1985; and

(4)   Schedule 5 to SI 2008/410 restates the disclosure requirements in respect of directors' remuneration and benefits that were previously set out in Part 1 of Schedule 6 to the CA 1985.

As with the small company regulations, the content of each Schedule to SI 2008/410 referred to above generally mirrors that in the equivalent Schedule to the CA 1985, except that definitions and other interpretations have been moved into a separate Schedule 10 to SI 2008/410. The disclosure requirements in Schedules 4 and 5 to SI 2008/410 also continue to apply to both Companies Act and IAS accounts (as under the CA 1985).

Minor amendments are made to both SI 2008/409 and SI 2008/410 by the Companies Act 2006 (Accounts, Reports and Audit) Regulations 2009[1] to correct an oversight in the definition of provisions in those regulations.

Regulation 4 to SI 2008/410 sets out a small number of disclosure exemptions for medium-sized companies. These retain the exemption from the disclosure on compliance with applicable accounting standards previously granted by s 246A(2) of the CA 1985 and introduce a new exemption from the disclosure of certain related party transactions (see above). However, the requirements of accounting standards on the disclosure of related party transactions (which are generally more extensive than those set out in the regulations) continue to apply. The regulations also retain the facility for a medium-sized company to deliver an abbreviated profit and loss account, although the detailed requirements are amended so that total turnover must always be disclosed separately (see para 6.33).

[1]   SI 2009/1581.

Group accounts

6.8 CA 2006, s 398 gives a small parent company the option to prepare consolidated group accounts but does not impose any obligation to do so. However, for accounting periods beginning on or after 1 April 2008, a small charitable company is subject to the requirements of charity law on the preparation and audit of accounts and the Charities (Accounts and Reports) Regulations 2008[1] require group accounts to be prepared and audited where the aggregate gross income of the group is more than £500,000 after eliminating all group transactions (see also para 6.37 below). Under s 399, all other parent companies (including those that qualify as medium-sized) must prepare consolidated accounts unless a specific exemption is available. This represents a significant change for medium-sized companies, which have generally been exempt from the requirement to prepare group accounts under the CA 1985. The following exemptions from the preparation of group accounts are retained from the existing legislation, subject to certain conditions:

(1)   Section 400 grants exemption where the parent is a member of a larger EEA group;
(2)   Section 401 grants exemption where the parent is a member of a larger non-EEA group; and
(3)   Section 402 grants exemption where all of the company's subsidiaries are eligible for exclusion from consolidation in Companies Act group accounts.

These exemptions, including the related conditions, re-enact ss 227(1), 227(8), 228, 228A and 229(5) of the CA 1985. A parent that qualifies for one of the exemptions can nevertheless prepare group accounts if it wishes.

CA 2006, ss 403–407 set out the general rules on the preparation of group accounts, including the IAS framework and the need for consistency within the group other than in exceptional circumstances. As with individual accounts (see para 6.7), Companies Act group accounts must comply with relevant regulations on the form and content of the consolidated balance sheet and profit and loss account and the detailed disclosures in the notes to the accounts. For accounting periods beginning on or after 6 April 2008, the detailed requirements are set out in:

(1)   Schedule 6 to the Small Companies and Groups (Accounts and Directors' Report) Regulations 2008;[2] and

(2)   Schedule 6 to the Large and Medium-sized Companies and Groups (Accounts and Reports) Regulations 2008.[3]

These new regulations generally restate the detailed requirements on the form and content of Companies Act group accounts previously set out in Schedule 4A to the CA 1985 with only minor amendments. The main change is that the regulations continue to require minority interests to be shown separately in the profit and loss account and balance sheet, but no longer specify the precise location or require the use of the heading 'minority interests'. This change has been made to facilitate the convergence of UK accounting practice with international requirements. In effect, the small company regulations enable a small parent company that prepares group accounts on a voluntary basis to take advantage of the small companies regime in preparing those accounts (provided that it also prepares its individual accounts under this regime). As with individual accounts, a small company can choose to comply with any corresponding provision of SI 2008/410 if it wishes. Schedules 2 and 3 to SI 2008/410 continue to set out certain adaptations of the group accounts requirements in the case of banking groups and insurance groups.

In the case of Companies Act group accounts, s 405 retains the previous rules on the inclusion and exclusion of subsidiaries from the consolidation, although some of these continue to be overridden by the more stringent requirements of FRS 2 'Accounting for Subsidiary Undertakings'. Section 409 deals with the disclosure of information about related undertakings, although the detailed requirements are once again set out in SI 2008/409 or SI 2008/410, as appropriate, and s 410 retains certain exemptions where the disclosures would otherwise be of excessive length.

[1]   SI 2008/629.
[2]   SI 2008/409.
[3]   SI 2008/410.

Parent company profit and loss

6.9 CA 2006, s 408 retains the exemption from publication of the parent company's individual profit and loss account, with a slight revision in the wording to clarify that this applies in all cases where group accounts are prepared under the Act, and not just where they must be prepared. There is an exemption from the separate disclosure of employee information in respect of the parent, but other disclosure exemptions currently granted by s 230 of the CA 1985 are not retained in the Act because the disclosures no longer form part of the primary legislation. They are set out instead in Regulation 3(2) of SI 2008/410, which provides that the individual profit and loss account of a parent company that falls within s 408 of the CA 2006 need not contain the information normally required by paragraphs 65 to 69 of Schedule 1 to SI 2008/410. Regulation 3(2) of SI 2008/409 includes a similar exemption in respect of the individual profit and loss account of a small parent company that prepares group accounts.

Off-balance sheet arrangements

6.10 CA 2006, s 410A, which was inserted by the Companies Act 2006 (Amendment) (Accounts and Reports) Regulations 2008,[1] introduces new accounts disclosure requirements in respect of off-balance sheet arrangements. These apply to both Companies Act and IAS accounts. If, in the financial year, the company is or has been party to arrangements that are not reflected in the balance sheet and, at the balance sheet date, the risks or benefits arising from those arrangements are material, the following details must be disclosed in the notes to the accounts:

(1)   the nature and business purpose of the arrangements; and
(2)   the financial impact of the arrangements on the company.

Information need only be given to the extent necessary to enable an assessment of the financial position of the company. Companies that qualify as small are exempt from this disclosure requirement and those that qualify as medium-sized are only required to give the details in (1) above.

In June 2008, the ASB issued a statement[2] noting that, following an enquiry, the Urgent Issues Task Force ('UITF') had been considering what constitutes an off-balance sheet arrangement for these purposes. Neither the UK legislation nor the underlying EU Directive[3] includes a definition of an off-balance sheet arrangement but guidance issued by the BERR[4] in June 2008 includes a non-exhaustive list, extracted from the Directive, of the types of transactions envisaged for disclosure. The UITF did not consider that it could issue formal guidance in the absence of a legal definition of an off-balance sheet arrangement but emphasised that disclosure is only required where material risks or benefits arise from the arrangements and to the extent necessary to enable the financial position of the company to be assessed. It also advised companies to consider the types of transaction envisaged by the Directive and the objective of the disclosure requirements.

[1]   SI 2008/393.
[2]   Available at http://www.frc.org.uk/asb/press/pub1643.html.
[3]   Directive 2006/46/EC.
[4]   'Guidance for UK Companies on Accounting and Reporting: Requirements under the Companies Act 2006 and the application of the IAS regulation'.

Employee and director disclosures

6.11 CA 2006, s 411 replaces s 231A of the CA 1985 on the provision of information on employee numbers and costs and applies to all companies other than those within the small company regime. Section 412 deals with the disclosure of directors' remuneration, but once again the detailed requirements are set out in:

(1)   Schedule 3 to the Small Companies and Groups (Accounts and Directors' Report) Regulations 2008;[1] and
(2)   Schedule 5 to the Large and Medium-sized Companies and Groups (Accounts and Reports) Regulations 2008.[2]

However, the main legislation retains the requirement for amounts paid to persons connected with a director, or a body corporate controlled by a director, to be included in the disclosures, and the duty for directors to provide the company with relevant information for disclosure purposes. Section 413 sets out disclosure requirements in respect of advances and credits granted to directors and guarantees entered into on behalf of directors by the company or its subsidiaries. The terminology and disclosure requirements are more straightforward than under the previous legislation. In the case of advances or credits, s 413 requires disclosure of the amount involved, the interest rate, the main conditions and any amounts repaid. In the case of guarantees, the disclosures include the main terms, the maximum potential liability for the company, and any amount paid or liability incurred. Totals must also be given for each of the monetary disclosures. There are no *de minimis* limits and the disclosure requirements apply to both Companies Act and IAS accounts. Comparatives should be given for all of these disclosures under the requirements of FRS 28 'Corresponding Amounts' or IAS 1 'Presentation of Financial Statements', as appropriate.

[1]   SI 2008/409.
[2]   SI 2008/410.

APPROVAL OF ACCOUNTS AND GOING CONCERN ISSUES

Approval and signature by directors

6.12 CA 2006, s 414 retains the previous requirements on the formal approval of individual and group accounts by the board and the signature of the company's balance sheet by a director on behalf of the board to evidence this approval. Where the accounts have been prepared in accordance with the small companies regime, a statement to this effect must be included in a prominent position above the director's signature.

The only significant change is the removal of the present requirement for the copy of the accounts delivered to the registrar to include the director's signature in manuscript on the balance sheet, although the name of the signatory must still be stated. This change has been made to prevent any unnecessary difficulties in the development of arrangements for the electronic delivery of annual accounts and reports to the registrar in due course. However, a manuscript signature continues to be required at present under the transitional provisions of the Companies Act 2006 (Commencement No 5, Transitional Provisions and Savings) Order 2007.[1] This transitional provision is due to be removed from 1 October 2009. From this date, the registrar will set the rules on the authentication of documents delivered to Companies House.

[1]   SI 2007/3495.

Importance of going concern

6.13 The economic downturn in the second half of 2008 and the early part of 2009 has heightened the awareness of the need for directors to give careful consideration to the issue of going concern when preparing and approving annual accounts, and has resulted in the publication of a number of new guidance documents. In November 2008, the Financial Reporting Council (FRC) published the following:[1]

(1)   'An Update for Directors of Listed Companies: Going Concern and Liquidity Risk' which draws together existing requirements and related guidance;
(2)   'Challenges for Audit Committees Arising from Current Economic Conditions' which summarises the key issues that directors and audit committees may need to consider in the present economic climate and sets out a number of detailed questions that may be relevant; and
(3)   a short report on the results of a recent study of the disclosures given by listed and AIM companies in respect of going concern and liquidity risk.

The FRC published a further guidance document for small companies, 'An Update for Directors of Companies that adopt the Financial Reporting Standard for Smaller Entities ('FRSSE'): Going Concern and Financial Reporting' in March 2009[1].

In December 2008, the Auditing Practices Board ('APB') issued Bulletin 2008/10 'Going Concern Issues During the Current Economic Conditions'[2] which is intended to be supplementary to APB Bulletin 2008/1 'Audit Issues when Financial Market Conditions are Difficult and Credit Facilities may be Restricted' which was published in January 2008. In particular, Bulletin 2008/10 includes an updated summary of the key risk factors that may affect going concern and issues that may have increased in significance in recent months.

[1]   All available at http://www.frc.org.uk/corporate/goingconcern.cfm.
[2]   Available at http://www.frc.org.uk/apb/publications/bulletins.cfm.

Directors' assessment

6.14 Directors must satisfy themselves that it is appropriate to prepare accounts on the going concern basis, although this requirement is not intended to provide any guarantee that the company will remain a going concern until the end of the next reporting period. The going concern assessment involves making a judgement at a particular point in time, based on the evidence available and reasonable assumptions about future events made at that time. Consequently, directors should document their knowledge of conditions and events, and the conclusions that they have drawn, as at the date of approval of the accounts, and the auditor should document his understanding of the relevant issues and his conclusions as at the date on which he signs his report, see para 6.44.

The FRC guidance recommends that directors plan their going concern assessment at an early stage and consider in particular what detailed information and analyses will need to be prepared. Early discussion of relevant issues with the company's auditor is also advised.

For some years, the main guidance on the assessment of going concern and related disclosures in the annual report and accounts[1] has been that issued in 1994 for directors of listed companies in connection with corporate governance reporting requirements. The FRC published an Exposure Draft of updated guidance in May 2009, having initially consulted on this in August 2008. In the light of the comments received in response to the initial consultation, together with feedback received in discussions with interested parties, the FRC concluded that the main guidance should incorporate the material in the recently-issued documents referred to at para 6.13 and should cover the full spectrum of UK companies rather than just listed companies. Consequently, the latest Exposure Draft 'Going Concern and Liquidity Risk: Guidance for Directors of UK Companies'[1] represents a complete revision and restructuring of the original guidance. It follows more closely the format and style of other FRC guidance documents by specifying four key principles with detailed guidance on their application in practice. Issues for directors of smaller companies are dealt with at the beginning of each section, followed by additional factors relevant to medium-sized and larger companies. Requirements that apply only to listed companies are highlighted in blue-shaded text. The guidance has also been drafted to cover a range of economic situations, on the basis that it is intended to remain in place for a number of years.

The objective of the guidance is to ensure that going concern assessments are made with appropriate diligence and that related disclosures are balanced, proportionate and understandable. Comments on the Exposure Draft are invited by 28 August 2009 and the FRC hopes to be in a position to issue the document in final form by mid-November 2009. Views are specifically invited on whether the revised guidance should apply for reporting periods ending on or after 31 December 2009.

[1]   Available at http://www.frc.org.uk/corporate/goingconcern.cfm.

Financing facilities

6.15 Both the FRC document 'An Update for Directors of Listed Companies: Going Concern and Liquidity Risk' and APB Bulletin 2008/10 note that, in the present climate, banks may be reluctant to provide positive confirmation that finance facilities will continue to be made available and emphasise that the absence of such confirmations does not necessarily cast doubt on an entity's ability to continue as a going concern. The reluctance of lenders to provide confirmation of finance facilities may extend to profitable businesses with only small borrowing requirements, and directors and auditors need to distinguish between situations where the reluctance is indicative of concerns specific to the entity and those where there are no indications of such concerns (for instance, where a lender has simply adopted a policy of not providing confirmations in respect of any customers).

Where there are potential concerns, the directors may be able to identify alternative strategies or funding to mitigate these. In this case the auditor will need to assess the likely effectiveness of the plans, and management's ability to carry them through, in deciding whether or not to include an emphasis of matter paragraph in his report or, in the most serious cases, issue a qualified report.

Additional attention may also need to be paid to the key assumptions used in the preparation of cash flow forecasts and related sensitivity analysis, and it may be necessary to consider a wider range of possible outcomes. Significant accounting and reporting judgements may also need to be reassessed (for instance, to identify whether any assets have become impaired or whether any accounting policies need to be revised as a result of the changing economic conditions).

Going concern disclosures

6.16 Accounting standards also require certain disclosures on going concern to be given in the accounts, particularly where there are material uncertainties. For listed companies, the Combined Code also requires directors to report that the business is a going concern, with supporting assumptions or qualifications where necessary. The overall conclusions from the study on going concern disclosures (see para 6.13) were that:

(1)   4 companies (13 per cent) provided very useful company specific information;

(2)   8 companies (27 per cent) provided some useful company specific information; and

(3)   17 companies (57 per cent) provided only general disclosures that were of limited usefulness.

The remaining company had no debt or substantial cash balances and so no liquidity risk disclosures.

It is clear that the FRC is looking for considerable improvements in disclosure as more companies begin to feel the effects of the present economic difficulties. One of the main criticisms is the tendency for relevant information to be disclosed in different places within the annual report and accounts, making it difficult for users to gain a comprehensive understanding of how liquidity issues impact on the business. Consequently, the FRC notes that it would be particularly helpful if all relevant disclosures could be brought together in one section of the annual report and accounts. Alternatively, the key disclosures should be summarised in a single note with a cross-reference to the other places where users can find more detailed information.

It is widely expected that there will be more disclosure of material uncertainties in respect of going concern in the coming reporting periods and that there will be an increase in the use of emphasis of matter paragraphs in auditor's reports (as required by CA 2006, s 495(4)(b) where relevant), see para 6.44.

The FRC documents and Bulletin 2008/10 also consider the need for going concern issues to be discussed in interim reports and preliminary announcements (where these are still issued on a voluntary basis).

The latest FRC Exposure Draft 'Going Concern and Liquidity Risk: Guidance for Directors of UK Companies' (see para 6.14) includes the following points of note in respect of disclosure:

(1)   where relevant, UK accounting standards and the FRSSE require disclosure of the fact that the review period considered by the directors is less than one year from the date of the approval of the financial statements, and the guidance proposes that the same disclosures should be given where accounts are prepared under IFRS;

(2)   the FRC proposes that a consistent approach should be taken in the case of interim financial reports that are required to give a true and fair view (as is the case for half-yearly financial reports prepared by listed companies under the FSA Disclosure and Transparency Rules) – consequently, directors would also need to disclose (where relevant) that their review has not extended to a period of at least twelve months from the date of approval of the interim financial statements.

DIRECTORS' REPORT AND DIRECTORS' REMUNERATION REPORT

Directors' report

6.17 CA 2006, ss 415–419 deal with the preparation of the directors' report and replace the previous requirements of the CA 1985 on this subject. They also incorporate certain additional requirements on the content of the business review, which apply only in the case of a quoted company.

The content of the annual business review is now driven by the requirements of the EU Accounts Modernisation Directive.[1] Changes to bring UK requirements into line with the Directive were introduced into the CA 1985 for accounting periods beginning on or after 1 April 2005 by the Companies Act 1985 (Operating and Financial Review and Directors' Report etc) Regulations 2005[2] and are retained in s 417 of the CA 2006, but with the additional disclosures for quoted companies referred to above. As a result, the legislation now provides that, to the extent necessary for an understanding of the development, performance or position of the company's business, the business review of a quoted company must include:

(1)   the main trends and factors likely to affect the future development, performance and position of the company's business;

(2)   information on environmental matters (including the impact of the company's business on the environment), the company's employees, and social and community issues – these disclosures should include details of the policies adopted and their effectiveness; and

(3)   information about persons with whom the company has contractual or other arrangements that are essential to the company's business.

If the review does not include information on any of the matters specified in (2) and (3), it must state which items have been excluded. The disclosure requirements in (3) were added at a late stage in the Bill's progress through

Parliament and gave rise to considerable debate when introduced.[3] In particular, they are intended to highlight any ethical issues arising from the company's contractual relationships with overseas suppliers. In the context of the preparation of a business review, the directors' duty to promote the success of the company should also be borne in mind (see para 3.17). Section 417 came into force on 1 October 2007 and applies for accounting periods beginning on or after that date.

As with annual accounts, most of the other detailed requirements on the content of the directors' report are now set out in regulations made by the Secretary of State rather than in the primary legislation, apart from the requirements for the report to state:

(1)   the names of those who have served as directors during the year;
(2)   the principal activities of the company during the course of the year; and
(3)   unless the company is subject to the small companies regime, the amount that the directors recommend for payment by way of dividend.

These disclosures are specified in s 416 of the CA 2006.

For accounting periods beginning on or after 6 April 2008, other requirements on the detailed content of the directors' report are set out in:

(1)   Schedule 5 to the Small Companies and Groups (Accounts and Directors' Report) Regulations 2008;[4] and
(2)   Schedule 7 to the Large and Medium-sized Companies and Groups (Accounts and Reports) Regulations 2008.[5]

These generally restate the requirements that applied under Schedule 7 to the CA 1985. The disclosure exemptions previously granted to small companies under s 246(4) of the CA 1985 are effectively retained in that the relevant disclosures are not required under the small companies regulations, and the limited exemption in respect of the disclosure of non-financial Key Performance Indicators previously granted to medium-sized companies under s 246A(2A) of the CA 1985 is retained in s 417(7) of the CA 2006. The main changes are:

(1)   an increase in the disclosure threshold for political donations from £200 to £2,000;
(2)   extension of the disclosure requirements on political donations to include donations to independent election candidates; and
(3)   an increase in the disclosure threshold for charitable donations from £200 to £2,000.

For accounting periods beginning on or after 29 June 2008, a listed company must include a corporate governance statement as a specific section of its directors' report, or must issue a separate corporate governance report published with and in the same manner as the directors' report (see para 6.68 below).

1   Directive 2003/51/EC of the European Parliament and Council amending Directives 78/660/EEC, 83/349/EEC, 86/635/EEC and 91/674/EEC on the annual and consolidated accounts of certain types of companies, banks and other financial institutions and insurance undertakings.
2   SI 2005/1011.
3   See 679 HL Official Report (5th series) GC165–172 (1 March 2006); 681 HL Official Report (5th series) cols 918–935 (10 May 2006) ; HC Official Report, SC D (Company Law Reform Bill), 13 July 2006, cols 686–708; 450 HC Official Report, cols 881–915 (18 October 2006); 686 HL Official Report, 2 November 2006, cols 453–471.
4   SI 2008/409.
5   SI 2008/410.

Disclosure exemption

6.18 Under s 417(10) of the CA 2006, information about impending developments or matters in the course of negotiation need not be disclosed in the business review if disclosure would, in the opinion of the directors, be seriously prejudicial to the interests of the company. Also, under s 417(11), the disclosures on contractual business arrangements need not include information about a person if that disclosure would, in the opinion of the directors, be seriously prejudicial to that person and contrary to the public interest. It should be noted that this exemption makes no reference to disclosure being seriously prejudicial to the company.

Additional disclosures for quoted companies

6.19 For accounting periods beginning before 6 April 2008, s 992 of the CA 2006 added a new Pt 7 of Sch 7 to the CA 1985, which requires certain additional disclosures to be given in the directors' reports of companies whose shares are publicly traded on a regulated market. The detailed disclosures include:

(1)   details of the company's capital structure;
(2)   any restrictions on the transfer of securities;
(3)   details of significant direct or indirect holdings of the company's securities;
(4)   details of any person who holds securities that carry special rights with regard to control of the company;
(5)   any restrictions on voting rights;
(6)   agreements that may result in restrictions on the transfer of securities or on voting rights;
(7)   any rules on the appointment and replacement of directors, or on amendment of the company's articles;
(8)   the powers of the directors, including any relating to the issuing or buying back of shares by the company;
(9)   any significant agreements that take effect, alter or terminate on a change of control following a takeover bid; and
(10)   any agreements for compensation for loss of office or employment as a result of a takeover bid.

The report must include any necessary explanatory material on these issues, and this material must also be included in, or provided with, any summary financial statement issued by the company.

These new disclosure requirements are introduced as a result of the EC Takeovers Directive[1] and apply to directors' reports for financial years beginning on or after 20 May 2006. As they are general disclosure requirements, designed to bring greater transparency to the market, they apply to all UK companies with voting shares traded on a regulated market, in London or elsewhere, irrespective of whether or not they are involved in a takeover. The disclosures were introduced initially by the Takeovers Directive (Interim Implementation) Regulations 2006[2] but these have now been revoked by the Companies Act 2006 (Commencement No 2, Consequential Amendments, Transitional Provisions and Savings) Order 2007[3] which brought into force Pt 28 (Takeovers) of the CA 2006, together with related provisions, on 6 April 2007.

For accounting periods beginning on or after 6 April 2008, disclosure continues to be required by paras 13 and 14 of Sch 7 to the Large and Medium-sized Companies and Groups (Accounts and Reports) Regulations 2008.[4]

[1]   Article 10 of EC Directive on Takeover Bids (2004/25/EC), see para 9.20.
[2]   SI 2006/1183.
[3]   SI 2007/1093.
[4]   SI 2008/410.

Disclosure to auditors

6.20 CA 2006, s 418 retains the requirement for the directors' report to include a statement to the effect that, for each person who is a director at the time that the directors' report is approved:

(1)   so far as that director is aware, there is no relevant audit information of which the company's auditors are unaware; and

(2)   he/she has taken all the steps that a director should have taken in order to become aware of any relevant audit information and establish that the auditors are aware of it.

Relevant audit information is defined as information needed by the auditors in connection with the preparation of their report on the annual accounts. In order to satisfy the requirement, each director should make appropriate enquiries of his/her fellow directors and of the company's auditors, and take such other steps required by the general duty of a director to exercise reasonable care, skill and diligence (see s 174 of the CA 2006, see para 3.28).

Approval and signature of directors' report

6.21 The requirement for the directors' report to be formally approved by the board and signed by a director or by the company secretary is retained in s 419 of the CA 2006. If, in preparing the report, advantage has been taken of the small companies' exemption, a statement to this effect must be included in a prominent position above the signature of the director or secretary. As with the annual accounts (see para 6.12 above), there is no longer a requirement under the legislation for the copy of the report delivered to the registrar to include a manuscript signature, although the name of the signatory must still be stated. However, a manuscript signature continues to be required at present under the transitional provisions of the Companies Act 2006 (Commencement No 5, Transitional Provisions and Savings) Order 2007.[1] This transitional provision is due to be removed from 1 October 2009. From this date, the registrar will set the rules on the authentication of documents delivered to Companies House.

The Companies Act 2006 (Accounts, Reports and Audit) Regulations 2009[2] insert a new section 419A into the CA 2006 to apply equivalent approval and signature requirements to any separate corporate governance statement that is prepared by a listed company (see para 6.68).

[1]   SI 2007/3495.
[2]   SI 2009/1581.

Directors' remuneration report

6.22 CA 2006, ss 420–422 retain the requirement for quoted companies to prepare an annual directors' remuneration report, with the Secretary of State empowered to make regulations specifying the detailed content of the report, how the information should be set out, and which elements should be subject to audit. The requirement for the directors' remuneration report to be formally approved by the board and signed by a director or by the company secretary is retained in s 422 but, as with the annual accounts (see para 6.12 above), there is no longer a requirement for the copy of the report delivered to the registrar to include a manuscript signature, although the name of the signatory must still be stated. However, a manuscript signature continues to be required at present under the transitional provisions of the Companies Act 2006 (Commencement No 5, Transitional Provisions and Savings) Order 2007.[1] This transitional provision is due to be removed from 1 October 2009. From this date, the registrar will set the rules on the authentication of documents delivered to Companies House.

For accounting periods beginning on or after 6 April 2008, detailed requirements on the content of the directors' remuneration report are set out in Sch 8 to the Large and Medium-sized Companies and Groups (Accounts and Reports) Regulations 2008.[2] These restate the requirements previously set out in Sch 7A to the CA 1985 (including the distinction between disclosures that are subject to audit and those that are not). The only change is a new requirement for the report to include a statement on how the pay and employment conditions of employees of the company or group were taken into account when determining directors' remuneration for the year. Introduction of this disclosure was deferred for a year, so that it applies for accounting periods beginning on or after 6 April 2009.[3]

1   SI 2007/3495.
2   SI 2008/410.
3   SI 2008/410, reg 2(3).

Directors' liability for false or misleading statements

6.23 CA 2006, s 463 sets out a clear statement of the liability of directors in respect of false or misleading statements made in the directors' report or the directors' remuneration report, and in any information derived from those reports that is included in a summary financial statement. A director is liable to compensate the company for any loss suffered by it as a result of any untrue or misleading statement made in such a report, or of the omission of anything which the legislation requires to be included, if:

(1)   he knew the statement to be untrue or misleading, or was reckless as to whether it was untrue or misleading; or

(2)   he knew the omission to be a dishonest concealment of a material fact.

However, there is no liability to any person other than the company as a result of reliance on information given in the report. Section 463 was brought into force on 20 January 2007 by the Companies Act 2006 (Commencement No 1, Transitional Provisions and Savings) Order 2006.[1]

It is hoped that the inclusion of this new 'safe harbour' provision will act as an encouragement for directors to provide more meaningful forward-looking information in statutory reports, and in the business review section of the directors' report in particular.

1   SI 2006/3428.

PUBLICATION OF ACCOUNTS AND REPORTS

Circulation of accounts and reports

6.24 CA 2006, ss 423–436 cover the publication and circulation of accounts and make a number of changes to the previous requirements, primarily as a result of recommendations made in the Company Law Review, see para 1.2. Under s 424, a private company must circulate copies of the accounts and reports to those entitled to receive them by the end of the period allowed for filing or by the date on which they are actually filed if this is earlier (see para 6.30). A public company must circulate copies at least 21 days before the meeting at which they will be laid (see para 6.28), although copies sent later than this will be deemed to have been duly sent if all of the members entitled to attend and vote at the meeting agree to this. However, there is no requirement to send copies to a person for whom the company does not have a current address. A company is considered to have a current address for a person if:

(1)   an address has been notified to the company by that person as one at which documents may be sent to him; and

(2)   the company has no reason to believe that documents sent to him at that address will not reach him.

This is designed to prevent companies having to continue to send documents to an address from which correspondence has previously been returned as undelivered or marked 'not known at this address', or an electronic equivalent.

Summary financial statements

6.25 CA 2006, ss 426–429 deal with the option to provide a summary financial statement to members rather than full accounts and set out separate requirements for unquoted and quoted companies. Detailed requirements on the form and content of a summary financial statement and on the consultation process with members continue to be set out in regulations. For accounting periods beginning on or after 6 April 2008, they are dealt with in the Companies (Summary Financial Statement) Regulations 2008.[1] There are no changes of substance in the new legislation, other than:

(1)   the introduction of a power for the regulations to provide for specified information to be sent with the summary financial statement, rather than included in it – and the new regulations specifically provide for the information on the company's capital structure and control required as a result of the EC Takeovers Directive (see para 6.19 above) to be included in the summary financial statement or to be sent out with it; and

(2)   an extension of the categories of persons to whom a summary financial statement may be sent in place of the full accounts to include indirect investors (as defined in s 146 of the CA 2006, see para 7.39).

The new regulations also make specific provision for a summary financial statement to be issued by a small company by referring to the detailed requirements of SI 2008/409 as well as those of SI 2008/410. However, for practical purposes, it seems unlikely that there would be any benefit to a small company in issuing a summary financial statement.

[1]   SI 2008/374.

Website publication by quoted companies

6.26 CA 2006, s 430 sets out new requirements for quoted companies to publish their annual accounts and reports on a company website. This change was also recommended in the Company Law Review. Annual accounts and reports must remain on the website until those for the subsequent financial period are published there and the legislation specifies the following additional requirements:

(1)   the website must be maintained by or on behalf of the company and must identify the company in question;

(2) access to the website, and the ability to obtain a hard copy of the information, must not be conditional on the payment of a fee or otherwise restricted, except so far as necessary to comply with other enactments or regulatory requirements in the UK or elsewhere;

(3) the information must be made available as soon as is reasonably practicable; and

(4) the information must be kept available throughout the period specified – however, a failure in this respect is disregarded if it is wholly attributable to circumstances that the company could not reasonably be expected to prevent or avoid, and provided that the relevant information was available for part of the period in question.

It is hoped that prompt publication of annual accounts and reports in this way will facilitate the exercise of the new right of members of a quoted company under s 527 of the CA 2006 to require website publication of a statement setting out any matter that they propose to raise at the next accounts meeting in relation to audit concerns (see para 6.57 below and also para 7.35).

Other publication issues

6.27 CA 2006, ss 431 (for unquoted companies) and 432 (for quoted companies) retain the previous provisions on the right of members and debenture holders to obtain a copy of the annual accounts and reports, and ss 433–436 retain previous requirements on the disclosure of the name of the signatory of the accounts, publication of the audit report with statutory accounts and the publication of non-statutory accounts. Section 435(7) clarifies that the provisions on non-statutory accounts do not apply to a summary financial statement. Section 251(7) of the CA 1985 previously stated that the requirements in respect of non-statutory accounts did not apply to a summary financial statement provided to entitled persons, but did not cover the situation where the statement was made available more widely, such as by publication on a website.

LAYING AND DELIVERY OF ACCOUNTS AND REPORTS

Laying of accounts and reports

6.28 CA 2006, ss 437 and 438 cover the laying of accounts and reports before the company in general meeting but apply only to public companies – as recommended in the Company Law Review, there is no requirement for private companies to go through this process for accounting periods beginning on or after 6 April 2008. In effect, the previous elective regime has now become the default regime for private companies. In the case of public companies, the legislation introduces the term 'accounts meeting' (which is defined in s 437(3) as the meeting at which the accounts and reports are laid before the members) and requires this meeting to be held no later than the end of the period allowed for filing the accounts and reports in question. As explained at para 6.30 below, this is reduced to six months from the end of the financial period in the case of a public company.

Members' approval of directors' remuneration report

6.29 CA 2006, s 439 retains the requirement for a quoted company to give its members the opportunity to vote on a resolution approving the directors' remuneration report. The vote is advisory only and does not impact on the contractual entitlement of directors to the remuneration shown but is intended to enable members to send a strong signal to the directors on the extent to which the board's remuneration policy is supported. Every person who is a director of the company immediately before the accounts meeting has a responsibility to ensure that the resolution is put to the vote, irrespective of whether or not they are actually in attendance at the meeting.

Filing of accounts and reports

6.30 CA 2006, ss 441–453 deal with the directors' duty to file annual accounts and reports with the registrar. Under s 442:

(1)   a private company is allowed a filing period of nine months from the end of the relevant accounting period – reduced from ten months under the CA 1985; and

(2)   a public company is allowed a period of six months from the end of the relevant financial period – reduced from seven months under the CA 1985.

The reductions were recommended in the Company Law Review on the basis of general improvements in technology and the speed at which information becomes out of date these days, together with the fact that UK filing periods are considerably more generous than those in other countries. Whether a company is a private or public company is determined by its status immediately before the end of the accounting period in question. As at present, separate rules continue to apply where a company's first accounting period extends for more than 12 months, and where an accounting reference period is shortened on a change of accounting date. The new filing periods apply in respect of accounting periods beginning on or after 6 April 2008.

The Companies Act 2006 (Accounts, Reports and Audit) Regulations 2009[1] amend ss 446 and 447 of the CA 2006 to require any separate corporate governance statement prepared by a listed company (see para 6.68) to be delivered to the registrar with the other reports and accounts.

[1]   SI 2009/1581.

Calculation of filing period

6.31 CA 2006, s 443 introduces a welcome change on the calculation of the period allowed for filing annual accounts and reports, which reverses the corresponding date rule established in *Dodds v Walker*.[1] The period allowed for filing will normally end with the date corresponding to the accounting date, but where this is the last day of the month, the filing period will end with the last day of the appropriate month. So, a public company with an accounting date of 30 June will have until 31 December (rather than 30 December) to file its accounts and reports.

[1]   [1981] 1 WLR 1027.

Late filing penalties

6.32 Penalties continue to apply under s 451 of the CA 2006 for a failure to comply with the filing requirements of the legislation, and the company continues to be liable to a civil penalty under s 453. New civil penalties have been introduced in respect of the late filing of accounts and reports on or after 1 February 2009 by the Companies (Late Filing Penalties) and Limited Liability Partnerships (Filing Periods and Late Filing Penalties) Regulations 2008.[1] These also amend s 242A of the CA 1985 so that the new penalties also apply to any accounts and reports prepared under that Act that are delivered late on or after 1 February 2009. The penalties have been amended to:

(1)   take account of inflation since 1992;
(2)   introduce a faster rate of increase in the penalties for companies who file their accounts and reports more than one month late; and
(3)   double the penalty for any company which files late, after having also filed late in the previous year.

As a result the following penalties apply with effect from 1 February 2009:

Period of delay	Public company penalty	Private company penalty
Not more than 1 month	£750	£150
More than 1 month but not more than 3 months	£1,500	£375
More than 3 months but not more than 6 months	£3,000	£750
More than 6 months	£7,500	£1,500

These penalties are doubled in any case where there was a failure to comply with the filing requirements in relation to the previous financial year and that financial year began on or after 6 April 2008.

[1]   SI 2008/497.

Abbreviated accounts

6.33 CA 2006, ss 444 and 445 set out the filing regimes for small and medium-sized companies. Where such companies prepare Companies Act accounts (as opposed to IAS accounts), the legislation retains the option for them to file abbreviated accounts but with detailed form and content requirements set out in regulations made by the Secretary of State. For accounting periods beginning on or after 6 April 2008, the requirements are set out in:

(1)   Schedule 4 to SI 2008/409 in the case of small companies; and
(2)   Regulation 4(3) of SI 2008/410 in the case of medium-sized companies.

The only significant change to the previous requirements is that the abbreviated profit and loss account of a medium-sized company must now show turnover separately (this was previously one of the figures that could be combined in the abbreviated profit and loss account).

Qualification as a medium-sized company or group is now covered in ss 465–467 of the CA 2006 but, as with small companies (see para 6.2), the only changes of substance are:

(1)   a company is now ineligible for qualification as a medium-sized company if it is a member of a group that includes a body corporate (other than a company) whose shares are admitted to trading on a regulated market (rather than a body corporate with the power to offer its shares or debentures to the public as under the CA 1985) – it should also be noted that the equivalent element of the definition of a small company (s 384) refers to shares admitted to trading on a regulated market in an EEA State, whereas s 467 includes no reference to the EEA; and
(2)   section 465(5) uses the more generalised definition of balance sheet total for both Companies Act and IAS accounts.

For accounting periods beginning on or after 6 April 2008, the qualifying conditions for medium-sized companies and groups set out in ss 465(3) and 466(4) of the CA 2006 are increased to the following by the Companies Act 2006 (Amendment) (Accounts and Reports) Regulations 2008:[1]

	Medium-sized company	Medium-sized group
Turnover of not more than	£25.9m	£25.9m net or £31.1m gross
Balance sheet total of not more than	£12.9m	£12.9m net or £15.5m gross
Number of employees not more than	250	250

The regulations also provide that, where the position in a preceding financial period needs to be considered in determining whether a company or group qualifies as medium-sized for an accounting period beginning on or after 6 April 2008, the higher thresholds may also be applied to that earlier year (but only for comparison purposes).

Where a small company files IAS accounts or Companies Act accounts that are not abbreviated accounts, but the directors still wish to take advantage of the option not to deliver a copy of the directors' report and/or the profit and loss account, s 444(5) requires the balance sheet to include a prominent statement that the accounts have been delivered in accordance with the provisions applicable to companies subject to the small company regime.

¹   SI 2008/393.

OTHER ACCOUNTS ISSUES

Other CA 2006 provisions

6.34   The remaining sections in Pt 15 of the CA 2006 set out:

(1)   the documents that must be delivered to the registrar by unquoted companies that do not qualify as small or medium-sized and by quoted companies (ss 446 and 447);

(2)   the conditions in respect of the filing exemption for unlimited companies (s 448);

(3)   the requirement for abbreviated accounts to include a special report from the auditor and to be formally approved and signed by the directors (ss 449 and 450);

(4)   the consequences of failure to file annual accounts and reports, including a power for the Secretary of State to make regulations on related penalties (ss 451–453) (see also 6.32 above); and

(5)   the regime for the voluntary and compulsory revision of accounts and reports (ss 454–462) – for accounting periods beginning on or after 6 April 2008, detailed requirements on the revision of accounts and reports are set out in the Companies (Revision of Defective Accounts and Reports) Regulations 2008.¹

There are also short sections covering the definition of accounting standards and other accounts expressions, the power of the Secretary of State to make further provision about accounts and reports by regulations, the preparation of accounts in euros and the position of banking partnerships. There are no changes of substance from existing requirements.

¹   SI 2008/373.

Overseas companies

6.35   Revision of the rules in respect of overseas companies has been under consideration for some time. An overseas company is currently defined as a limited company incorporated outside Great Britain but with a business presence in Great Britain, and separate regimes apply in respect of the filing of accounts, depending on whether that presence is a place of business or a branch. A DTI (now BERR) consultation document issued in 1999 considered the problems that arise from the present requirements and recommended the introduction of a single registration scheme for overseas companies, based on the requirements that currently apply in respect of a UK branch. The proposals were considered further during the Company Law Review. This continued to recommend a single registration scheme, with the framework set out in the primary legislation and the details implemented by secondary legislation, and also proposed that:

(1)   an overseas company should be required to file the annual accounts and reports which its home state requires it to prepare and publish; or

(2)   where the home state does not have accounts requirements, the Secretary of State should be empowered to require the filing of accounts prepared in accordance with prescribed regulations.

Section 1044 of the CA 2006 now defines an overseas company as a company incorporated outside the UK and s 1049 sets out provisions to enable the Secretary of State to make detailed regulations on the preparation and delivery of accounts by overseas companies that are required to register under the Act. Section 1050 empowers the Secretary of State to make similar regulations in respect of credit or financial institutions incorporated (or otherwise formed) outside the UK and Gibraltar but which have a UK branch.

A further consultation document was issued in February 2007 and the Government's response to the issues raised was published in December 2007, together with draft regulations under the CA 2006. In June 2008, the Government published a summary of its responses to the issues raised during this consultation process, together with an updated draft of the new regulations. These are intended to apply to overseas companies as defined in the CA 2006 and the main objective continues to be the establishment of a single regulatory regime covering both UK branches and UK places of business of overseas companies. The proposed regime is based on the current registration and reporting requirements for an EU branch of an overseas company in order to maintain compliance with the 11th EC Company Law Directive,[1] but the aim has been to keep obligations for overseas companies to a minimum, whilst ensuring the availability of transparent information about businesses operating in the UK. In particular, overseas companies will be able to prepare accounts in accordance with IAS or, where applicable, in accordance with the law of their parent state (subject to certain condition on the content of those accounts). Separate provisions will continue to be made for credit and financial institutions and for other companies. The Overseas Companies Regulations 2009 (currently available in draft form) are intended to apply to overseas companies with a UK establishment (as defined in the regulations) with effect from 1 October 2009.

[1]   Directive 89/666/EEC.

AUDIT EXEMPTION

Audit exemption regime

6.36   CA 2006, s 475 sets out the requirement for annual accounts to be audited, unless the company qualifies for one of the exemptions available to a small company (s 477) or a dormant company (s 480), or is exempt from Pt 16 of the Act on the basis that it is a non-profit-making company that is subject to public sector audit (see para 6.38 below). The new legislation generally maintains the current audit exemption regime (with the exception of the special provisions relating to charitable companies – see 6.37 below), including the right of members representing 10 per cent or more of the nominal value of the issued share capital (or 10 per cent or more of the members, if the company does not have a share capital) to require an audit to be carried out. Where advantage is taken of audit exemption, there continues to be a requirement for the balance sheet to include a statement by the directors that:

(1)   the members have not required the company to have the accounts for that year audited; and
(2)   the directors acknowledge their responsibilities for complying with the requirements of the Act with respect to accounting records and the preparation of accounts.

Charitable companies

6.37 Significant changes have been made to the audit exemption regime for charitable companies. For accounting periods beginning before 1 April 2008, under company law, a company that is a charity will usually meet the total audit exemption conditions if:

(1)   it qualifies as a small company for that year under company law;
(2)   its gross income for the year is not more than £90,000; and
(3)   its balance sheet total for the year is not more than £2.8m.

Also, for these accounting periods, a charitable company will usually meet the report conditions under company law if:

(1)   it qualifies as a small company for that year under company law;
(2)   its gross income for the year is more than £90,000 but not more than £500,000; and
(3)   its balance sheet total for the year is not more than £2.8m.

If these conditions are met, the company will be exempt from the audit requirement for that year, provided that the directors arrange for a special report on the company's accounts to be made to the members by a reporting accountant.

For accounting periods beginning on or after 1 April 2008, small charitable companies are removed from the audit exemption provisions of company law and are brought instead within the scope of the external scrutiny requirements of charity law as a result of changes made by:

(1)   the Companies Act 2006 (Commencement No 6, Saving and Commencement Nos 3 and 5 (Amendment)) Order 2008;[1] and
(2)   the Charities Act 2006 (Charitable Companies Audit and Group Accounts Provisions) Order 2008.[2]

This is to ensure that the same scrutiny requirements apply to all charities, irrespective of whether they are incorporated or unincorporated. Under the new regime, the accounts of a charitable company must be subject to full audit where:

(1)   gross income is more than £500,000; or
(2)   gross income is more than £100,000 and the aggregate value of the charity's assets is more than £2.8m – however, for accounting periods beginning on or after 1 April 2009, these thresholds are increased to £250,000 and £3.26m respectively by the Charities Acts 1992 and 1993 (Substitution of Sums) Order 2009[3].

The Charities (Accounts and Reports) Regulations 2008[4] also require a parent charity to prepare group accounts where the gross income of the group is more than £500,000 after eliminating all group transactions from income from the year and to have those accounts audited. The following accounts scrutiny requirements apply to other charitable companies:

(1)   the trustees of a charitable company with gross income of more than £10,000 (increased to £25,000 by SI 2009/508 for accounting periods beginning on or after 1 April 2009) but not more than £500,000 may elect for an independent examination in place of a full audit – where gross income is more than £250,000, the independent examiner must be from one of the recognised professional bodies specified in the legislation, and the examiner's report must state the qualification held; and
(2)   the accounts of a charitable company with gross income of less than £10,000 (increased to £25,000 by SI 2009/508 for accounting periods beginning on or after 1 April 2009) will not require any independent scrutiny.

The most significant impact of this change will be on charitable companies with gross income between £10,000 and £90,000. The accounts of such companies have generally been exempt from any form of external scrutiny under company law, but they will in future require an independent examination under charity law. However, the increase of the lower threshold to £25,000 for accounting periods beginning on or after 1 April 2009 will mean that the smallest of these charities continue to benefit from the exemption in future.

However, a charitable company that requires an audit under company law (for instance, where it is ineligible for the exemptions granted to small companies or the directors do not elect to take advantage of audit exemption) remains subject to the CA 2006 audit requirement, and the charity law accounts scrutiny provisions no longer apply.

The above requirements apply in respect of charities registered in England and Wales. Similar but slightly different requirements apply in respect of charities registered in Scotland. In particular, where the directors of a charitable company that is entered on the Scottish Charity Register do not elect to take advantage of audit exemption under company law, the accounts must be audited under both company law and Scottish charity law.

APB Bulletin 2009/1 'Auditor's Reports – Supplementary Guidance for Auditors of Charities with 31 March 2009 year ends'[5] sets out detailed guidance for auditors on reporting in respect of accounting periods that begin on or after 1 April 2008 but before 6 April 2008 and includes a useful matrix of the accounts and audit requirements that apply in each case, together with the legislative source. However, it deals only with audit requirements and so does not cover the independent examination options that may be available in certain cases. Bulletin 2009/1 covers a relatively narrow time period but needed to be issued because of the slight difference in the respective implementation dates of the changes for charitable companies (1 April 2008) and the accounts provisions of the CA 2006 (6 April 2008). Updated guidance will be issued in due course to take account of the impact of the requirements of the CA 2006 on charitable companies for accounting periods beginning on or after 6 April 2008.

1   SI 2008/674.
2   SI 2008/527.
3   SI 2009/508.
4   SI 2008/629.
5   Available at http://www.frc.org.uk/apb/publications/pub1891.html.

Companies subject to public sector audit

6.38 CA 2006, ss 482 and 483 introduce new provisions to allow a public sector auditor to audit non-profit-making public sector bodies that are constituted as companies. Companies exempted from the normal audit requirement by these sections are not subject to the Fourth EC Company Law Directive. In the case of a group, the exemption is only available if every company in the group is non-profit-making. Where the directors take advantage of the exemption, the company's balance sheet must include a clear statement of the fact that it is entitled to the exemption.

APPOINTMENT OF AUDITORS

Appointment of auditors: private companies

6.39 The new legislation retains broadly similar requirements to those in the CA 1985 on the appointment of auditors, although it sets out separate provisions for private and public companies to reflect the fact that private companies are no longer required to lay the accounts before the members in general meeting (see para 6.28 above). In the case of a private company, therefore, unless the company qualifies for audit exemption (see para 6.36) and the directors propose to take advantage of this, s 485 requires auditors to be appointed before the end of the period of 28 days beginning with:

(1)   the end of the time allowed for sending out the accounts and reports for the previous financial year; or

(2)   if earlier, the date on which those accounts and reports were actually sent out.

The appointment should normally be made by the shareholders and by ordinary resolution. The directors continue to be allowed to make an appointment at any time before the company's first accounts meeting, following any period when the company qualified for audit exemption and so had not appointed auditors, or to fill a casual vacancy. Under s 486, the Secretary of State retains the power to appoint auditors where a private company fails to do so within the period allowed, and the company must give notice to the Secretary of State within one week of the end of that period that the power has become exercisable. Section 487 clarifies that newly appointed auditors do not take office until the previous auditors have ceased to hold office.

Although most of Pt 16 of the CA 2006 came into force on 6 April 2008, ss 485–488 (see also para 6.40) came into force on 1 October 2007, together with Pt 13 of the CA 2006, which deals with meetings and resolutions.

Reappointment of auditors: private companies

6.40 Under the CA 1985, a private company can elect to dispense with the annual appointment of auditors, in which case the auditors in office are deemed to be reappointed each year. The CA 2006 removes the requirement for a formal election to be made and s 487 provides that, where a private company has not made an appointment by the end of the period allowed for appointing auditors, any auditor already in office is deemed to be reappointed unless:

(1)   the auditor was appointed by the directors rather than the members;
(2)   the company's articles require actual reappointment;
(3)   the deemed reappointment is prevented by the members – under s 488, 5 per cent of the members (or less if the articles so provide) can give notice to the company that the auditor should not be reappointed;
(4)   the members resolve that the auditor should not be reappointed; or
(5)   the directors resolve that no auditor should be appointed for the financial year in question (ie because an audit of the accounts is unlikely to be required).

This is without prejudice to other provisions of the CA 2006 on the removal and resignation of auditors.

Appointment of auditors: public companies

6.41 In the case of a public company, s 489 of the CA 2006 requires auditors to be appointed each year before the end of the meeting at which the accounts and reports for the previous financial year are laid. The appointment should normally be made by the shareholders and by an ordinary resolution. The directors continue to be allowed to make an appointment at any time before the company's first accounts meeting, following any period when the company qualified for audit exemption and so had not appointed auditors, or to fill a casual vacancy. As with private companies, s 490 retains the power of the Secretary of State to appoint auditors where the company fails to do so within the period allowed, and the company must give notice to the Secretary of State within one week of the end of that period that the power has become exercisable. Section 491 clarifies that, without prejudice to other provisions of the CA 2006 on the removal and resignation of auditors:

(1)   newly appointed auditors of a public company do not take office until the previous auditors have ceased to hold office; and

(2)   auditors of a public company cease to hold office at the conclusion of the accounts meeting next following their appointment, unless they are formally reappointed.

Terms of appointment

6.42 Professional auditing standards require auditors to ensure that the respective rights and responsibilities of the directors and the auditors in relation to the annual accounts are set out in formal terms of engagement between the company and the auditors. This is to help ensure that those respective responsibilities are clearly understood and so prevent any potential misunderstandings.

A DTI (now BERR) consultation document[1] published towards the end of 2003 tackled the difficult issue of the liability of company directors and company auditors. The Companies (Audit, Investigations and Community Enterprise) Act 2004 subsequently introduced certain changes in respect of directors' liability (which are retained in ss 234–238 of the CA 2006) but made no changes in the case of auditors. However, the Government indicated that it would consider the introduction of a system to allow auditors to limit their liability by contract with the shareholders if it was clear that this would enhance competition and also improve audit quality (see para 6.59–6.64 below). The DTI White Paper 'Company Law Reform', published in March 2005, developed the proposals further and suggested a number of additional initiatives to improve audit quality and audit value and intended to balance the proposed limitation of liability. These initiatives included the publication of audit engagement letters, and s 493 of the CA 2006 now empowers the Secretary of State to make regulations requiring the disclosure of the terms on which a company auditor is appointed, remunerated or performs his duties. Regulations made under this section will be able to:

(1)   require disclosure of a copy of any written terms or a written memorandum of any terms that are not in writing;

(2)   specify the time and place of such disclosure; and

(3)   require the place and means of disclosure to be stated in the notes to the accounts, the directors' report or the auditors' report.

However, no regulations have been made under this section as yet.

[1]   Director and Auditor Liability: A Consultative Document.

Auditor remuneration

6.43 CA 2006, s 492 retains the existing provisions that allow the remuneration of the auditors to be fixed by whoever appoints them and s 494 retains provisions to enable the Secretary of State to make regulations on the disclosure of the nature of the services provided to the company and its associates by the auditors and their associates and of the related remuneration. The regulations can specify that disclosure must be given in the notes to the accounts, in the directors' report or in the auditors' report. Section 494 mirrors the provisions introduced by C(AICE)A 2004 as s 390B of the CA 1985. New disclosure requirements under this section were introduced by the Companies (Disclosure of Auditor Remuneration) Regulations 2005[1] for accounting periods beginning on or after 1 October 2005. These made significant changes to the disclosure of fees for both audit and non-audit services, particularly in the case of group accounts, and required a detailed analysis of fees for non-audit services to be given in the notes to the accounts. For accounting periods beginning on or after 6 April 2008, these regulations are repealed and replaced by the Companies (Disclosure of Auditor Remuneration and Liability Limitation Agreements) Regulations 2008.[2] The new regulations restate the existing disclosure requirements in respect of auditor remuneration with two minor changes:

(1)   they require the auditor of a medium-sized company, if requested, to provide the Secretary of State with details of the remuneration received for the following services, if the information has not been given voluntarily in the notes to the accounts:
   •   assurance services other than the auditing of the company's accounts;
   •   tax advisory services; and
   •   other services; and
(2)   they introduce a new disclosure exemption for certain smaller fees for services provided by distant associates of the auditor (as defined in para 4 of Sch 1 to SI 2008/489) – this exemption relates only to fees classified as relating to 'other services' and such remuneration is not disclosable if it does not exceed either £10,000 or one per cent of the total audit remuneration received by the company's auditor in its most recent financial year, ending no later than the financial year of the company to which the accounts relate.

The Institute of Chartered Accountants in England & Wales ('ICAEW') has published guidance on the practical implications of the current disclosure requirements in TECH 06/06 'Disclosure of Auditor Remuneration' (available from the ICAEW website at http://www.icaew.co.uk). A revised version of the initial guidance was published in July 2007.

[1]   SI 2005/2417.
[2]   SI 2008/489.

AUDITOR REPORTING

Auditor's report on annual accounts

6.44 CA 2006, s 495 sets out detailed requirements on the form and content of the auditor's report on the annual accounts and essentially repeats the requirements previously set out in s 235 of the CA 1985 in relation to the annual accounts, but with the opinion required from the auditor framed in a slightly different way. In particular, the report must include:

(1)   an introduction identifying the accounts that have been audited and the financial reporting framework applied;

(2)   a description of the scope of the audit, identifying the auditing standards in accordance with which the audit was conducted;

(3)   a clear statement of the auditors' opinion on whether the accounts give a true and fair view of:
- the company's state of affairs at the end of the financial year;
- the company's profit or loss for the financial year; and
- where relevant, the state of affairs of the group at the end of the financial year, and of its profit or loss for the financial year, so far as concerns the members of the company;

(4)   the auditor's opinion on whether the accounts have been properly prepared in accordance with the relevant financial framework; and

(5)   the auditor's opinion on whether the accounts have been prepared in accordance with the requirements of the CA 2006 (and, where relevant, Article 4 of the IAS Regulation).

The report must be qualified or unqualified, and must include a reference to any matters to which the auditors wish to draw attention by way of emphasis without qualifying their report.

In practice, the requirements of International Standard on Auditing (UK & Ireland) 700 (ISA (UK & Ireland) 700) and the guidance set out in related Auditing Practices Board ('APB') Bulletins must also be taken into account. A revised version of this standard, which makes some significant changes to the form and content of auditor's reports, applies for accounting periods beginning on or after 6 April 2008 and ending on or after 5 April 2009 (see para 6.47 below). The APB also issued Bulletin 2008/8 'Auditor's Reports for Short Accounting Periods in Compliance with the United Kingdom Companies Act 2006' (ie accounting periods which begin on or after 6 April 2008 but end before 5 April 2009) in September 2008. This takes two example reports from latest guidance on auditor reports under the CA 1985 (APB Bulletin 2006/6 'Auditor's Reports on Financial Statements in the United Kingdom') and presents a marked-up revision to achieve compliance with the reporting requirements of the CA 2006.

Auditor's report on directors' report

6.45 Requirements in relation to the audit of the directors' report are set out in a separate section of the CA 2006, although this was previously dealt with in s 235 of the CA 1985 together with the requirements in respect of the annual accounts. Section 496 of the CA 2006 requires the auditor to state in his report whether, in his opinion, the information given in the directors' report is consistent with the accounts for the relevant financial year. Once again, for practical purposes, the requirements of auditing standards (in particular, ISA (UK & Ireland) 720) and related APB pronouncements must also be taken into account.

The Companies Act 2006 (Accounts, Reports and Audit) Regulations 2009[1] insert new sections 497A and 498A into the CA 2006 to apply similar audit requirements to any separate corporate governance statement that is prepared by a listed company and to require an auditor to report on any failure to prepare a corporate governance statement where relevant (see para 6.68).

[1]   SI 2009/1581.

Auditor's report on directors' remuneration report

6.46   CA 2006, s 497 deals with the auditor's report on the auditable part of the directors' remuneration report prepared by a quoted company. Once again, this retains the previous requirements and requires the auditor to state whether, in his opinion. the auditable part of the directors' remuneration report has been properly prepared in accordance with the Act.

Changes under ISA (UK & Ireland) 700 revised

6.47   The APB issued an Exposure Draft of a proposed revision of ISA (UK & Ireland) 700 in August 2008. This followed on from an earlier Discussion Paper that explored some of the concerns over the clarity and usefulness of the present style of report. Institutional investors generally want the auditor's report to be more informative, but accounts preparers are keen for the report to be shorter and less ambiguous. The APB considers that the coming period provides an opportunity for the UK to take a new approach and so to help influence international thinking. Consequently, the APB has now revised ISA (UK & Ireland) 700 in a way that facilitates, but does not require, the use of a shorter form of auditor's report.

ISA (UK & Ireland) 700 (revised)[1] was published in March 2009 and makes significant changes to the form and content of auditor's reports. It applies to the audits of UK companies for accounting periods beginning on or after 6 April 2008 and ending on or after 5 April 2009. In the case of other UK entities, it will apply for accounting periods ending on or after 15 December 2010. The APB plans to make a further announcement in respect of Irish companies once the legal position in Ireland has been clarified.

Under the revised standard, the section of the report previously headed 'Basis of Opinion' is changed to 'Scope of the Audit' and auditors are offered three alternative approaches:

(1)   the inclusion of a cross-reference to a 'Statement of the Scope of an Audit' set out on the APB website;

(2)   the inclusion of a cross-reference to a 'Statement of the Scope of an Audit' set out elsewhere within the annual report; or

(3)   the inclusion of a short prescribed description of the scope of an audit within the report.

The APB is actively encouraging auditors to discuss with their clients the approach that they plan to take. However, in view of the phased approach to implementation of the standard, only descriptions of the scope of a UK company audit (one for a publicly traded company and one for a non-publicly traded company) are currently included on the APB website. The APB plans to monitor the extent to which the option to refer the website description is used in practice and will then assess whether there is a need to provide equivalent statements for other entities.

The APB published four illustrative reports alongside the standard, covering both publicly traded and non-publicly traded companies, all of which present separately:

(1)   the auditor's opinion on the financial statements, with individual presentation of the various elements of the opinion required under section 495(3) of the CA 2006 (see para 6.44);

(2)   the auditor's opinion on other matters prescribed by company law (ie whether the directors' report is consistent with the financial statements and, in the case of a quoted company, whether the directors' remuneration report has been properly prepared); and

(3)   matters on which the auditor is required to report by exception – in the case of listed companies, this includes the auditor's role in relation to corporate governance disclosures.

The description of the auditor's responsibilities is also reduced in length, and some of the material previously included here is moved to the section at the end of the report detailing matters on which the auditor is required to report by exception and stating, where relevant, that there are no issues that the auditor needs to raise in respect of these. The report also includes a specific reference to the fact that the auditor is required to comply with APB Ethical Standards for Auditors. The brief statement on the directors' responsibilities is now amended to refer specifically to their responsibility for being satisfied that the accounts give a true and fair view.

The APB has also published a new set of example auditor's reports on the accounts of UK companies in Bulletin 2009/2 'Auditor's Reports on Financial Statements in the United Kingdom'[2]. These also apply for accounting periods beginning on or after 6 April 2008 and ending on or after 5 April 2009. Those in Bulletin 2006/6 (see para 6.44) continue to apply for all accounting periods that begin before 6 April 2008, including any that extend for more than a year and so end on or after 5 April 2009.

The APB is continuing to undertake further research to help identify how the auditor's report could be made more informative.

1   Available at http://www.frc.org.uk/apb/publications/pub1901.html.
2   Available at http://www.frc.org.uk/apb/publications/pub1965.html.

Duties of auditors

6.48 CA 2006, s 498 retains the existing provisions on the duties of auditors and sets out an auditor's duty to form an opinion on whether:

(1)   adequate accounting records have been kept by the company and adequate returns have been received from any branches not visited (see para 6.5);

(2)   the company's individual accounts are in agreement with the accounting records and returns; and

(3)   in the case of a quoted company, the auditable part of the directors' remuneration report is in accordance with the company's accounting records and returns.

As under the CA 1985, if the auditor is not satisfied on any of the above points, he must include an appropriate statement in his report. Section 498 also retains the requirement for the auditor to report, where relevant, that he has failed to obtain all the information and explanations that he considered necessary, and for him to include in his report any information on directors' remuneration, benefits or compensation for loss of office that has not been given in the annual accounts or directors' remuneration report, so far as he is reasonably able to do so. However, there is no specific requirement under s 498 for the auditor to make good any missing information in respect of advances, credits and guarantees involving directors. Finally, where the directors have prepared accounts and reports in accordance with the small company regime when, in the opinion of the auditor, they were not entitled to do so, s 498(5) requires the auditor to state this fact in his report on the accounts.

For accounting periods beginning on or after 6 April 2008 and ending on or after 5 April 2009, the APB has changed the way in which matters on which the auditor is required to report by exception are explained and dealt with in the report (see para 6.47).

Rights of auditors

6.49 CA 2006, ss 499–502 retain the current CA 1985 provisions on the auditor's rights to information. Section 502 sets out the auditor's right of access at all times to the company's books, accounts and vouchers (in whatever form) and his right to require appropriate information and explanations from any officer or employee of the company, any person accountable for the company's books and records, any subsidiary undertaking incorporated in the UK, together with its officers, employees and auditors, and any person who fell within one of these categories at the time to which the auditor's enquiries relate. Section 500 details the auditor's rights in relation to overseas subsidiaries and s 501 repeats the offence of knowingly or recklessly making a statement to an auditor that is misleading, false or deceptive in a material particular. (See also para 6.20 above on the requirement for directors to disclose all relevant information to the auditor). Section 502 retains the auditor's right to receive all communications supplied to the members of a private company in respect of a written resolution, to receive all notices and other communications in respect of any general meeting of the company, and to attend and speak at such a meeting.

Signature of auditor's report

6.50 CA 2006, s 503 requires the auditor's report to state the name of the auditor and to be signed and dated. The Act also provides that, where the auditor is a firm, the report should be signed by the senior statutory auditor in his/her own name, for and on behalf of the audit firm. In other words, for accounting periods beginning on or after 6 April 2008, the audit engagement partner with overall responsibility for the audit must sign the audit report in his/her own name as well as that of the firm. This change implements one of the requirements of the EC Statutory Audit Directive[1] (see para 6.65 below). Section 504(3) provides that the liability of an individual is not increased simply as a result of being identified as the senior statutory auditor.

The legislation specifies that the individual identified as the senior statutory auditor must be eligible in his/her own right for appointment as auditor of the company (ie he/she must satisfy all relevant legal and professional requirements).

The names of both the audit firm and the senior statutory auditor must be included in published copies of the accounts. However, s 506 includes provisions enabling the name of the auditor and of a senior statutory auditor to be withheld where:

(1)   the company considers that there are reasonable grounds to indicate that disclosure would create, or be likely to create, a serious risk that the auditor, the senior statutory auditor or any other person would be subject to violence or intimidation and has resolved that the name(s) should not be disclosed; and

(2)   the company has given notice of the resolution to the Secretary of State, as set out in the legislation.

The new requirement applies to all auditor's reports issued under company law, including those on revised accounts and reports and the special auditor's report on abbreviated accounts filed by small and medium-sized companies. The Auditing Practices Board ('APB') has issued detailed guidance on the new requirements in Bulletin 2008/6 'The Senior Statutory Auditor under the United Kingdom Companies Act 2006'.[2] The Bulletin considers some of the practical issues that may arise from the new requirements and emphasises in particular that another partner or responsible individual is not permitted to sign a report for and on behalf of the senior statutory auditor. Audit firms may therefore need to have contingency plans in place to deal with a situation where the senior statutory auditor is not available to sign the report.

1   Article 28.1 of Directive 2006/43/EC.
2   Available at http://www.frc.org.uk/apb/publications/bulletins.cfm.

New offences by auditors

6.51 CA 2006, s 507 creates a new criminal offence of knowingly or recklessly causing an auditor's report on a company's annual accounts to:

(1)   include any matter that is misleading, false or deceptive in a material particular; or

(2)   omit a statement required by the legislation in respect of:
- accounts not agreeing with the accounting records and returns;
- necessary information and explanations not being obtained; or
- the directors of a small company wrongly taking advantage of the exemption from the preparation of group accounts.

The section applies as follows for accounting periods beginning on or after 6 April 2008:

(1)   where the auditor is an individual, to that individual and any employee or agent who is eligible for appointment as auditor of the company; and

(2)   where the auditor is a firm, to any director, member, employee or agent who is eligible for appointment as auditor of the company.

CA 2006, s 508 sets out provisions enabling the Secretary of State to issue guidance to relevant regulatory and prosecuting authorities on dealing with potential offences in connection with an auditor's report. Regulatory and prosecuting authorities are defined as the recognised supervisory bodies, bodies concerned with accounting standards, the Director of the Serious Fraud Office, the Director of Public Prosecutions, the Director of Public Prosecutions for Northern Ireland and the Secretary of State. Section 509 sets out similar provisions for Scotland, where the Lord Advocate is empowered to issue relevant guidance and the relevant regulatory authorities are defined as recognised supervisory bodies, bodies concerned with accounting standards and the Secretary of State.

The wording of this aspect of the legislation gave rise to considerable debate during the passage of the Bill through Parliament and the accountancy profession raised a number of concerns over the potential implications, including the possibility of increased audit costs for companies, an increase in the number of qualified audit reports and the possibility that auditors could find themselves criminally liable as a result of making an honest mistake. Attempts were made to replace the words 'knowingly or recklessly' with 'dishonestly and fraudulently' but these were unsuccessful. The Government maintains that recklessness has a significantly higher threshold than ordinary negligence or carelessness and that, in order to be caught by the offence, an auditor would need to have been aware that acting or, more likely, failing to act would carry certain risks and to have decided to proceed, regardless of this. In other words, an individual cannot be reckless inadvertently. It has also made clear its intention that prosecution should be used only in the most serious cases.

CHANGES IN AUDIT APPOINTMENTS

Change of auditor

6.52 Shareholders retain the right to remove an auditor before the end of his term of office but can only do so by ordinary resolution at a meeting of the company (CA 2006, s 510). Such a resolution requires special notice and it should be noted that even a private company will need to hold a general meeting in order to pass the resolution (ie it cannot be dealt with as a written resolution). There is no other way in which an auditor can be removed before his term of office has expired, unless he chooses to resign. The legislation retains the existing requirements on the auditor's right to receive a copy of the notice of the intended resolution, to make written representations to the company and to speak at any general meeting at which it is proposed to fill the vacancy or at which his term of office would otherwise have expired.

It should also be noted that, for accounting periods beginning on or after 6 April 2008, under CA 2006, s 994(1A), the removal of an auditor on the grounds of divergent opinions on accounting treatments or audit procedures, or on any other improper grounds, is treated as being unfairly prejudicial to the interests of some part of the company's members, so that a member can petition for relief under CA 2006, s 994. In effect, this change implements one of the requirements of the EC Statutory Audit Directive (see para 6.65).

CA 2006, ss 514 and 515 deal respectively with the procedure for a private company to appoint a new auditor by means of a written resolution on the expiry of the term of office of the current auditor; and the procedure for any company (public or private) to appoint a new auditor at a general meeting on the expiry of the term of office of the current auditor.

Sections 518–521 of the CA 2006 also retain:

(1) the existing provisions on the rights of a resigning auditor;
(2) an obligation for an auditor to make a formal statement of any circumstances connected with his ceasing to hold office for any reason (or where relevant, in the case of an unquoted company, a statement that there are no circumstances that need to be drawn to the attention of the members or creditors of the company);
(3) an obligation for the company to send a copy of the auditor's statement to every person entitled to receive a copy of the accounts or, where appropriate, to apply to the court and notify the auditor of this application; and
(4) an obligation for the auditor to send a copy of his statement to the registrar, unless he has received notification from the company of an application to the court.

Similarly, ss 512 and 517 retain an obligation for the company to notify the registrar of any resolution removing an auditor from office or of any notice of resignation received from the auditor.

Additional notification requirements by auditors

6.53   The new legislation also imposes certain additional notification requirements on an auditor who ceases to hold office on or after 6 April 2008. These
apply to all major audits (see below), irrespective of why the auditor ceases to
hold office, and in any other case where an auditor ceases to hold office before
the end of his term of office (ie where he has resigned or has been dismissed).
In these situations, s 522 requires the auditor to:

(1)   notify the appropriate audit authority that he has ceased to hold office;
(2)   accompany that notification with a copy of the statement of the
      circumstances connected with his ceasing to hold office that has been
      made to the company; and
(3)   if this statement is to the effect that there are no circumstances that
      need to be brought to the attention of the members or creditors of the
      company, provide a statement of the reasons for ceasing to hold office.

A major audit is defined in s 525 as a statutory audit of a listed company or of
any other entity in which there is a major public interest. In the case of a
major audit, notification to the appropriate audit authority must be made at
the same time as the auditor's statement is deposited at the company's
registered office. In other cases, the timing of notification is to be decided by
the audit authority but will not be earlier than the depositing of the statement
with the company. For major audits, the appropriate audit authority is the
Secretary of State or a body to which functions relating to the supervision of
statutory auditors have been delegated (currently the Professional Oversight
Board ('POB')), and in other cases it is the relevant supervisory body.

The POB has issued statutory guidance on what constitutes a major audit for
these purposes, together with additional guidance to help auditors deal with
the new notification requirements (see para 6.55 below). APB Bulletin 2008/9
'Miscellaneous Reports by Auditors Required by the United Kingdom Companies Act 2006', which provides examples of an auditor's statement on
ceasing to hold office, also recommends that, where an auditor who ceases to
hold office before the end of his term of office is acting on the basis that the
audit is a 'major audit', he should advise the company of this in order to
clarify the company's obligation to notify POB of the change. In other cases,
the auditor should advise the company of his relevant supervisory body for
notification purposes.

Additional notification requirements by the company

6.54   CA 2006, s 523 introduces a further requirement for the company to
notify the appropriate audit authority in any case where the auditor ceases to
hold office before the expiry of his term of office and to provide either:

(1)   a statement by the company of the reasons for the auditor ceasing to
      hold office; or
(2)   where relevant, a copy of the statement by the auditor of the circum-
      stances connected with his ceasing to hold office that need to be
      brought to the attention of the members or creditors of the company.

This notification must be given no later than 14 days after the date on which the auditor deposits his statement at the company's registered office. The POB has issued guidance to help companies deal with the new notification requirements (see para 6.55 below).

POB guidance on notification

6.55 The new notification requirements apply in any relevant case where the auditor ceases to hold office on or after 6 April 2008 and the POB has issued guidance in the form of flowcharts and related notes[1] to help both auditors and companies identify who should be notified, how the notification should be made, and what it should cover. The POB documentation sets out statutory guidance on what constitutes a major audit for these purposes and includes audits of the following in the definition:

(1)   all UK incorporated companies with equity and/or debt securities admitted to the Official List, and any group including such an entity;
(2)   all UK incorporated AIM or PLUS-quoted companies;
(3)   unquoted companies with either:
  •   group turnover in excess of £500 million; or
  •   group turnover in excess of £100 million and group long-term debt in excess of £250 million;
(3)   unquoted companies or groups that are subsidiaries of foreign parent companies and where the turnover of the UK company or group is in excess of £1,000 million; and
(4)   charitable companies with income in excess of £100 million.

Subsidiary companies of any of the above may also be treated as major audits in order to avoid the need for notification to more than one authority.

In the case of a major audit, the POB requires the notification to:

(1)   state who has signed it and in what capacity, and provide appropriate contact details;
(2)   give the company's number and the address of its registered office; and
(3)   include the year end of the company's last audited accounts.

In other cases, where notification must be made to the recognised supervisory body with which the auditor is registered, the POB directs auditors and companies to the ICAEW website for further guidance on this at present, noting that the other recognised supervisory bodies may provide similar guidance in due course.

[1]   Available at http://www.frc.org.uk/pob/regulation/notification.cfm.

Informing the accounting authorities

6.56 CA 2006, s 524 requires the appropriate audit authority, on receiving notice from an auditor or a company under ss 522 or 523 respectively, to inform the accounting authorities (unless these are the same as the audit authority) and, if the audit authority thinks fit, to forward a copy of the statement or statements accompanying the notice. The accounting authorities are defined as the Secretary of State and any person authorised for the purposes of s 456 of the Act (revision of defective accounts: persons authorised to apply to the court). The body currently authorised for this purpose is the Financial Reporting Review Panel.

Members' rights

6.57 Subject to certain conditions and for accounting periods beginning on or after 6 April 2008, members of a quoted company can require the company to publish on a website a statement setting out any matter that they propose to raise at the next accounts meeting in relation to:

(1)   the audit of the company's accounts (including the auditor's report and the conduct of the audit) that are to be laid at that meeting; or

(2)   any circumstances connected with the company's auditor ceasing to hold office since the previous accounts meeting.

The notice of the accounts meeting must draw attention to the possibility of a statement being placed on the website under these provisions (see also para 7.35).

Under s 527, once the company has received such a request from members holding at least 5 per cent of the total voting rights or from at least 100 members with a relevant right to vote and who hold shares on which there has been paid up an average sum, per member, of at least £100, it must comply with the request within three working days and keep the information available until after the meeting to which it relates. The company must also forward the statement to the company's auditor not later than when it is made available on the website. Section 527(5) provides protection for the company if members seek to abuse this right, by enabling the company or any other aggrieved person (such as the company's auditor) to apply to the court.

Access to Statutory Audit Working Papers

6.58 For accounting periods beginning on or after 6 April 2008, as a result of UK implementation of the EC Statutory Audit Directive (see para 6.65 below), an auditor who has ceased to hold office is required to give his successor access to his audit working papers. Outgoing auditors have always been encouraged to enable the change of auditor to proceed smoothly, but access to audit working papers has generally not been allowed, due primarily to liability concerns. The new requirement is now specified as one of the required rules of the recognised supervisory bodies[1] and applies to statutory audits (as defined in s 1210 of the CA 2006). The change is intended to maintain audit efficiency and cost-effectiveness on a change of auditor, and also to help reduce any potential risks that might arise.

The Audit and Assurance Faculty ('AAF') of the Institute of Chartered Accountants in England & Wales ('ICAEW') has issued practical guidance on this in Technical Release AAF 01/08 'Access to Information by Successor Auditors'.[2] The successor auditor should have been formally appointed as auditor before making any request, and is expected to be specific about the information requested and to avoid making unnecessary requests. The outgoing auditor should set out in writing the basis on which information will be provided and should copy this to the company. Successor auditors are restricted in how they can use the information provided, and in particular should not comment on the quality of the outgoing auditor's work unless they have a legal or professional obligation to do so.

[1] Paragraph 9(3)(c) of Sch 10 to the CA 2006.
[2] Available at http://www.icaew.com/index.cfm/route/159730.

AUDITOR LIABILITY LIMITATION AGREEMENTS

Limitation of auditor's liability

6.59 With effect from 6 April 2008, CA 2006, s 532 retains the general prohibition against a company exempting or indemnifying its auditor from any liability in connection with negligence, default, breach of duty or breach of trust in respect of the audit of the company's accounts, except as permitted by:

(1)   Section 533 in respect of an indemnity for the costs of successfully defending proceedings; or
(2)   Sections 534–538 which set out new provisions in respect of liability limitation agreements.

It should be noted that s 533 no longer allows a company to purchase or maintain insurance for its auditors against any relevant liabilities, as was previously permitted by s 310(3) of the CA 1985.

A liability limitation agreement is defined as an agreement that seeks to limit the liability owed to a company by its auditor in relation to the audit of its accounts. The agreement can cover any liability for negligence, default, breach of duty or breach of trust but it cannot cover more than one financial year and so must specify the year to which it relates. The limitation must also be fair and reasonable, taking into account in particular:

(1)   the auditor's responsibilities;
(2)   the nature and purpose of the auditor's contractual obligations to the company; and
(3)   the professional standards expected of the auditor.

The legislation does not require the agreement to be framed in any particular way and states specifically that the limit on the amount of the auditor's liability need not be a sum of money, or a formula, specified in the agreement. However, the Secretary of State is empowered to make regulations that require or prevent the inclusion of specified provisions, although the Government has indicated that this power will only be used if problems emerge or there is evidence that the provisions are being misused.

Authorisation by the members

6.60 A liability limitation agreement must be authorised by the members but can be put into place by an ordinary resolution unless the company's articles require a higher majority (or unanimity). It can also be withdrawn by ordinary resolution at any time before the company enters into the agreement or before the beginning of the financial year to which it relates. In the case of a private company, an agreement may be authorised:

(a)   by the company passing a resolution, before it enters into the agreement, which either waives the need for approval or approves the principal terms of the agreement; or

(b)   by the company passing a resolution granting approval of the agreement after it has been entered into.

Similar arrangements apply in the case of a public company, except that the agreement must always be approved by the members (ie authorisation cannot be achieved by waiving the need for approval). In the case of advance approval, the principal terms must include the type of act or omission covered, the financial year to which the limitation relates and the limit to which the auditor's liability is subject.

Accounts disclosure

6.61 CA 2006, s 538 requires the fact that the company has entered into a liability limitation agreement with its auditors to be disclosed as prescribed in regulations to be made by the Secretary of State. The Companies (Disclosure of Auditor Remuneration and Liability Limitation Agreements) Regulations 2008[1] apply for accounting periods beginning on or after 6 April 2008 and require certain disclosures to be given in the notes to the accounts for the financial year to which the agreement relates or, if the agreement was entered into too late for the information to be disclosed in those accounts, in a note to the accounts for the following year. The following information must be disclosed:

(1)   the principal terms of the agreement – these are defined in s 536(4) of the CA 2006 as:
- the kind(s) of acts or omissions covered;
- the financial year to which the agreement relates; and
- the limit to which the auditor's liability is subject; and

(2)   the date of the resolution approving the agreement or, in the case of a private company, waiving the need for shareholder approval.

[1]   SI 2008/489.

FRC Guidance

6.62 The Financial Reporting Council ('FRC') issued practical guidance on the use of auditor liability limitation agreements in June 2008.[1] This has been developed by a working group which included representatives of companies and investors as well as the accountancy profession, and it sets out illustrative examples of the principal terms of auditor liability limitation agreements and specimen resolutions for both private and public companies. Whether a liability limitation agreement is fair and reasonable is an issue that must be assessed in the particular circumstances of each case and, ultimately, would be for the courts to decide in the event of a dispute. Consequently, the FRC guidance does not attempt to determine what is fair and reasonable but illustrates the various approaches that companies and their auditors might take and the issues to consider in each case. For example, an agreement could:

(1) base the liability limitation on the auditor's proportionate share of responsibility for any loss;
(2) set the limit purely by reference to the fair and reasonable test;
(3) set a cap on the auditor's liability, expressed either as a monetary amount or based on an agreed formula; or
(4) use a combination of some or all of the above.

It also emphasises that the existence of a liability limitation agreement does not reduce or otherwise affect the legal and professional obligations of the auditors and that the detailed provisions of the CA 2006, and in particular those relating to shareholder approval, must be properly complied with for the agreement to be effective.

[1] 'Guidance on Auditor Liability Limitation Agreements' – available at http://www.frc.org.uk/publications/pubs.cfm.

Issues for Directors to Consider

6.63 Directors must be satisfied that it is in the company's best interest to enter into a liability limitation agreement – for instance, in order to secure the appointment of an auditor that is particularly well suited to meet its requirements. The FRC guidance includes a section on the issues that directors should take into consideration and emphasises that their duties are the same as those in respect of any other contract entered into on behalf of the company. In particular, they need to understand the nature of the proposed agreement and its practical implications, although the FRC also notes that it is not unusual for companies to enter into agreements with suppliers of goods and services that include limitations, or even exclusions, of liability.

Directors should also consider whether the company is subject to any other laws or regulations that might preclude entry into such an agreement. For instance, additional considerations may apply if the company operates in certain sectors or has overseas interests.

The FRC guidance looks in detail at how a liability limitation agreement will interrelate with the auditor's other terms of engagement and some of the related timing issues that may arise over signature of the engagement letter and shareholder approval of the limitation agreement. Generally, the significance of these issues will increase with the size and complexity of the company's shareholder base. Timing issues may also be particularly relevant in the case of a group, where directors will need to consider whether approval by subsidiaries should be put into place before or after holding company approval. Group situations may also be complicated by the involvement of more than one audit firm and the inclusion of foreign companies.

Shareholder considerations

6.64 Directors will also need to consider whether the company's shareholders have any particular policies on such agreements. For instance, the Association of British Insurers and the National Association of Pension Funds have already indicated that, in the case listed and other publicly traded companies, their members should only support agreements that provide for proportionate liability unless there are compelling reasons why this is not appropriate. The Institutional Shareholders' Committee ('ISC') has also issued a statement on what institutional investors are likely to expect from companies[1] and notes that they will generally be supportive of agreements that provide for proportional liability, but not those that include a fixed cap. The ISC also emphasises that the legislation is permissive rather than compulsory and that neither directors nor shareholders should feel under any obligation to enter into a liability limitation agreement. The ISC sees the move very much as part of a wider process to maintain and improve audit quality and is keen that directors and audit committees should be able to demonstrate that there is a clear benefit to the company where such an agreement is proposed.

The ISC also emphasises that investors will expect companies to use the specimen principal terms provided in the FRC guidance and to be prepared to disclose and explain any proposed divergence from these. Early consultation with shareholders is advised in all cases, but especially where the FRC guidance is not being followed.

[1] Available at http://www.institutionalshareholderscommittee.org.uk/library.html.

IMPLEMENTATION OF THE EC STATUTORY AUDIT DIRECTIVE

Main changes under the Directive

6.65 The EC Statutory Audit Directive was formally adopted in May 2006 and came into effect on 28 June 2006, replacing the EC Eighth Company Law Directive which previously formed the basis for a large part of current UK company law requirements on the audit of individual and group accounts. Member states were given until June 2008 to implement the requirements of the new Directive, which is considerably broader in scope than its predecessor, although current practice in the UK is already in line with many of the Directive's requirements. The main changes affecting UK statutory audits are:

(1)   a requirement for the audit report to be signed in the name of at least one individual audit partner on behalf of the firm – for accounting periods beginning on or after 6 April 2008, CA 2006 provides for the senior statutory auditor to sign the report on behalf of the audit firm (see para 6.50 above);

(2)   a requirement that the dismissal of statutory auditors is only permitted on proper grounds (see para 6.52 above);

(3)   a requirement for an outgoing auditor to provide all relevant information to the incoming auditor (see para 6.58 above);

(4)   a requirement for information on fees receivable by the auditors of medium-sized companies in respect of non-audit services to be provided when requested (see para 6.43 above);

(5)   more stringent statutory requirements on group audits, covering in particular the documentation of reviews of audit work performed by third country auditors – it is expected that these requirements will be adequately met by the adoption of a UK and Ireland version of IAS 600 (revised) 'The Audit of Group Financial Statements' in due course;

(6)   a requirement for auditors of listed entities to publish an annual transparency report (see para 6.66 below); and

(7)   a requirement for companies whose shares are publicly traded to have a body responsible for carrying out the audit functions specified in the Directive (see para 6.67 below).

As a result of changes made by the Company Reporting Directive[1], there is also a new requirement for companies whose shares are publicly traded to make a formal statement on compliance with the corporate governance code that applies or has been voluntarily adopted, and the main features of the company's internal control and risk management systems in relation to financial reporting and (where relevant) the preparation of consolidated accounts (see para 6.68 below).

[1]   Directive 2006/46/EC.

Transparency reporting by listed company auditors

6.66 In April 2007, the POB issued regulations on the publication of transparency reports by auditors of listed companies and other public interest entities under powers transferred to it under the CA 2006. The Statutory Auditors (Transparency) Instrument 2008[1] came into force on 6 April 2008 and introduces the term 'transparency auditor' which is defined as 'a statutory auditor that has made an audit report on the annual accounts of one or more public interest entities at any time during the financial year of that statutory auditor'. A public interest entity is defined as an issuer whose shares are admitted to trading on a regulated market, and the audit of which is a statutory audit under s 1210 of the CA 2006. The transparency reporting requirements apply for financial periods beginning on or after 6 April 2008, and an auditor covered by the requirements must prepare a transparency report for each financial year in which an audit report has been issued on a public interest entity. The Instrument specifies the minimum content of the report, but auditors are free to provide additional information on a voluntary basis if they wish. The minimum contents include:

(1)   details of the legal structure and ownership of the auditor and of any network to which it belongs;

(2)   details of the auditor's governance structure;

(3)   a description of the auditor's internal control system and a statement on its effectiveness;

(4)   details of when the last formal monitoring of the auditor's performance took place;

(5)   a list of the public interest entities for which an audit report has been signed in the period, although information may be omitted to the extent that it would create, or be likely to create, a serious risk of violence or intimidation – the regulations also offer the option of the auditor making these details available separately on its website, provided that the transparency report provides a clear link to the relevant details;

(6)   details of the auditor's independence practices and procedures, together with confirmation that these have been subject to internal review;

(7)   a statement on the auditor's policies and practices to ensure that statutory auditors maintain their technical and professional skills;

(8)   financial information for the year, which must include an indication of the importance of statutory audit work; and

(9)   information on the basis for partner remuneration.

The report must be made available on a website maintained by, or on behalf of, the auditor not later than three months after the end of the financial year to which it relates and must remain on the website for a period of at least two years from the end of that three-month period.

In June 2009, the POB published the results of a review of the 2008 transparency reports prepared on a voluntary basis by a number of the larger audit firms in advance of the new statutory requirement[2]. The POB emphasises that it does not want to prescribe a particular template or format for transparency reports, but notes that there are a number of significant differences in approach, content and level of detail in the voluntary reports. Whilst the POB concludes that firms have generally sought to meet the spirit as well as the letter of the future requirements, it identifies a number of areas where it considers that disclosure could be improved.

[1]   Available at http://www.frc.org.uk/pob/regulation/oversight.cfm.
[2]   'Transparency Reporting by the Largest UK Audit Firms: Commentary on 2008 Reports' available at http://www.frc.org.uk/pob/publications/pub1991.html.

Audit committee requirement for listed companies

6.67 The requirement for public-interest entities to have an audit committee has been implemented in the UK through the FSA Disclosure and Transparency Rules ('DTRs') and applies for accounting periods beginning on or after 29 June 2008. For these accounting periods, under DTR 7.1, a listed company must have a body responsible for monitoring:

(1)   the financial reporting process;
(2)   the effectiveness of the company's internal control, internal audit (where applicable) and risk management systems;
(3)   the statutory audit of the annual and consolidated accounts; and
(4)   the independence of the external auditor, and in particular the provision of any additional services to the company.

The relevant body must have at least one independent member and at least one member with competence in accounting and/or auditing (although these requirements may be met by the same individual), and the company must issue a statement identifying the body and how it is composed. This can be done as part of the company's annual corporate governance reporting or can be made publicly available by other means.

Corporate governance reporting by listed companies

6.68 The requirements on corporate governance reporting have also been implemented through the FSA DTRs and apply for accounting periods beginning on or after 29 June 2008. Under DTR 7.2, a listed company must include a corporate governance statement as a specific section of its directors' report, or must issue a separate corporate governance report published with and in the same manner as the directors' report. The minimum contents of the statement include:

(1)   a reference to the corporate governance code to which the entity is subject, or which it has voluntarily applied – the report must state where this code is made available to the public and explain any departures from the code, together with its reasons for them;
(2)   the main features of the company's internal control and risk management systems in relation to the financial reporting process and, where relevant, the process for preparing consolidated accounts;
(3)   a description of the composition and operation of the company's administrative, management and supervisory bodies and their committees; and
(4)   the information required by paragraph 13 of Schedule 7 to SI 2008/410 (see para 6.19) in respect of:
    ● significant holdings in the company's securities;
    ● any person holding securities with special rights with regard to control of the company;
    ● any restrictions on voting rights;
    ● any rules on the appointment or replacement of the directors or on amendment of the company's articles; and
    ● the powers of the company's directors.

Where a company takes up the option of issuing a separate corporate governance report, it must either include the disclosures in (4) above in that report or include a cross-reference to the directors' report where the relevant details are provided.

Where a listed company includes the corporate governance statement as part of its directors' report, the statement will automatically be approved by the directors and delivered to the registrar as part of that report and will be covered by the auditor's opinion on consistency between the directors' report and the annual accounts. However, the CA 2006 does not currently cover a situation where a listed company takes up the option to prepare a separate corporate governance report. The Companies Act 2006 (Accounts, Reports and Audit) Regulations 2009[1] amend the legislation to introduce equivalent requirements in this situation. In particular:

(i) new sections 472A and 538A define a corporate governance statement and a separate corporate governance statement for accounts and audit purposes respectively;

(ii) new section 419A requires any separate corporate governance statement to be approved by the board of directors and signed on behalf of the board by a director or by the company secretary;

(iii) sections 446 (unquoted companies) and 447 (quoted companies) are amended to require any separate corporate governance statement to be delivered to the registrar with the other reports and accounts and to state the name of the person who signed the statement on behalf of the board;

(iv) new section 497A requires the auditor to state whether, in his opinion, the information given in a separate corporate governance statement in compliance with DTR 7.2.5 (internal control and risk management systems in respect of financial reporting) and DTR 7.2.6 (capital structure) is consistent with the accounts; and

(v) new section 498A provides that, where a company is required to prepare a corporate governance statement and no such statement is included in the directors' report:
 * the auditor must ascertain whether such a statement has been prepared; and
 * if it appears to him that no such statement has been prepared, he must state that fact in his report on the annual accounts.

The new provisions apply for accounting periods beginning on or after 29 June 2008 that have not ended before 27 June 2009 (the date on which the regulations came into force). The Explanatory Memorandum published with the regulations notes that the Auditing Practices Board may develop additional guidance on the auditor's role in relation to corporate governance statements.

[1] SI 2009/1581.

STATUTORY AUDITORS

Summary

6.69 New provisions on statutory auditors are set out Pt 42 of the CA 2006. These restate, with certain modifications, the provisions currently set out in Pt 2 of the Companies Act 1989 ('CA 1989') and equivalent Northern Ireland legislation. Most of the changes are based on the requirements of the EC Statutory Audit Directive (see para 6.65 above). In particular, the new legislation:

(1)   extends the categories of auditors that are subject to regulation and makes provision for the registration and regulation of auditors who audit companies incorporated outside the EU but listed in the UK – such auditors may or may not be based in the UK;

(2)   provides for the Comptroller and Auditor General and regional Auditors General to carry out statutory audits and sets out provisions on the regulation and supervision of their functions as a statutory auditor.

Part 42 of the CA 2006 came into force on 6 April 2008. Only the most significant changes are outlined here.

Statutory auditors

6.70 CA 2006, s 1210 defines a statutory auditor as including:

(1)   auditors appointed under Pt 16 of the CA 2006;
(2)   those who audit building societies, banks, insurance undertakings and insurers that are friendly societies or industrial and provident societies;
(3)   those appointed under the Insurance Accounts Directive (Lloyd's Syndicate and Aggregate Accounts) Regulations 2004;[1] and
(4)   a person appointed as auditor of a prescribed person under a prescribed enactment authorising or requiring the appointment.

The Secretary of State is also empowered to add auditors of other persons to the list.

[1]   SI 2004/3219.

Register of auditors

6.71 CA 2006, s 1239 retains the provisions of s 35 of the CA 1989 in respect of the register of auditors but extends them to cover all persons eligible for appointment as a statutory auditor and third country auditors who apply to be registered here. The Secretary of State is required to make regulations for the maintenance of the register and s 1239 specifies the details that must be included for each person's entry in the register. The regulations can provide for certain elements of the register to be kept by different persons (for instance, that an oversight body should maintain the details for registered third country auditors whilst the recognised supervisory bodies maintain the details for other statutory auditors). The Secretary of State is permitted to disapply certain limited requirements in respect of third country auditors, for instance to take account of the fact that they are already subject to appropriate supervision in their own country. Detailed requirements are now set out in the Statutory Auditors and Third Country Auditors Regulations 2007.[1]

[1]   SI 2007/3494, as amended by the Statutory Auditors and Third Country Auditors (Amendment) Regulations 2008, SI 2008/499.

Information available to the public

6.72   CA 2006, s 1239 continues to provide for regulations to specify that information in the register of auditors should be made available to the public on request and for a charge to be made for inspection of the register or for the provision of copies of specified entries. Section 1240 sets out new provisions enabling the Secretary of State to make regulations obliging statutory auditors to disclose information on their ownership, governance, internal controls in respect of audit quality and independence, turnover and the entities for whom they have acted as statutory auditor. This allows for transparency reporting by the auditors of listed companies under the requirements of the EC Statutory Audit Directive (see para 6.66 above).

Chapter 7

SHAREHOLDER COMMUNICATIONS, RESOLUTIONS AND MEETINGS

Carol Shutkever

INTRODUCTION

7.1 The provisions in the Companies Act 2006 ('CA 2006') relating to company communications, resolutions and meetings are substantially different from the regime in the Companies Act 1985 ('CA 1985'). Some of these changes are deregulatory but some add additional requirements and new shareholder rights, particularly for listed companies. In addition, the CA 2006 for the first time makes certain rights available to the underlying owners of shares rather than just the registered holders. One of the four stated company law reform objectives of the CA 2006 was 'enhancing shareholder engagement'. The changes relating to shareholder rights, including the rights of beneficial owners who are not on the register, reflect that aim.

The provisions relating to shareholder meetings and shareholder rights in the CA 2006 have already been amended in order to reflect the EU Shareholder Rights Directive.[1] The Directive has been implemented in the UK via the Companies (Shareholders' Rights) Regulations 2009[2] (the 'Shareholder Rights Regulations'), which made amendments to Pt 13 of CA 2006 with effect from 3 August 2009. The Directive requires Member States to impose particular requirements relating to meetings on companies that have voting shares admitted to trading on a regulated market in any EEA state. The changes made by the Shareholder Rights Regulations therefore primarily relate only to those companies. However a number of the changes relate to all companies. A new definition of a 'traded company' has been inserted in Pt 13 (s 360C) to reflect the new provisions applying just to those companies. It is unfortunate that the complexity of Pt 13 has been increased by this definition being similar to, but not the same as, the definition in Pt 13 of a 'quoted company' (ss 361 and 385; the definition covers companies listed in the EEA and companies admitted to trading on the New York Stock Exchange or NASDAQ). The concept of quoted companies has been retained and is used to impose a separate set of requirements on those companies.

The requirements relating to shareholder resolutions, shareholder meetings and company communications are found in a range of provisions scattered across the CA 2006 which need to be looked at together to understand their full effect. The provisions relating to resolutions and meetings are largely contained in Pt 13 of the CA 2006. The provisions relating to communications by companies are set out in Pt 37 (supplementary provisions) and Schs 4 and 5. Part 8 contains general provisions about company members and Pt 9 deals separately with the exercise of members' rights.

1   2007/36/EC.
2   SI 2009/1632.

COMPANY COMMUNICATIONS

7.2 The communications provisions in the CA 2006 were bought into force with effect from 20 January 2007 under the Companies Act 2006 (Commencement No 1, Transitional Provisions and Savings) Order 2006.[1]

The provisions relating to communications which came into force on that date are the provisions in ss 1143–1148 and s 1168 of the CA 2006 and the provisions in Schs 4 and 5. The provisions in ss 308, 309 and 333 of Pt 13 of the Act regarding notices of meetings also came into force on that date because of their link to the communications provisions. The provisions in the CA 1985 which were inserted by the Companies Act 1985 (Electronic Communications) Order 2000 in relation to electronic communications, in particular in relation to notice of meetings and proxies sent in electronic form (in ss 369 and 372), were repealed with effect from 20 January 2007.

1   SI 2006/3428.

The location and scope of the communications provisions

7.3 There is a completely new approach to the provisions on company communications in the CA 2006. The specific and piecemeal provisions that were in the 1985 Act have been replaced by general provisions about communications by and to companies, in particular in relation to communications in electronic form.

The general provisions dealing with communications by companies are contained in ss 1143–1148 in Pt 37 of the CA 2006 (supplementary provisions). This then refers the reader to Schs 4 and 5 of the CA 2006 which set out the provisions applying to all documentation supplied to or by a company.

There are, in addition, specific provisions in other parts of the CA 2006 relating to communications. In particular Pt 13 of the CA 2006 (dealing with resolutions and meetings) sets out both the ability to use electronic communications (for example for requisitions by shareholders) and also the requirements when electronic communications are used for communications relating to meetings (for example requirements in relation to notices of meeting being made available via a website).

A key aspect of the scope of the communications provisions in the CA 2006 is that, under s 1143 of the CA 2006, the provisions on communications in ss 1144–1148 and Schs 4 and 5 have effect 'for the purposes of any provisions of the Companies Acts that authorises or requires documents or information to be sent or supplied by or to a company'. This has two consequences:

- The communications provisions do not apply to all communications to and from a company – only ones authorised or required by the Companies Acts. Therefore, although the provisions do not just cover communications with a shareholder but also apply to any communications by a company with any third party, s 1143 limits the effect of this.
- It means that any references in the Companies Acts to a requirement to send or deposit a document can include a communication in electronic form provided that the requirements of Sch 4 or 5 (as relevant) are complied with.

For the purposes of the communications provisions, a company includes any body corporate (s 1148(1)).

Section 1144 of the CA 2006 describes the application of Schs 4 and 5 on communications:

- Schedule 4 sets out the manner in which documents or information sent or supplied *to* a company must be sent or supplied.
- Schedule 5 sets out the manner in which documents or information to be sent *by* a company must be sent or supplied.

Under s 1144(3), if documents or information are sent or supplied by one company to another then the provisions in Sch 5 rather than Sch 4 apply. This is the case even if the sender is for example a company that is a shareholder of the recipient company, because it is still treated as a communication *by* a company. However, the fact that the communications provisions only cover, as described above, documents authorised or required to be sent to companies pursuant to the Companies Acts limits the effect of this extension of the definition.

Interaction between a company's articles and the communications provisions

7.4 The communications provisions in the CA 2006 override any contrary provision in a company's articles[1] except in the few limited cases (for example s 1147 – see para 7.9 below) in which the provisions are expressly made subject to any contrary provision in the articles. They give the company power to communicate in the manner provided for in Sch 5 irrespective of a more restrictive provision in the articles (with the exception of the use of deemed acceptance of communications via a website for which Sch 5 expressly requires a provision in the articles or an authorising resolution – see para 7.6 below).

However this power only applies to the extent of the documents covered by the communications provisions. As described above, the communications provisions apply to communications authorised or required to be sent to or by a company under the Companies Acts. If a company wants to use electronic communications in relation to all documents and information sent to shareholders and not just those provided for under the Companies Acts, it should include an express provision in its articles covering all communications with shareholders.

[1]   See DTI Explanatory Notes to the CA 2006, para 1465.

Communications sent by companies

7.5 The CA 2006 is intended to make it easier for companies to communicate with their shareholders electronically. This was stated by the Government to be one of the key cost savings for traded companies arising as a result of the CA 2006. In particular, the new provisions provide an ability to communicate with shareholders by means of a website, both by specific agreement and as a default position.

Under the CA 1985, as a result of amendments made by the Companies Act 1985 (Electronic Communications) Order 2000, certain types of communications with shareholders were permitted to be made electronically by way of specific provisions setting out the requirements for electronic communication. Table A also includes provisions to allow electronic communications which (under the CA 1985 provisions now repealed) applied if the company's articles did not expressly provide for it. There were no general provisions about communications with shareholders and no provisions about communications with other third parties.

The approach taken in the CA 2006 is to have general provisions about any communications authorised or required to be sent under the Companies Act by or to a company, rather than including specific provisions about electronic communications for each type of document. There is also no equivalent to the concept in the CA 1985 of the Table A provisions applying if the company's articles do not contain any provisions about electronic communications. This is because the general provisions in the CA 2006 apply irrespective of provisions in a company's articles and therefore override any contrary provisions in the articles.

The provisions about communications by companies are set out in Sch 5 of the CA 2006 and the key aspects of these as regards electronic communications are described in paras 7.6 and 7.7 below.

The Institute of Chartered Secretaries and Administrators ('ICSA') has issued guidance on how companies should deal with the new e-communications provisions in the CA 2006 in practice.[1]

There are also some important general provisions and definitions in ss 1145–1148 and 1168 of the CA 2006:

- Under s 1145 there is a general right for a shareholder to receive a hard copy version of any document sent to him by the company in electronic form. The company must send the hard copy within 21 days of a request from the shareholder.
- Section 1168 of the CA 2006 defines what is meant by document being sent in 'hard copy form' or in 'electronic form' for the purposes of the CA 2006, including Schs 4 and 5:
    - Under s 1168(2) a document is sent in hard copy form if it is supplied in a paper copy or similar form capable of being read.
    - Under s 1168(3), a document or information sent or supplied in electronic form if it is sent or supplied:
      (a) by electronic means (for example by email or fax); or
      (b) by any other means while in electronic form (for example sending a disk by post).
- There is then a further definition in s 1168(4) of what is meant by document or information sent or supplied by electronic means which refers to information sent and received by means of electronic equipment for the processing or storage of data and entirely transmitted, conveyed and received by wire, radio, optical means or other electromagnetic means.
- In all cases when a document is sent or supplied in electronic form it must be done in a manner which will enable the recipient to read it and to retain a copy of it (s 1168(5)). This means being capable of being read by the naked eye, including maps and images.
- Section 1146 allows a company to specify how a document sent or supplied in electronic form should be authenticated. If it does not do so then a statement by the sender as to his identity is sufficient if the company has no reason to doubt it.
- Under s 1148(1) 'address' for the purposes of the company communication provisions includes any number or address given for purposes of sending or receiving documents by electronic means.

[1]   ICSA Guidance on Electronic Communications with Shareholders 2007 (Ref 160207).

Website communications by companies

7.6 Under Pt 4 of Sch 5 to the CA 2006, a company can use website communications with:

- any shareholder who expressly agrees with the company to receive communications in that form; and
- provided that the company has the necessary general shareholder authority (see below), any shareholder who is deemed to have so agreed because he fails to respond to a request from the company for agreement to website communications.

This applies to all forms of communications (including notices of meetings and other documentation such as annual reports) falling within the communications provisions under s 1143, that is all documents or information authorised or required by the Companies Acts to be sent or supplied by or to a company. There are similar provisions applicable to communications with holders of debt securities.

In order to make use of the website default route, that is the ability to treat shareholders as having deemed to have given their agreement to website communications if they do not respond, there are a series of steps that a company needs to take. The requirements, which are set out in Pt 4 (in particular para 10) and Pt 6 of Sch 5 to the CA 2006, are as follows:

- The default power can only be used to the extent that the members of the company have resolved that the company may send or supply documents or information to members by making them available on a website or the articles contain a provision to that effect.
- The company must write to shareholders asking for their consent to receive all or any communications via a website. The notice to shareholders must comply with the requirements set out in para 10 of Sch 5. If the company does not receive a response within 28 days then that can be taken as an agreement to receive communications in that way.
- Consent can be requested by the company in relation to all or any communications from the company.
- Each shareholder may only be asked once every 12 months whether he is prepared to accept communications by means of a website so as to be subject to the deemed consent provisions if he fails to respond within 28 days. Companies may still want to contact each new member about communication methods when they first are put on the register, but they could just ask new shareholders if they want to positively elect for email or website communication, so that the 12 month period for requesting website acceptance is not triggered at that time (otherwise there will be a different time limit for each new shareholder). The ICSA guidance on electronic communications (referred to in para 6.5 above) recommends that shareholders are asked no more than once every two years.
- Conversely, a shareholder who is deemed to have given consent need not be asked to renew it every year. The consent can be in perpetuity until revoked by an express notice to the company from the shareholder.
- Unless the articles of the company provide otherwise, the agreement or deemed agreement of all joint holders must be obtained to receive communications via the website, although the documentation and notifications can just be sent to the first named holder.

Once a shareholder is deemed to have agreed to communications via a website using the procedure described above, or has expressly agreed to accept communications via a website, then the following provisions in Sch 5 apply to the method of communicating with the shareholder:

- The communication with the shareholder can be made by the document being made available on the company's website. However, the company must in addition provide the shareholder with a notification in hard copy (or email if the shareholder has specifically consented to email communication in accordance with the requirements set out in para 7.7 below) of the availability of the document on the website. The notification must notify the shareholder of the presence of the document or information on the website, the address of the website and where and how it can be accessed on the website.

- In relation to notices of meeting, there is a further requirement, set out in s 309 of the CA 2006, that the notification of availability must state that it concerns a notice of the meeting and specify the place, date and time of the meeting.
- The notification is deemed to have been given, or the document to have been sent, on the date on which the shareholder is sent the notification or, if later, the date on which the document appears on the website.
- The document must stay on the website during the period required by a specific provision in the CA 2006 relating to that documentation or in the absence of such a specific provision for at least 28 days. Under s 309, notice of availability of a notice of a shareholder meeting must stay on the website from the date of notification to the conclusion of the meeting.
- As mentioned in para 7.5 above, shareholders always have a right to ask for a hard copy of anything that has been sent to them in electronic form.
- Shareholders can always revoke their deemed or express agreement to communications via the website by notice to the company at any time.
- Unless the articles provide otherwise, then on the death or bankruptcy of a member, the company can continue to supply documentation or information in the manner in which the documentation had previously been supplied, until such time as an address in the UK supplied by a person claiming on death or bankruptcy is supplied instead, in which case that address must be used.

A shareholder may agree to receive documentation or information in electronic form either generally or specifically under Sch 5. There is nothing in Sch 5 preventing a company (in relation to either actual or deemed acceptance of website communications) from requiring that a shareholder either accepts or is deemed to accept all communications electronically (by email or website) or has to receive them all in hard copy. Consent can be given generally or specifically but there is no requirement that a request must give those options. It is up to a company to decide whether to have a more complicated arrangement in which shareholders are allowed to elect for certain documentation (report and accounts for example) to be received via a website, but receive the remainder in hard copy. The company can also, in the notice, reserve the right to send a hard copy at any time.

Email communications by companies

7.7 In relation to communications from companies by email to shareholders, there is still a requirement (under para 6(a) of Sch 5 of the CA 2006) for a specific opt in by individual shareholders. This is largely because, in any event, the company needs to obtain their email address in order to send information to them in that way. Companies can, as was the case under the CA 1985, write to shareholders to ask them whether they wish to provide an email address for all or any communications rather than receiving documentation in hard copy. The requirements are set out in Pt 3 of Sch 5. This could include receiving an email notification, rather than hard copy notification, of the availability of a document on a website.

A company can, under para 6(b) of Sch 5, be deemed to have accepted email communications but only to the extent provided for in the Companies Acts – as described in para 7.8 below in relation to the equivalent provision in Sch 4.

The provisions in Pt 6 of Sch 5, described in para 7.6 above in relation to website communications, as regards joint holders and the effect of death and bankruptcy apply equally to email communications.

Email addresses are likely to change more frequently than postal addresses, for example as a result of a change in internet provider. Traded companies will therefore need to have effective methods agreed with their registrars of keeping track of shareholders' email addresses.

Communications sent to companies

7.8   Schedule 4 to the CA 2006 applies to communications sent to companies. However, as mentioned in para 7.3 above, communications from one company to another fall under Sch 5 rather than Sch 4. This is because they will always also be a communication *from* a company and s 1144 provides that Sch 5 rather than Sch 4 is the Schedule that takes precedence in that case. It is therefore the provisions in Sch 5 that determine how communications are sent by a company pursuant to the provisions of the Companies Acts even if the sender is a shareholder in the recipient.

The key provision in Sch 4 is that a person may communicate with the company in electronic form if the company has agreed that the document may be sent or supplied in that form or has deemed to have so agreed by a provision in the Companies Acts.

There are specific provisions in the CA 2006 which create a deeming provision in relation to the company accepting communications at an electronic address.

Under s 333 of the CA 2006, where a company has given an electronic address in a notice calling a shareholder meeting, it is deemed to have agreed that any document or information relating to proceedings at that meeting may be sent by electronic means to that address. Also in s 333, where a company has given an electronic address in an instrument of proxy sent in relation to the meeting then it is deemed to have agreed that any document or information may be sent by electronic means to that address. In each case this is subject to any limitations set out in the notice or proxy. There are specific requirements in s 333A as regards the provision by traded companies of an electronic address for proxies (see para 7.21 below for further details).

Under s 298 of the CA 2006, where a company has given an electronic address in any document containing or accompanying a proposed written resolution, then the company is deemed to have agreed that any document or information relating to that resolution may be sent by electronic means to that address.

There are also provisions in the CA 2006 specifically allowing certain documents to be sent in electronic form which would seem to apply irrespective of a company's agreement (because they would amount to a contrary provision for the purposes of s 1143 on the application of the general communications provisions). In particular the provisions relating to shareholder requisitions (described in paras 7.29–7.36 below) permit requisitions to be sent to the company in electronic form (although they make no provision as to which electronic address the requisition should be sent to).

It may be thought advisable for a traded company to provide a general address to which a document or information may be sent to it or served on it by electronic means and to make that address available on the company's website. Companies will need to decide whether they use a general email address for all purposes, perhaps an address provided by their registrars, or whether they wish to use different email addresses for different purposes. For example, the new provisions relating to an ability to send documentation such as requisitions in an electronic form means that companies may want to specify the email address that can be used for this purpose on its website. In any event, there should be systems and controls in place agreed between the company and its registrars as to how communications sent to any specified email address are to be monitored and responded to.

Service of documents by and on companies

7.9 The supplementary provisions in Pt 37 about documents and information include deemed service provisions.

As regards service of documents by companies, under s 1147 (which is in force) if documents and information are sent or supplied by a company either:

- by post to an address in the United Kingdom; or
- by electronic means

then, subject to the application of the contrary provisions referred to below, the document or information is deemed to have been received by the recipient 48 hours after it was sent. The period of 48 hours (s 1147(5)) does not include non-working days (as defined in s 1173).

Where the documentation or information is sent by means of website then it is deemed to have been received when the material was first made available on the website or, if later, when the recipient received notice of the fact that material is available on the website (s 1147(4)).

These deeming provisions are subject to two contrary provisions:

- where the documents or information are sent or supplied by a company to its members, to any contrary provision in the company's articles of association or, in the case of debenture holders, to any contrary provision in the constitution of the debenture;
- in the case of persons other than members or debenture holders, to any contrary provision in a contract between the company and that person.

The provision therefore creates a default provision as to when documents sent by a company are deemed to have been received in the absence of a provision in the articles, terms of debenture or contract. There was no equivalent in the CA 1985. At first sight it appears very wide, applying to any type of document or information sent by a company to any third party. However its scope is limited by the wording in s 1143 (referred to in para 7.3 above) which limits the effect of the company's communications provisions, including s 1147, to provisions of the Companies Acts that authorise or require documents to be sent or supplied by or to a company.

CA 2006, s 1147 has the effect of overriding s 7 of the Interpretation Act 1978, which provides that where a statute requires a document to be served by post then the service is deemed effective at the time at which the letter would have been delivered in the ordinary course of post. There is however no provision in s 1147 in relation to posting to an address overseas and, in that respect, s 7 of the Interpretation Act 1978 would still apply (subject always to contrary provision in the articles).

Companies are therefore likely to want to exclude s 1147 by including an express provision in their articles covering all communications to shareholders as regards when the notice or document is deemed to have been received according to the method by which it is sent. In particular, companies may wish to provide that a notice or document sent by post is deemed to be received on the next day. Under Table A (Art 115) notices of meeting are deemed to be delivered 48 hours after posting (including non-working days). However this only covers notices, whereas s 1147 covers all documents and information sent by a company to any person unless there is a contrary provision in the articles.

It might be thought that s 1147 could catch communications sent by companies which are shareholders in a company as well as communications by a company to its shareholders. However, it is unlikely that this is what is intended. Section 1147 is expressed to apply to communications sent 'by' a company whereas s 1143, on the scope of the communications provisions, applies to communications required or authorised to be sent 'by or to' a company. It would be anomalous if a corporate shareholder returning a proxy by post were fixed with the deemed receipt time in the CA 2006 whereas an individual shareholder was not. The fact that the articles are only expressed to override s 1147 in relation to documents supplied by the company to its members also suggests it was not intended to cover communications by corporate shareholders to the company because there would be no possibility of overriding it in that case.

As regards service of documents on companies, s 1139 (which is not yet in force because it is not part of the communications provisions) provides that a document may be served on a company registered under the CA 2006 by leaving it at or sending it by post to:

- in the case of a UK company, the company's registered office (with special provision for service of proceedings in England and Wales for companies registered elsewhere in the UK); or
- in the case of an overseas company, the registered address of a person authorised to accept service of documents, or failing that, any place of business of the company in the UK.

This replicates the provisions previously in ss 695 and 725 of the CA 1985 in establishing a place for service of notice for all UK registered companies.

There is then a separate, and new, provision in s 1140 for service of documents on directors and others, which allows service at that person's registered address.

SHAREHOLDER MEETINGS AND RESOLUTIONS

7.10 Part 13 of the CA 2006 deals with shareholder meetings and resolutions. It was brought into force on 1 October 2007 under The Companies Act 2006 (Commencement No 3, Consequential Amendments, Transitional Provisions and Savings) Order 2007[1] (the 'Third Commencement Order'). As mentioned in para 7.1 above, Pt 13 has already been amended by the Shareholder Rights Regulations in order to implement the EU Shareholder Rights Directive. The ICSA has issued guidance on the changes resulting from the implementation of the Directive.[2]

Part 13 covers how resolutions are to be passed (Chapter 1), the procedure for written resolutions (Chapter 2), the procedure for resolutions at meetings, including proxies and corporate representatives (Chapter 3), the requirements for public company AGMs (Chapter 4), the additional requirements imposed on quoted companies (Chapter 5), the requirements as to records of resolutions and meetings (Chapter 6) and supplementary provisions, including the computation of notice periods (Chapter 7).

The approach to shareholder resolutions and meetings in Pt 13 of the CA 2006 is quite different from the CA 1985. The provisions in Pt 13 apply to impose an obligation or confer a power on a company not withstanding any contrary provisions about meetings in its articles, except where the relevant provision is made expressly subject to contrary provision in the articles.[3]

Companies and their advisers need to look carefully in each case at whether or not the new provisions are subject to any contrary provisions in a company's articles, or alternatively override any contrary provisions in a company's articles (in some cases, the position as regards contrary intention has been reversed compared to the CA 1985). A number of the provisions that appear in Table A but not in the CA 1985 itself have been changed into statutory provisions in the CA 2006. The changes mean that existing companies that retain Table A articles (in the form prior to the 2007 amendments to Table A) will find that many of the provisions relating to resolutions, meetings and communications will be inconsistent with the provisions in the CA 2006. In some cases the CA 2006 will override them (for example as regards the rights of proxies) and in other cases the provision in the articles will mean that a relaxation in the CA 2006 (for example the shorter minimum notice period for special resolutions) cannot be used until the articles are changed.

¹   SI 2007/2194.
²   ICSA guide on changes resulting from the implementation of the Shareholder Rights Directive (Ref 090729).
³   See DTI Explanatory Notes to the CA 2006, para 522.

Shareholder resolutions

7.11 Section 281 of the CA 2006 provides that a resolution of the members of a private company must be passed as a written resolution in accordance with Chap 2 of Pt 13 or at a meeting of members and that a resolution of the members of a public company must be passed at a meeting of members (with Chap 3 of Pt 13 setting out the provisions which apply to meetings of members). The intention is that resolutions may only be passed in the manner provided for in s 281.[1] The CA 1985 did not include any equivalent provision.

Section 281(4) of the CA 2006 does however preserve the principle in *Re Duomatic*[2] and provides that nothing in Pt 13 affects:

'any enactment or rule of law as to:
  (a)   things done otherwise than by passing a resolution
  (b)   circumstances in which a resolution is or is not treated as having been passed, or
  (c)   cases in which a person is precluded from alleging that a resolution has not been duly passed.'

Resolutions of members can, as was the case under the CA 1985, be passed, as ordinary resolutions, with a 50 per cent majority (s 282) or as special resolutions with a 75 per cent majority (s 283). See para 7.19 below in relation to the impact of these provisions on the chairman's casting vote.

The concept of extraordinary resolutions (which under the CA 1985 had to be passed by a 75 per cent majority in the same way as a special resolution but could be passed on 14 rather than 21 days' notice) does not exist in the CA 2006. Very few resolutions were in any event passed as extraordinary resolutions. Resolutions to vary class rights have been changed to special resolutions under the CA 2006 (see para 7.26 below) and references in the Insolvency Act 1985 to extraordinary resolutions of members have also been changed to special resolutions. A transitional provision in the Third Commencement Order[3] preserves existing references in articles of association and contracts to extraordinary resolutions and states that they are to be treated as if s 378 of the CA 1985 applied to them (and they continue to need to be filed).

Under s 281(3) of the CA 2006, where a provision of the Companies Acts requires a resolution of the members but does not specify what kind of resolution is required, then the default is that an ordinary resolution is required unless the company's articles require a higher majority. Where a provision specifies that an ordinary resolution is required then, according to the DTI Explanatory Notes to the CA 2006,[4] the articles will not be able to specify a higher majority. Anything that can be done by ordinary resolution may also be done by special resolution (s 282(5)).

Section 301 provides that a resolution is validly passed at a general meeting if the notice of the meeting and resolution and procedure at the meeting are dealt with in accordance with both Chap 3 (and 4 if relevant) of Pt 13 and the articles, thus ensuring compliance with the mandatory procedural provisions in Chap 3 and with the articles.[5] The equivalent provision in the CA 1985 (s 378(6)) only applied to extraordinary and special resolutions and referred to compliance with the procedures set out in the Act or the articles.

The concept of, and procedures for, elective resolutions of private companies which were set out in the CA 1985 are removed completely in the CA 2006. This is because the statutory requirements covered by elective resolutions in the CA 1985, for example the dispensation from the requirement to hold an AGM, do not apply at all to private companies under the CA 2006.

There is a new express statutory power for directors to convene a shareholder meeting (s 302).

[1] See DTI Explanatory Notes to the CA 2006, para 523.
[2] [1969] 2 Ch 365.
[3] SI 2007/2194, Sch 3, para 23 (as amended by SI 2007/3495).
[4] See DTI Explanatory Notes to the CA 2006, para 523.
[5] See DTI Explanatory Notes to the CA 2006, para 545.

Written resolutions

7.12 The CA 2006 sets out a detailed statutory process for the passing of written resolutions by a private company. The general provisions about resolutions in Chap 1 of Pt 13 include provisions about written resolutions as well as resolutions passed at meetings. The procedure for passing a written resolution is then set out in Chap 2 of Pt 13.

The key deregulatory change is that under the CA 2006 a written resolution can be signed by the same majority as a resolution passed at a meeting, that is 50 per cent for an ordinary resolution (s 282(2)) and 75 per cent for a special resolution (s 283(2)), whereas under the CA 1985 the statutory procedure required unanimity. This reflects the policy that a written resolution procedure can operate just as well as a meeting as a way of passing shareholder resolutions. There is a move from the CA 1985 assumption that private companies will take shareholder decisions via a meeting to a recognition that most private companies are likely to wish to operate solely by written resolutions.

A written resolution has the same effect as a resolution passed at a general meeting (s 288(5)). There are two exceptions (s 288(2)), which are that the written resolution procedure in the CA 2006 cannot be used to remove a director from office under the power in s 162, or to remove an auditor before the expiration of his period of office using the power under s 510. The special procedures for certain types of written resolutions (for example share buy backs and directors' service contracts) which in the CA 1985 were set out in Sch 15A, are in the CA 2006 set out with the relevant provision in the Act as an express provision relating to approval of that matter by written resolution.

The are procedural requirements which must be complied with in order to pass a written resolution. These are set out mainly in Chap 2 of Pt 13 (ss 288–299) but also elsewhere in Pt 13. The procedures are:

- A written resolution must be circulated if it is proposed (s 288(3)) either by the directors of the company (under s 291) or by members holding 5 per cent of the voting rights or any lower percentage specified in the articles (under s 292). See para 7.34 below in relation to this power for members to requisition a written resolution.

- A copy of the resolution must be sent to every member entitled to vote on the resolution (s 291(2)) even though it is not necessary for every member to agree to the resolution. The articles cannot override this. This contrasts with the requirement in the CA 2006 for notices of meeting to be sent to all shareholders which is subject to any contrary provision in the articles (s 310(4)). So the articles can for example, exclude the right of overseas holders to receive a notice of meeting (see para 7.17 below) but not a copy of a written resolution.

- The resolution must be accompanied by a statement as to how to signify agreement to the resolution (s 291(4)).

- The resolution must also be accompanied by a statement as to the date by which the resolution must be passed if it is not to lapse (s 291(4)).

- Copies of the resolution and accompanying statements can be circulated in either hard copy or in electronic form (s 291(3)) (subject to compliance with the electronic communications provisions described in paras 7.2–7.8 above).

- The resolution must be sent at the same time (as far as reasonably practicable) to all members entitled to vote on the resolution or, if it is possible to do so without undue delay, by submitting the same copy or a series of copies, to each eligible member in turn (s 291(3)). The date it is first sent out to any members is defined as the circulation date (s 290).

- The written resolution is passed when the required majority of eligible members (that is the members entitled to vote on the circulation date – s 289) signify their agreement to it (s 296). In contrast to the written resolution procedure in the CA 1985, this can be by indicating agreement otherwise than by signing.

- On a written resolution, each member has one vote in respect of every share held by him, subject to any provision in the company's articles (s 284). The articles cannot provide for different voting rights on a written resolution than a member has on a poll (s 285A) (see also para 7.19 below in relation to the provisions in the CA 2006 about voting).

- The resolution lapses if it is not passed within the time specified in the articles or, if there is no time specified, within 28 days of the circulation date (s 297).
- When the written resolution is to be passed as a special resolution, then the resolution must expressly state this in order to be passed validly as a special resolution (s 283(3)). This removes an area of uncertainty that existed under the CA 1985, which did not include any specific requirement for a written resolution to state that it was to be passed as a special resolution.
- A copy of the written resolution must be sent to the company's auditors. Under s 502(1), the company's auditor is entitled to receive all communications relating to a written resolution that are required to be supplied to a member of the company by Chap 2 of Pt 13. This is the equivalent of s 390(2) of the CA 1985. However the provision in s 381B of the CA 1985 requiring the resolution to be sent to the auditors at or before the time the written resolution is circulated has not been repeated in the CA 2006 and it is therefore no longer specifically part of the process requirements for passing a written resolution.

Failing to comply with the procedures as to the form and manner of circulation of the resolution which are set out in s 291 (or s 293 for resolutions put forward by the shareholders) is a criminal offence for every officer of the company but does not invalidate the resolution (ss 291(7) and 293(7)).

As mentioned above, the CA 2006 specifically requires written resolutions to be passed in accordance with the procedures in Pt 2 (s 281). In particular, there is no saving for a separate power to pass resolutions in accordance with a power in the articles.

When the statutory written resolution procedure was first added to the CA 1985 by the Companies Act 1989 (ss 381A–381C of the CA 1985), one of the issues that immediately arose was whether or not the written resolution procedure set out in the CA 1985 overrode any power in a private company's articles to allow a company to pass a resolution unanimously in writing (as set out, for example, in Art 53 of Table A) so that the procedure in the CA 1985 had to be followed notwithstanding the power in the articles. In particular, there was a concern that the written resolution procedure in the CA 1985 contained additional requirements (including a requirement to notify an auditor seven days before the written resolution of the fact that the resolution was to be passed). As a result, the Deregulation (Resolutions of Private Companies) Order 1996[1] was passed which provided that the written resolution procedure did not prejudice any power conferenced by a company's articles. This position has not been replicated in the CA 2006. The concept of a saving for a provision allowing written resolutions in the articles, at least where the articles provide for written resolutions by unanimous consent, was considered during the passage of the Bill through Parliament but was rejected by the Government.

The written resolution procedure in the CA 2006 therefore overrides any power in the articles. In particular the procedure in the CA 2006 relating to the form of the resolution, the statements to accompany it and the requirement to send a copy to the auditor are required to be complied with irrespective of any general power in the articles, including the Table A Articles, allowing a written resolution to be passed (although the problem from the original 1989 Act provision of a seven-day waiting period for sending copies to the auditors, which was repealed by the 1996 Deregulation Order, has at least not been repeated in the CA 2006).

The requirement to follow the statutory procedure rather than a power in the articles could create confusion and a risk of non-compliance. This is particularly the case given that Table A included (prior to the October 2007 changes to Table A, as described below) a power to pass resolutions in writing. Although a reliance by a private company on the power in the articles resulting in a failure to follow the additional procedures in s 291 will not invalidate the resolution, breach is a criminal offence. It is also unclear what the inter-relationship is between the provisions on written resolutions and s 357 on the records of decisions by sole members – whether this would allow a sole member not to follow the written resolution procedure.

It is important to note, however, that the Government's view[2] is that the written resolution procedure in the CA 2006 need only be complied with where it is being used in order to pass a resolution required by an enactment to be passed as a special resolution or an ordinary resolution. Where the resolution is to be passed pursuant to a separate requirement in a company's articles of association for a resolution on that matter, and is not required by any enactment, then the written resolution may be passed using the power in the articles and the articles can determine the percentage required to pass the resolution.

The CA 2006 does not contain a statutory procedure for a written resolution by a public company. This was also the case in the CA 1985. Under the CA 1985 regime it was still regarded as possible for public companies to pass written resolutions if authorised by their articles of association. However, the difference in the CA 2006 is that (as described in para 7.11 above) s 281(2) is a new provision stating that a resolution of a public company 'must' be passed at a meeting of the members. This would therefore, at least in relation to resolutions required under the Companies Acts, override any provision in a public company's articles allowing the company to pass written resolutions, even if unanimous. It can, nevertheless, be argued that even though a public company is not given the power in the CA 2006 to pass a written resolution, the saving in s 281(4) for the *Duomatic* principle (see para 7.11 above) could in theory be used in relation to a unanimous written resolution passed by a public company. This would, however, be subject to the limits of the *Duomatic* principle, especially where the procedures for the relevant resolution in the Act are there to protect creditors, and to the fact that the EU Second Company Law Directive[3] requires resolutions of public companies relating to share capital to be passed at a general meeting.

Under s 300 of the CA 2006, a company's articles cannot prevent a resolution required by an enactment from being passed as a written resolution. This means that the articles cannot require a meeting, rather than a written resolution, for any shareholder approval required by any enactment. The provisions of s 281(3) (see para 7.11 above) will also apply to written resolutions so that where the CA 2006 is silent as to the type of resolution required, the resolution can be an ordinary resolution unless the articles provide for a higher percentage. Table A originally contained a provision giving the company power to pass shareholder resolutions in writing by unanimous argeement. This was removed from Table A with effect from 1 October 2007, to reflect the commencement of Part 13 of the CA 2006. For companies incorporated prior to that date using Table A articles, it is not thought that this provision in Table A, giving a power to pass resolutions in writing by unanimous agreement, creates a restriction on the company's ability to pass resolutions in writing with less than unanimous consent using the statutory powers in Chap 2 of Pt 13. This is because it can be argued that it is a power in the articles rather than a restriction and can therefore run alongside the statutory power and does not override it (no guidance or transitional provision has been issued in relation to this Table A article).

1   SI 1996/1471.
2   450 HC Official Report (5th series), col 978 (18 October 2006).
3   77/91/EEC.

Notice of general meetings

7.13 The amendments to Pt 13 by the Shareholder Rights Regulations have made the provisions in the CA 2006 relating to notices of meeting very complex.

Length of notice of meeting

7.14 There are statutory minimum notice periods for each type of shareholder meeting. However it is important to note that the articles may, in the case of all or any particular type of meeting, provide for a longer period of notice (for example Art 38 of Table A) and this will then override the statutory minimum (s 307(3) and s 307A(6)).

AGMs for public companies, and AGMs for traded companies even if private, must be held on at least 21 days' notice (s 307(2) and s 307A(1)) (see also para 7.18 below).

Subject to the special provisions for traded companies described below, the CA 2006 provides that all other meetings (including AGMs of private companies that are not traded companies) can be held on 14 days' notice irrespective of whether or not a special resolution is to be proposed at the meeting (s 307(1) and (2)).

As a result of the amendments made by the Shareholder Rights Regulations, there are special provisions about notice periods for traded company general meetings (s 307A). The statutory default minimum notice period for traded company general meetings (but not class meetings) that are not AGMs for both ordinary and special resolutions is 21 days instead of 14 days (with the exception of certain meetings relating to matters covered by the Takeovers Directive, for which there is a 14 day minimum period). The notice period can be reduced from 21 days to 14 days if two conditions are met. Firstly, the company must allow shareholders to vote 'by electronic means accessible to all members' having the right to vote. This is stated to be satisfied if a facility is available to all members to appoint a proxy by means of a website. Secondly, shareholders must pass a special resolution at the AGM every year approving the shortening of the notice period.

As was the case under the CA 1985, if the business to be conducted at the meeting is business which under the Companies Acts requires special notice, then 28 days' notice must be given to the company of the intention to move the resolution (s 312). The period for the company to give notice of the resolution requiring special notice when it cannot be sent out with the notice of meeting is 14 days (s 312(3)).

Under the CA 2006 the percentage required for consent to short notice of a meeting is 90 per cent rather than the 95 per cent provided for in the CA 1985 for a private company (unless the articles provide for a higher percentage up to 95 per cent), but for a public company it remains at 95 per cent (s 307(6)). This does not apply to AGMs for which (as was the case under the CA 1985) unanimity is required (s 337) or to any general meetings of traded companies, which are not permitted to be held on short notice at all (s 307A).

See para 7.25 below in relation to length of notice for a reconvened meeting following an adjournment.

CA 2006, s 360 provides that, in relation to the specific provisions in Pt 13 requiring notices to be given, including the notice periods for meetings in s 307 and s 307A, the reference to the notice period is to be calculated on a clear days basis:

'excluding—
    (a) the day of the meeting; and
    (b) the day on which the notice is given ...'

This is a new provision. It did not appear in the CA 1985, although it is a provision in the Table A Articles. It creates a calculation of the minimum notice period which cannot be overridden by the articles. The CA 1985 contained no statement as to how the notice periods for general meetings were to be calculated. However, Art 38 of Table A provides for 'clear days' notice', which is defined in Art 1 of Table A as being the period excluding the day when the notice was given or deemed to be given and the day for which it is given or on which it is to take effect. The provision in the CA 2006 covers the question of clear days for all companies and overrides any provision in the articles because it determines the calculation of the minimum statutory length of notice for meetings. The reference to the date on which the notice is 'given' tracks the wording in Table A but it would have been better if the wording were clearer, given that in other provisions in the Act there are references to a notice being 'sent' (for example s 310) and s 1147 provides for when a notice is deemed to have been 'received'. However, it does appear that it is the date that the notice is deemed to have been received, and not the date that the notice is sent out, that is the date it is 'given' and therefore the relevant date for the purposes of the calculation in s 360 (this is the interpretation that has been followed for the corresponding provision in Table A regarding the calculation of clear days). The date of deemed receipt of the notice will be determined by the articles, or if the articles are silent, by reference to s 1147 in the CA 2006 (see para 7.9 above).

Method of giving notice of meeting

7.15 Sections 308, 309 and 333 of the CA 2006 in relation to notices of shareholder meetings were brought into force on 20 January 2007 at the same time as the communications provisions. Sections 309 and 333 relate to the use of electronic communications for notices and are described in paras 7.6 and 7.8 above. Section 308 provides that notice of a general meeting must be given in hard copy or electronic form or by means of a website. This is in contrast to s 370 of the CA 1985 which provided that notice of meeting was to be given in accordance with the provisions in the articles or, failing that, in accordance with Table A. It appears that one effect of s 309 is that a notice of meeting, at least in relation to resolutions required under the Companies Acts, is no longer permitted to be given by newspaper advertisement which is sometimes provided for as a fallback in the articles (for example if there is a postal strike).

Content of notice of meeting and website information

7.16 Section 311 of the CA 2006 states that the notice of meeting must include the time, date and place of the meeting and the general nature of the business that is to be dealt with at the meeting.

In the case of traded companies, s 311(3) (inserted by the Shareholder Rights Regulations) sets out a specific list of information which must also be included in the notice of meeting. This includes a statement as regards the rights to vote at the meeting, the procedures that need to be complied with to attend and vote at the meeting, details in relation to proxy forms and a statement of the right of members to ask questions (see para 7.24 below).

Paragraph 7.21 below explains what information needs to be included in notices of meetings about proxy rights and paras 7.29–7.36 below explain what information needs to be included in notices of meetings about requisition rights.

A traded company is also required, under s 311A (also inserted by the Shareholder Rights Regulations) to include specific information on a website in advance of the general meeting. This includes details in relation to the shares in the company (such as total voting rights) and a copy of the notice of the meeting. This information must be available on the website during the period from the date on which the notice of the meeting is given until the conclusion of the meeting. In addition, quoted and untraded companies are required to include details on their website in relation to any polls taken at the meeting (see para 7.20 below).

Who the notice of meeting needs to be sent to

7.17 Under s 310 of the CA 2006, a notice of meeting must be sent to all members. This is expressly subject to any provision in the company's articles (s 310(4)). In contrast, under s 370(2) of the CA 1985, a notice of meeting was, subject to anything contrary in the articles, required to be served on any member who was entitled to receive them under the Table A provisions. Table A only requires notices to be sent to members who have provided an address in the UK or who have provided an electronic address (Art 112). Therefore the presumption is reversed. Under the CA 1985, unless the articles provide otherwise, notices only needed to be sent to those entitled to receive notice under the Table A provision whereas under the CA 2006, unless the articles provide otherwise, notices must be sent to all members. Section 310(4) also allows articles to continue to provide that a member need not receive notice if the company no longer has a valid address for that member.

There is a new express statutory statement that an accidental failure to give notice of a meeting, or of a resolution to be proposed at a meeting, to one or more persons will not, subject to any contrary provisions in the company's articles, invalidate the meeting (s 313).

Annual General Meetings

7.18 The requirements for Annual General Meetings ('AGMs') are set out in Chapter 4 of Pt 13.

All public companies, and all private companies that are traded companies, are required to hold an AGM.

AGMs of public companies (and of private companies that are traded companies) still require at least a 21-day notice period under s 307(2) and s 307A(1) of the CA 2006. Consent to short notice must be unanimous and is not in any event permitted for a company that is a traded company (s 337).

The AGM for a public company must (s 336(1)) be held within six months of the year end (for a private company that is a traded company the deadline is nine months). This deadline is the replacement for the provision in the CA 1985 (in s 366) for AGMs to be held no more than 15 months apart. There is no separate time limit as there was under the CA 1985, for holding of an AGM in the first two years of incorporation. If as a result of shortening an accounting reference period, the deadline cannot be complied with, there is no breach provided the AGM is held within three months of giving the shortening notice (s 336(2)).

For private companies (with the exception of traded companies), there is no longer any requirement for an AGM or any requirements about timings for AGMs. Private companies may however still have annual general meetings if they wish to do so. Furthermore, where a private company's articles refer expressly to a requirement to hold an annual general meeting, then under the transitional arrangements for the CA 2006[1] the company will (unless it had previously passed an elective resolution dispensing with AGMs) continue to be required to have an AGM until such time as it changes its articles (indirect references such as directors retiring by rotation at AGMs will not trigger the obligation; only an express requirement).

1   SI 2007/2194, as amended.

Voting at general meetings

7.19 Section 284 of the CA 2006 contains the provisions about voting by members at general meetings. Subject to any contrary provision in the company's articles (s 284(4)), each member has one vote per share. Section 284 provides specifically for one vote per share on a written resolution (see para 7.12 above) and one vote per member on a show of hands. There are then specific additional provisions in s 285 in relation to voting by proxies (see para 7.21 below), in s 285A in relation to voting on written resolutions (see para 7.12 above) and in s 323 in relation to voting by corporate representations (see para 7.22 below).

There are restrictions on the ability of a traded company to impose limits on share transfers prior to a meeting (so called 'share blocking') and as regards the use of record dates for voting at the meeting. Under s 360B, inserted by the Shareholder Rights Regulations, the articles of a traded company cannot impose any restriction on share transfers during the period of 48 hours (excluding non-working days) before the meeting and cannot restrict a member's ability to vote based on whether the shares had previously been dealt with in a particular way.

The time for determining the right to vote at the meeting (s 360B(2)) must in the case of a traded company be not earlier than the time 48 hours before the time of the meeting (excluding non-working days).

There is a new statutory default position (reflecting the Table A position), subject to any contrary provision in the articles, that only the vote of the senior joint holder may be counted (s 286).

One concern about the effect of ss 281 and 282 when passed was that, because they required an ordinary resolution to be passed by a 'simple majority' of the members voting, they did not allow for a chairman's casting vote. They are also not expressed to be subject to contrary provisions in the articles. However, there was then a saving provision in the Third Commencement Order[1] so that companies that had a provision for a chairman's casting vote in their articles prior to 1 October 2007 could validly retain it (and could reinsert it even if removed after that date). Traded companies were then excluded from this transitional provision as a result of an amendment made to the Third Commencement Order by the Shareholder Rights Regulations. In a final twist, the amendments to s 282 made by the Shareholder Rights Regulations seem to mean that a casting vote is permitted (at least on a show of hands) because s 282(3) now just refers to a majority of the votes cast by those entitled to vote (although the wording on voting by a poll has not changed and the position in that case remains unclear).

Under amendments made by the Shareholder Rights Regulations, the 2006 Act states (s 360A) that nothing in Pt 13 shall be taken to preclude shareholders from participating in a general meeting, that is to attend, speak and vote, by electronic means in order to allow a meeting to be held even though all of the participants are not present together in the same place. In the case of a traded company, if this facility is used, there is a requirement that the facility is made only subject to such restrictions as are necessary to ensure identification and the security of the electronic communications. The provision in s 360A is unfortunately couched in negative rather than positive terms, that is that Pt 13 does not preclude the use of electronic means, rather than expressly permitting it. This leaves it unclear as to the extent to which pre-existing common law on the conduct of meetings and when something can be a 'meeting' still applies.

All companies are also permitted to allow shareholders to vote on a poll in advance of the meeting (s 322A). In the case of traded companies this may only be made subject to requirements necessary to ensure identification.

[1]   SI 2007/2194, Sch 3, para 23A, as inserted by SI 2007/3495 Sch 5, para 2.

Polls

7.20 Under s 321 of the CA 2006, the articles cannot provide that a demand for a poll must be made by more than five members, or members holding more than 10 per cent of the voting rights, and cannot exclude the right to demand a poll except on election of the chairman and adjournment of the meeting. This is the same as under s 373 of the CA 1985. Proxies are given a statutory right to join in the demand for a poll under the CA 2006 (s 329).

Section 322 expressly provides that on a poll a member entitled to more than one vote need not, if he votes, use all his votes, or cast all his votes in the same way.

Under s 341 of the CA 2006, if a quoted or traded company holds a poll, then it must include certain information on its website. In the case of traded companies, the information required (as a result of the changes made by the

Shareholder Rights Regulations) is more detailed and includes, for example, the proportion of the company's share capital represented by the votes cast, the number of votes withheld and the subject matter of the poll. The information must be made available as soon as reasonably practicable (and in the case of a traded company in any event by the end of sixteen days after the day of the meeting or if later the day after the declaration of the result of the poll) and be kept available for at least two years (s 353).

Importantly, there is also a right for members of a quoted company to requisition an independent report on a poll. This is described in para 7.36 below.

Proxies

7.21 The rights of proxies appointed by shareholders are enhanced in the CA 2006. This reflects the policy of enfranchising the underlying owners of shares.

Section 324 of the CA 2006 states that a member of a company is entitled to appoint a proxy to exercise all or any of his rights to attend and speak and vote at a meeting of the company. A member can appoint more than one proxy provided that each proxy is appointed to exercise the rights attached to different shares held by him (s 324(2)).

Articles may confer more extensive rights on proxies (s 331) but cannot restrict the statutory rights of proxies set out in the CA 2006.

Section 324A requires proxies to vote in accordance with any instructions given by the member. This was inserted as a result of the changes made by the Shareholder Rights Regulations but it applies to all companies. It is an unusual provision for the CA 2006 in that it imposes an obligation on an individual rather than on a company. However, arguably it is just a statutory statement of the position that would exist (by virtue of contract or of fiduciary duties) at common law in any event. There are no stated statutory consequences either for the proxy or for the company (in terms of any affect on the validity of the vote) if the requirement is not followed.

Under s 285 of the CA 2006 (as amended by the Shareholder Rights Regulations), there are specific provisions about voting by proxies. On a show of hands, subject to any contrary provision in the articles, each proxy has one vote unless he has been appointed by more than one member, and is instructed by at least one member to vote against and one member to vote for, in which case he has one vote for and one vote against the resolution (s 285(1) and (2)). On a poll, a proxy can exercise all of the voting rights that a member could have exercised, provided that when a member appoints more than one proxy, the proxies together cannot exercise more extensive voting rights than could have been exercised by the member in person (s 285(3) and (4)).

Proxies have a right to join in demanding a poll and there are specific provisions about how a demand by a proxy is treated (s 329). This right will override any contrary provision in the articles.

The position of proxies in relation to quorum requirements (s 318) is described in para 7.23 below.

Companies must include in all notices of meeting a statement informing the members of their rights to appoint a proxy under s 324, including multiple proxies, and, if relevant, any more extensive rights conferred by the articles (s 325). Breach is a criminal offence for the officers of the company (but does not invalidate the meeting). See para 7.39 below as regards how this applies for underlying owners with information rights.

As mentioned in para 7.8 above, where a company provides an electronic address in an instrument of proxy it is deemed to have permitted any information relating to the meeting to be sent to that address (subject to any limitations set out in the proxy form).

A traded company must provide an electronic address for receipt of documentation relating to proxies (s 333A, inserted by the Shareholder Rights Regulations). This is not the same as the concept in s 307A in relation to length of notice of meeting (described in paragraph 7.14 above). It is thought that it could for example just be an email address or could be a CREST proxy facility, even though only CREST members can access it.

Traded companies cannot impose any requirements about provision of information on appointment of a proxy except those relating to identification and instructions to the proxy (s 327(A1)), inserted by the Shareholder Rights Regulations). Traded companies must require proxy appointments and termination of appointment to be in writing (s 327(A1) and 330(A1)), although as a matter of interpretation this may involve electronic means such as CREST.

The articles cannot require proxies to be returned more than 48 hours before the time of the meeting (s 327). Whereas under the CA 1985 the 48 hours was an absolute period, under the CA 2006 non-working days are excluded when calculating the earliest deadline that can be specified in the articles. Most companies currently specify a period of 48 hours in their articles for the proxy deadline (and it is the period specified in Art 62 of Table A). To make use of the ability to add non-working days to the 48-hour cut-off time, the articles would need to be amended.

Section 327 also covers the time for return of a proxy in circumstances in which a poll is taken. In the case of a poll taken more than 48 hours after it is demanded, the articles cannot require the proxy form to be received earlier than 24 hours before the time appointed for the taking of the poll (s 327(2)(b)). There is a separate provision in s 327(2)(c) in relation to a poll taken not more than 48 hours after it was demanded, which states that articles cannot require proxies to be delivered earlier than the time at which the poll was demanded. However, s 327(2)(c) has not been brought into force because of concerns about how it would operate in practice.

The CA 2006 also provides that the minimum notice period for the termination of a proxy appointment cannot be more than 48 hours before the meeting, excluding working days (s 330). In contrast, the CA 1985 did not include any provision about notice of termination (and Art 63 of Table A provides for notice of termination to be received at any time before the meeting).

Corporate representatives

7.22 Under s 323 of the CA 2006 a corporation can appoint a person or persons to act as its representative at a meeting of the company. A corporate representative is in the same position as a member attending the meeting and therefore has the same rights as a member to attend, be counted in the quorum and vote (s 323(2) of the CA 2006).

One issue which often arose under the CA 1985 is whether or not a member could appoint more than one corporate representative for any meeting. This is clarified under s 323 of the CA 2006 which provides that a member can appoint one or more corporate representatives to attend a meeting. However, s 323(4) originally provided that if a member appointed more than one person as a corporate representative and the representatives exercised their power at the meeting in different ways, then the power was treated as if it had not been exercised. The effect seemed to be that if a single corporate representative was appointed, he could vote blocks of shares in different ways on a poll, but that if multiple corporate representatives were appointed, then they each had to vote all of the shares held by the company they represented in the same way on a poll. Revisions were therefore made to s 323 under the Shareholder Rights Regulations. Section 323(4) now provides that the limit to the power of multiple corporate representatives only applies if they exercise a power in respect of the same shares in the company (this is the same as the concept for proxies voting on a poll, as described in para 7.21 above). This therefore allows multiple corporate representatives to vote in different ways on a poll, provided that the number of votes that they are casting does not exceed the number of votes held by the member that they represent. In addition, s 323 has been amended so that on a vote on a show of hands 'each authorised person has the same voting rights as the corporation would be entitled to' (s 323(3)). It appears that this would apply to give them each one vote even if there are more of them than the number of shares held by the corporation because s 323(4) does not apply to s 323(3). It is thought, although the wording is unclear, that if a representative is appointed by more than one corporation, he still has the same voting rights on a show of hands as he would if he were appointed by a single corporation, because he is just given the same 'same' voting rights, rather than there being any suggestion that the voting rights should be added together.

Quorum at general meetings

7.23 The quorum for general meetings is two unless the articles provide otherwise or the company is a single member company, for which there is a quorum of one (s 318). Section 318 is expressed to be subject to any contrary provision in the articles. This replicates the position under the CA 1985. However, whereas the default position under the CA 1985 (s 370(4)) was that two members personally present were a quorum (which therefore included a corporate representative but not a proxy), s 318 of the CA 2006 provides as the default provision that a proxy can be counted in the quorum as a qualifying person. However, if there are two corporate representatives or two proxies representing the same member then they cannot both count in the default quorum (s 318(2)). The wording in s 318 and the Explanatory Notes is not clear, but it would appear logical that, even though they cannot both be counted in the quorum, one of them could be.

Questions at general meetings

7.24 There is a statutory right for shareholders to ask questions at meetings of traded companies (s 319A). This was inserted by the Shareholder Rights Regulations. For all other companies the right to ask questions is not statutory but is based on common law and on any provisions in the articles of association. Under s 319A, a traded company must cause to be answered any question relating to the business of the meeting unless one of the exceptions applies. These exceptions include if it would be undesirable in the interests of the company or the good order of the meeting that the question be answered or if it would involve disclosure of confidential information. This new statutory requirement will give a chairman of a meeting less flexibility than he has in the past when dealing with questions at general meetings, and he will need to be confident that one of the exceptions applies before refusing to answer a question, or stating that he wishes to move to a vote with no more questions. (The exception for the 'good order' meeting should provide scope for calling an end to questions if there has already been a considerable number and the business of the meeting is being prevented from being conducted because of the quantity of questions).

Adjournments

7.25 Section 332 of the CA 2006 provides that a resolution passed at an adjourned meeting is deemed to have been passed on the day it has actually passed and not any earlier date (this is the same as the position under s 381 of the CA 1985).

There is, with one exception, no prescribed statutory notice period for reconvening an adjourned meeting – the method of adjourning and reconvening the meeting is a matter for the articles. The only exception is when a traded company meeting is adjourned for lack of a quorum. In that case, the original minimum period of notice applies to reconvening the meeting, unless the business of the meeting stays the same and the meeting is reconvened not less than 10 days later (s 307A(6), as inserted by the Shareholder Rights Regulations).

Class meetings and variation of class rights

7.26 The requirements in the CA 2006 relating to resolutions and meetings are extended to class meetings by ss 334, 281 and 352. As was the case under the CA 1985 there are two exceptions to this principle of the same provisions applying (which are set out in s 334 of the CA 2006), that is the right to demand a poll (one holder for class meetings) and the quorum (one third for class meetings). In addition, most (but not all) of the additional requirements that apply to general meetings of traded companies, such as those relating to the length and content of the notice, do not apply to class meetings of traded companies (s 334(2) and 334(2A)).

The provisions relating to the method of varying class rights are set out in Chap 9 of Pt 17 (ss 629–640) of the CA 2006 dealing with classes of shares.

The variation of class rights provisions largely replicate the provisions in the CA 1985 but there are some changes of detail. The basic provision that class rights may be varied in accordance with the articles of association or failing that with the consent in writing of 75 per cent of the holders of that class or a 75 per cent majority at a meeting (with the resolution now being a special resolution rather than an extraordinary resolution) remains the same (s 630 of the CA 2006 and s 125 of the CA 1985). The provisions have been extended to cover companies without a share capital. The abolition of the ability to put class rights in the memorandum (with any existing provisions deemed to become part of the articles) means that the provisions about varying class rights in the memorandum are no longer relevant. The provisions from the CA 1985 regarding the right of holders to object to the variation are also replicated in the new Act.

How do the provisions in s 630(4) regarding consent in writing from three quarters of the holders of the class interact with the provisions in Pt 13 on written resolutions? Under the CA 2006, all resolutions of private companies can be passed as written resolutions with the same majority as those passed at a meeting and s 281 provides that a written resolution, including of a class, must be passed in accordance with Chap 2 of Pt 13. However, given that s 630(4) requires 'consent in writing' rather than a resolution (see also s 281(4) which provides that Pt 13 does not effect any provision as to things done other than by passing a resolution) it can be argued that the provisions in Chap 2 of Pt 13 do not apply in determining how the written class consent should be obtained and that the articles can also just refer to consent in writing without following the statutory written resolution procedure.

Records of shareholder meetings and resolutions

7.27 Under the CA 2006, records of general meetings and class meetings and copies of written resolutions must be kept for at least 10 years (s 355 and 359). Under the CA 1985 there was (in s 382) just an unlimited obligation to keep records.

Under s 502 of the CA 2006, as was the case under the CA 1985, the auditor of the company is entitled to receive all notices of other communications relating to general meetings and to attend any general meetings of the company. As mentioned in para 7.12 above, an auditor is also entitled to receive a copy of any communications relating to a written resolution.

Members of a company are entitled to inspect the records of meetings and resolutions free of charge and (on payment of a fee) to ask for a copy of them (s 358). This replicates the position in the CA 1985.

The provisions relating to the filing of resolutions at Companies House are not dealt with in Pt 13. Instead the general provisions about filing of resolutions (in s 380 of the CA 1985) are to be found in ss 29 and 30 of the CA 2006, which are in Chap 3 of Pt 3 dealing with a company's constitution. The general position regarding which resolutions must be filed at Companies House, including special resolutions, is very similar to the position under the CA 1985.

Disclosure of voting by institutions

7.28 Part 44 of the CA 2006 gives the Government a power to pass regulations requiring institutional shareholders to disclose whether and how they have voted shares in traded companies (s 1277). The Government has said that it does not intend to put forward regulations as part of the implementation process for the CA 2006 in order to impose these requirements and that it will only do so in future if there is a failure by investors to take voluntary measures to increase voting levels and voting disclosure.

SHAREHOLDER REQUISITION RIGHTS

7.29 The shareholder requisition rights that were in the CA 1985 have been retained in similar form in the CA 2006 and, in addition, shareholders of quoted and traded companies have been given new requisition rights in the CA 2006.

As described in para 7.41 below, under the CA 2006 some, but not all, of the requisition rights are also able to be exercised by underlying owners under the provisions in Pt 9 of the CA 2006. These are the requisitions for circulation of a resolution at an AGM, circulation of a matter for consideration at an AGM, circulation of a member's statement for a meeting, an independent report on a poll and the website publication of audit concerns.

All of the requisition rights may be exercised by sending a requisition in either hard copy form or in electronic form (see paras 7.2–7.8 above in relation to the communications provisions in the CA 2006).

The requisition rights for shareholders in each type of company are as follows:

Requisition of a general meeting by members of any type of company (s 303)

7.30 Under s 303 of the CA 2006, shareholders holding at least five per cent of the paid up voting share capital in a company can requisition a general meeting. The figure in s 303 was originally ten per cent, but was reduced to five per cent by the amendments made by the Shareholder Rights Regulations.

The procedure regarding requisitioning the meeting is set out in ss 303 and 304 and is mostly the same as it was under the CA 1985 in terms of the process and the consequence of failing to hold the meeting. There are two substantive changes. First, there is an explicit right for shareholders to put forward the text of the resolution to be proposed at the meeting. Second, under the CA 2006 the resolution is treated as having not been properly requisitioned if it would be ineffective if passed (whether because it is inconsistent with the company's constitution or otherwise) or if it is defamatory or is frivolous or vexatious (s 303(5)). This creates a new explicit power for companies to refuse to agree to a requisition on these grounds. In the past case law has limited the requisition right if it related to a matter which could not be validly passed as a resolution, but the provision in s 303 makes the position clearer.

Requisition of a resolution at an AGM by members of a public company (s 338)

7.31 Shareholders holding at least five per cent, of the total voting shares, or being at least 100 in number and holding shares on which there has been paid up an average sum per member of at least £100, may, under s 338 and 339 of the CA 2006, requisition a resolution to be put to an annual general meeting of a public company (this is the same as in s 376 of the CA 1985). For private companies, this right has been removed to reflect the fact that annual general meetings are no longer required for private companies.

CA 2006, s 338 specifically requires the voting rights test to be by reference to those entitled to vote on the relevant resolution rather than, as under the CA 1985, the meeting as a whole.

A significant change for public companies is that, if a requisition is received before the end of the financial year preceding the meeting, the cost of circulating the resolution falls to the company rather than the members (s 340).

There is a new requirement in s 337(3) (inserted by the Shareholder Rights Regulations) that if the notice of AGM of a traded company that is a public company is sent out more than six weeks before the meeting, it must include a statement of this requisition right.

As in the case with the requisition of a general meeting, a company does not need to act on a requisition in relation to a resolution which would be ineffective if passed, or is defamatory, frivolous or vexatious (s 338(2)).

Requisition of a matter to be raised at an AGM by members of a traded company (s 338A)

7.32 In the case of a traded company, in addition to requisitioning a resolution at an AGM, shareholders can requisition a 'matter' for consideration at an AGM (s 338A, and 340A), added by the Shareholder Rights Regulations). The percentage required is the same as that for requisitioning a resolution at an AGM; that is the shareholders holding at least five per cent of the total voting shares or being at least 100 in number and holding shares with an average sum paid of at least £100. There is the same exception for defamatory, frivolous and vexatious matters. The timing and costs provisions (s 340B) are also the same as those for requisitioning a resolution at an AGM and there are the same requirements about including a statement of the right in the notice of meeting (s 337(3)). The requisition must be accompanied by a statement setting out the grounds for the request.

Requisition of circulation of statement by members of any type of company (s 314)

7.33 Shareholders with at least five per cent of the voting rights, or being at least 100 in number and holding shares on which there has been paid up an average sum per member of at least £100, may under s 314 of the CA 2006 requisition the circulation of a statement of up to 1,000 words to those entitled to receive the notice of a meeting about any resolution or business to be dealt with at that meeting. This applies to any type of company.

This substantially replicates the position in s 376 of the CA 1985. Again, the two substantive changes are that the qualifying voting rights must now specifically relate to the relevant resolution (s 314(3)) and that if a requisition for the circulation of a statement at an annual general meeting is received before the financial year end then the expenses are to be borne by the company rather than the requisitionists (s 316).

Under s 317, a company may apply to court for an order that it does not need to circulate the statement because the rights under s 314 are being abused. In contrast to the right to refuse to respond to a requisition under ss 303 and 338 (as described above), the abuse provision in s 317 cannot be used without an application to the court. Section 317 provides a wider right to object than the

184

provision in the CA 1985 (s 377) which required the abuse to be for the purpose of seeking publicity for a defamatory manner whereas s 317 refers to any abuse of the right.

Requisition of the circulation of a written resolution and accompanying statement by members of a private company (s 292)

7.34 There is a right in s 292 of the CA 2006 for shareholders in a private company to requisition the circulation of a written resolution (which is linked to the new concept of written resolutions for private companies being entirely equivalent to holding a meeting). This did not exist under the CA 1985. The required percentage is five per cent of the voting rights, or any lower percentage specified in the articles (s 292(5)). Circulation is at the expense of the requisitionists (s 294). The company has 21 days to circulate the first copy of the resolution (s 293(3)). There is also a right to have a statement of no more than 1000 words circulated with the resolution (s 292(3)). The limits on the requisitions under ss 303 and 314 of the CA 2006 in relation to ineffective, vexatious or abusive requisitions are replicated for written resolution requisitions (ss 292(2)) and 295).

Requisition of a statement on a website about audit concerns by members of a quoted company (s 527)

7.35 Part 16 of the CA 2006 contains a requisition right in relation to audit that did not appear in the CA 1985. Under s 527, shareholders in a quoted company (as defined in ss 385 and 531) holding at least five per cent of the total voting shares, or being at least 100 in number and holding shares on which there has been paid up an average sum per member of at least £100, can require the company to publish on a website a statement setting out any matter relating to the audit of the company's accounts that are to be laid before the next meeting or any circumstance relating to an auditor ceasing to hold office since the previous meeting that the member proposes to raise at the meeting.

The requisition has to be received at least one week before the relevant meeting. It has to be made available by the company on the website within three working days of receipt of the request and then kept available until after the meeting to which it relates. The company has to forward a copy of the statement to its auditor when it puts the statement on its website. The expenses of dealing with the requisition must be met by the company and not the requisitionists (s 529(2)).

The company or auditor can apply to court for an order that it is not required to comply because the right is being abused (s 527(5)).

The notice of the meeting at which the accounts are to be laid must draw attention to, and include specified particulars about, this requisition right (s 529(1)).

Requisition of an independent report on a poll by members of a quoted company (s 342)

7.36 There is also a new requisition right in the CA 2006 for members of a quoted company (as defined in ss 361, 385 and 531) in relation to polls (ss 342–354).

Shareholders holding at least 5 per cent of the voting shares, or being at least 100 in number and holding shares on which there has been paid up an average sum per member of at least £100 can requisition an independent report on a poll (s 342).

The key details of this right are:

- The requisition can be received either before the meeting or up to one week after the meeting (s 342(4)). This means that, at every meeting, the possibility of a requisition must be catered for in terms of the poll procedure.
- The right applies to class meetings as well (s 352).
- The company must appoint an independent assessor to prepare the report and the appointment must be made within one week after the requisition is received (s 343(2)).
- An independent assessor cannot be an officer or employee of the company or any associated company, or a person connected with them, and cannot be a person who has any other role in relation to the poll (s 344). It cannot therefore be the registrar of the company. It could be an auditor of the company, if the auditor has no other role in the poll (s 344(2)).
- The independent assessor must prepare a report (s 347) as regards the procedures for the poll, votes cast, validity of proxies and compliance with ss 325 and 326 of the CA 2006 in relation to proxies.
- The assessor has the right to attend the meeting and to receive any information that he requires from the company in order to fulfil his role (ss 348 and 349).
- If a requisition is made before the meeting it does not mean that a poll has to be held at the meeting. If no poll is actually held then the directors do not have to obtain a report (s 343(6)).
- The details of the fact of the appointment of the assessor and the report of the independent assessor must be made available on the company's website (s 351). They must be put on as soon as reasonably practicable and kept on for two years (s 353).

There is no provision in the CA 2006 as to the effect of any irregularities raised in the report as regards the procedures at the meeting or the poll. However, a shareholder may, for example, wish to use the results of the investigation as evidence that a resolution was not properly passed in accordance with s 301.

EXERCISE OF MEMBERS' RIGHTS – RIGHTS OF UNDERLYING OWNERS

7.37 Part 9 of the CA 2006 sets out important rights for beneficial owners of shares who are not on the shareholder register because their shares are held in the name of a nominee. These also came into force on 1 October 2007 under the CA 2006 Third Commencement Order. In particular, companies whose shares are traded on a regulated market, must give information rights to underlying owners if requested to do so by the members who hold shares on their behalf.

It has always been a basic tenent of UK company law that a company's relationship with its members is based on who is named in the register of members as the registered holder of the shares. This was reflected in the provisions in the CA 1985 to the effect that the memorandum and articles constitute a contract between the company and its members (s 14) and that no notice of trust is to be entered on the share register (s 360). Both of these provisions are replicated in the CA 2006 (s 33 and s 126 respectively).

However, one of the themes relating to shareholder engagement during the company law review process was how to enfranchise indirect holders. In particular, a large proportion of shares in traded companies are now held via nominees rather than directly by the underlying owners, in part because of the effect of the CREST system under which only a CREST member can hold shares in uncertificated form via CREST. In the original version of the Companies Bill, as it was introduced into Parliament, these concerns were dealt with largely just by way of the enhanced rights of proxies. There was also in the original version of the Bill a provision, in what is now Pt 9 of the CA 2006, stating that where articles of association provided generally for a person nominated by a member to enjoy all or any of the rights of the member, then anything required or authorised to be done in the CA 2006 by the member could also be done by the nominated person. However, during the passage of the Bill in Parliament, the issue of the rights of those holding via nominees became a controversial one. In the House of Lords, an amendment was passed so that, rather than allowing articles to state the members could appoint another person to enjoy all or any of the rights of members, all listed company articles were deemed to have a provision to that effect. The protests resulting from this sweeping and significant change, both in terms of its practicalities and its substance, led to a compromise position put forward by the Government which found its way into the final version of the CA 2006.[1] Under the compromise, the ability of members of listed companies to nominate another person to exercise a member's rights was restricted to information rights but Pt 9 was also expanded to refer to other aspects of the exercise of rights by members.

In the final version of Pt 9 in the CA 2006, there are four types of provisions relating to the exercise of rights:

- Rights arising as a result of a provision in a company's articles – this applies to all companies.
- Information rights where a person holds shares on behalf of another person and nominates that person to enjoy those rights – this only applies to companies whose shares are admitted to trading on a regulated market.
- The ability to exercise rights over shares in different ways – this applies to all companies.

- The ability for certain shareholder requisition rights to be exercised by underlying owners – this applies in accordance with the type of companies to which the requisition rights apply.

[1] HC Official Report, SC D (Company Law Reform Bill), 20 July 2006, cols, 887–903.

Effect of provision in a company's articles (s 145)

7.38 Under s 145 of the CA 2006, where a company's articles contain a provision enabling a member to nominate another person to enjoy or exercise all or any specified rights of the member, then anything required or authorised by any provision of the Companies Acts to be done by or in relation to the member shall, or may instead be, done by or in relation to the nominated person as if he were a member of the company. In particular this includes the right to requisition a general meeting, to receive notice of meeting and to act as proxy. It is still however the case that only the registered holder can enforce the rights against the company and only the registered holder can transfer the shares (s 145(4)).

This provision was included because of concerns about the validity of existing provisions of this nature in articles of association, in order to put their validity beyond doubt. The provision only applies where a company's articles include a provision or provisions to that effect. It is therefore voluntary for use by companies of any type. Care, however, needs to be taken that companies do not inadvertently trigger a s 145 right and that s 145 does not override a company's intended purpose when including provisions in articles of association relating to underlying owners. Therefore, if for example a company includes provisions in its articles giving underlying owners a right to attend and speak at meetings, or giving rights to ADR holders, these will need to be carefully assessed to ensure that s 145 does not have unintended consequences or result in an extension of the rights beyond that which is intended. Companies may wish to specifically exclude the effect of s 145 in relation to these provisions and set out the specific rights and requirements in their articles rather than relying on the deeming provision in the CA 2006.

Nomination of persons to enjoy information rights (s 146)

7.39 Under s 146 of the CA 2006, a member of a company whose shares are admitted to trading on a regulated market (this is a different definition to the definition of traded company in Pt 13 of the CA 2006 and includes companies with non-voting traded shares) who holds shares on behalf of another person may nominate that person to enjoy information rights.

Information rights are defined in s 143(3) as 'the right to receive a copy of all communications that the company sends to its members generally or to any class of its members that includes the person making the nomination'. Specifically this is stated to include the right to receive the report and accounts (s 146(3)(b)).

CA 2006, ss 147–150 then set out details of how the information rights are to operate. The sections are short on detail and leave a range of questions unanswered. It is up to companies and their registrars to interpret the provisions, and operate them, in a practical way within the spirit of the provisions. In practice, to date these provisions have not imposed the level of additional burden that was originally feared. That is because the take up of information rights has been low and there are only a handful of organisations operating as nominees who are actively using the information rights route for the underlying owners that they represent.

Breach of the provisions does not invalidate any notice or other action by the company relating to the communication and nor is it a criminal offence. Furthermore, only members of the company themselves can enforce the right – the underlying holder does not have any right to do so (s 150).

The following are the key details of the information rights and how they operate:

- The reference to communications sent to members 'generally' is intended to exclude personalised communication. For example, dividend vouchers, provisional allotment letters on rights issues and share certificates do not need to be copied to the person nominated by the holder because they are personalised for the particular shareholder, by reference to the shareholder's name and the number of shares he holds, rather than being communications sent to members generally.
- The nominated person has a right to receive the information in addition to the member himself – not instead of the member.
- The right is to receive all communications (s 146(5)). Neither the company nor the shareholder nor the nominated person has a right to restrict it to some types of communications only.
- The right only applies to a person who holds shares 'on behalf of' another person, that is a nominee for that person. There is however no provision allowing a company to test whether or not the person nominated is the beneficial owner of the share and in practice it will just have to assume the nominations it receives are valid.
- There is no obligation on a member to make a nomination and no right for the underlying owner to nominate himself. The nomination is at the choice of the registered holder (but he may be obliged to do so in his contract with the underlying owner) and the company only has to respond to a nomination by the registered holder.
- A member cannot nominate more persons than he has shares because if more are nominated than there are shares then the effect of the nomination, for all of the persons nominated, is suspended (s 148(5)). So a person holding 100 shares can nominate 100 persons but no more.
- If the person nominated to receive communications wishes to receive them in hard copy then he is required to ask the person making the nomination to notify the company of that fact before the nomination is made and provide an address to which copies may be sent (s 147(2)). The shareholder making the nomination then notifies the company of the request to receive hard copies when it gives the company details of the nominated person (s 147(3)). Again, there is no method of a

189

company determining whether this procedure has been followed. It just has to act upon notices received from the shareholder to the effect that certain nominated persons wish to receive hard copies.

- If a person is nominated to receive information rights and the shareholder does not state that the nominated person wishes to receive communications in hard copy then the default position is that the nominated person can receive communications via the company's website (s 147(5)).

- A nominated person may at any time ask to receive a hard copy of a particular document that he has already been provided with electronically (ss 146(3)(b) and 147(6)).

- The provisions in the CA 2006 relating to communications with shareholders electronically apply to the persons nominated to receive information rights as they do to shareholders (s 147(4)). Therefore, for example, it is possible to write to the nominated persons every 12 months to see whether they still wish to receive a hard copy and, if they do not respond, the default position of communication via the website applies.

- There is an overriding default provision under which a company may write to a person nominated to receive information rights every 12 months to enquire whether he wishes to continue to have information rights (s 148(7)). If the company receives no response within 28 days the nomination ceases to have any effect.

- Where there is a choice as to the type of communication being received by a member, for example whether or not a summary financial statement is to be received rather than the full annual report and accounts, it is necessary to go through the same procedure in relation to the person nominated to receive information (s 146(4)). This is irrespective of the choice made by the shareholder making the nomination.

- The right to receive information can be terminated at any time at the request of the member or the nominated person (s 148(2)). The nomination also ceases if either the member or the nominated person dies or becomes bankrupt or is wound up (s 148(3)).

- The right to information theoretically also ceases if a member ceases to hold the shares on behalf of the nominated person because the s 146(2) right would no longer apply. However there is no requirement for the member or the nominated person to notify the company to this effect. Therefore, unless the member ceases to be the registered holder, or the company receives a voluntary notification of the termination, the company will need to continue to assume that the member is holding on behalf of the nominated person.

- Any provision in a company's articles in relation to communications with members has 'a corresponding effect (subject to any necessary adaptations) in relation to communications with a nominated person' (s 150(3)). In particular, there is a specific statement that where entitlement to receive information or documentation is determined by reference to a record date, then that record date also applies to a nominated person (s 150(4)). This means that a company can rely on provisions in its articles without needing to make specific provision in its articles about persons entitled to information rights. For example, where the articles allow a company to exclude holders in overseas jurisdictions from receipt of notices, then that can also apply to the information rights of the nominated person.

- A notice of meeting which is copied to a person who has been nominated to receive information rights, must be accompanied by a statement that the person nominated may have a right under an agreement between him and the member to have someone appointed as proxy for the meeting and that he may have a right to give instructions to the member as to the exercise of votes (s 149).

- The statement in the notice of meeting as to the member's rights in relation to the appointment of proxies must either be omitted from the copy of the notice sent to the nominated person or must state that the rights relating to proxies do not apply to a nominated person (s 149(3)). This is to avoid confusion as to who may appoint a proxy. In the absence of anything specific in a company's articles to the contrary, the appointment of a proxy may only be by the member and not by the nominated person. The nominated person may have a right under his arrangements with the shareholder to direct the shareholder as to who should be appointed as proxy and how the proxy should vote but he does not himself have the right to appoint a proxy.

Exercise of rights in different ways (s 152)

7.40 There is a general provision in s 152 stating that where a member holds shares in a company (of any type) on behalf of more than one person then the rights attached to the shares, either under the articles or pursuant to any enactment, need not all be exercised and, if exercised, need not all be exercised in the same way.

The section then goes on to say that if a member decides to utilise this right he should inform the company as to the extent to which he is exercising the rights and the extent to which they are exercised in each way.

This is a very general and wide provision. It was inserted partly as a result of pressure from private client investment groups who wanted to ensure that, for corporate actions by traded companies, members had a right to elect in different ways to reflect the wishes of those on whose behalf they held shares but it goes wider than that concept and also covers private companies as well.

In order to comply with s 152, companies need to ensure that when they are conducting corporate actions, for example B share schemes and scrip dividend arrangements, shareholders are always able to elect in different ways in relation to parts of their shareholding.

One issue arising from this new provision is how it interrelates with specific provisions in articles and shareholders' agreements limiting the exercise of rights by members, given that it applies to all types of companies. During the debate on this provision in the House of Lords,[1] Lord Sainsbury confirmed that s 152 could override a more restrictive right in the articles. The example given was where articles provide for pre-emption rights to operate on an all or nothing basis and Lord Sainsbury said that s 152 would operate to override that provision and allow a member to exercise the right in part if (and only if) he held shares on behalf of more than one person. However, Lord Sainsbury went on to say that because the section only covers rights attaching to the shares, it does not effect rights in shareholders' agreements. It would therefore be possible for shareholders to contract to limit the right that would otherwise apply under s 152 by way of a specific provision in a shareholders' agreement. So, in the example of pre-emption rights, the rights and restrictions could be set out in the shareholders' agreement so as to bind the shareholders only to exercise the pre-emption rights as a whole.

The provision would also not apply where the transaction is between a third party and the shareholder, rather than an exercise of the rights attaching to the shares. For example, on a takeover, it would still be possible for the bidder to require a choice of consideration to be taken in relation to the whole of a particular shareholding.

[1]   686 HL Official Report (5th series) col 448 (2 November 2006).

Exercise of requisition rights by underlying holders (s 153)

7.41 Specific requisition rights are singled out in s 153 as being rights which can be exercised by persons who are not members of the company but on whose behalf shares are being held. These are the circulation of a statement for a meeting, circulation of a resolution for an AGM, circulation of a matter for consideration at an AGM, requiring an independent report on a poll and requiring publication of audit concerns (see paras 7.29–7.36 above for details of these rights).

In each case, the requisition may be made by at least 100 persons on whose behalf voting shares are being held. The shares which are being held on their behalf must have an average sum paid up per requisitionist of at least £100. This is to match the 100 person test in the relevant requisition right. There can be a mixture of registered holders and underlying owners to meet the 100 person test.

The percentage voting rights qualification for the relevant requisition rights is not referred to in s 153 and so can still only be used by registered holders and not by underlying owners having a right to direct those votes.

The requisition must state the name of the member of the company who holds shares on behalf of the person making the requisition. The member must be holding the shares on behalf of that person in the course of business. The requisition must also state that the person making the requisition has the right to instruct the member how to exercise the voting rights attaching to the share.

In order to prevent multiple counting for the same shares, if the shares are held on behalf of persons jointly, then only one of those underlying owners can make the request and count towards the 100 persons and the registered holder cannot count in the 100 if the underlying owner is already being counted. The company has a right to demand such evidence as it may reasonably request that the requirements in s 153 are satisfied.

SHARE REGISTERS

7.42 The provisions in the CA 2006 relating to share registers are in Chaps 2 and 3 of Pt 8 (which contains general provisions about members of a company).

In relation to maintenance of the share register there are some changes of detail compared to the CA 1985 including a reduction in the length of time required for keeping entries of past members from 20 years to 10 years (s 121) and in the case of joint holders a statement that only one address should be shown (s 113). The provisions regarding branch registers (in Chap 3) are the same as under the CA 1985.

In relation to the inspection and copying of share registers there are some important changes in the CA 2006. There is a new requirement that the person asking to inspect or copy must give their name and state the purpose for which the information is to be used (s 116). The company has a new right (s 117) to apply to court for an order that it does not have to comply with the request on the basis that it is not for a 'proper purpose'. There is no provision as to what a 'proper purpose' means. ICSA has issued guidance on this provision, including examples of what should constitute a proper purpose and what is likely to be an improper purpose.[1] It is important to note that the company cannot just refuse to comply because it believes the request is not for a proper purpose. It is up to the company to apply to court within five working days if it does not want to comply with the request – if it does not do so and does not comply with the request then it has committed an offence.

The inclusion of the new provision on proper purpose reflects concern about the misuse of shareholder lists for boiler room scams and activist campaigns. The requirements regarding the content of company annual returns in the CA 2006 also limit the information to be included about shareholder addresses for the same reason.

[1]   ICSA Guide on Access to the Register of Member: the Proper Purpose Test (Ref 090114).

DISCLOSURE OF INTERESTS IN SHARES

7.43 The rules relating to disclosure of interests in shares were originally a matter for company law, with the relevant provisions set out in the CA 1985. However following the implementation of the EU Market Abuse Directive in July 2005, and then the EU Transparency Directive in January 2007, the CA 1985 provisions have been repealed and replaced by rules issued by the Financial Services Authority which are set out in the Disclosure and Transparency Rules ('DTRs') in the FSA Handbook.

The rules on disclosure of substantial interests in shares are set out in DTR 5 (these are the provisions that replace CA 1985 ss 198–209). DTR 5 applies to listed companies and to UK incorporated plcs that have their shares admitted to trading on a prescribed market, including AIM and PLUS Markets. For other public companies, previously covered by the CA 1985 disclosure of interests regime, there are no continuing provisions about disclosure of interests.

For those with interests in UK incorporated companies, the requirement in DTR 5 is to disclose to the company any interest in voting shares which exceeds or falls below three per cent and every one per cent threshold change thereafter. Interests in voting rights can arise either directly (that is as a shareholder) or indirectly (for example as beneficial owner) or via financial instruments that give a right to acquire shares carrying voting rights. Disclosure must be made to the company within two trading days on the FSA's prescribed form. In the case of listed companies, this must be filed with the FSA at the same time as it is sent to the company. The company is then required to disclose the information received via a Regulatory Information Service (RIS) announcement by the end of the trading day following receipt of the notification.

Only the power for a public company to investigate interests in its own shares has been left as a company law matter. This power was originally set out in CA 1985 s 212 and is now in Pt 22 of the CA 2006, with s 793 being the replacement for s 212. The test of interests in shares for the purposes of Pt 22 is the same as it was in the CA 1985, rather than using the new tests of voting interests in DTR 5. The definition of an interest in shares for the purpose of Pt 22 is set out in s 820. It includes where a person enters into a contract to acquire shares or, not being the registered holder, is entitled to exercise any right, or control the exercise of any right, conferred by the shares (whether or not that right is subject to conditions). It also extends to having a right to call for delivery of the shares or having a right to acquire an interest in, or being under an obligation to take an interest in shares. Certain family interests and corporate interests are treated as a person's interest for this purpose (ss 822 and 823 of the CA 2006).

There are separate requirements in the FSA rules in DTR 3 about disclosure of interests in shares by directors. The provisions previously in s 324 of the CA 1985, which required directors of public companies to disclose their interests to the company itself, have been repealed and have not been replaced in the CA 2006. The disclosure of dealing obligations in DTR 3 principally apply to any UK incorporated company that has securities admitted to trading on any EEA regulated market. Under DTR 3, directors and other persons discharging managerial responsibilities (and their connected persons) must notify the company in writing of the occurrence of all transactions conducted on their own account in the shares of the company, or derivatives or any other financial instruments relating to those shares, within four business days of the day on which the transaction occurred. The company must then itself notify a RIS of any information notified to it under DTR 3.

KEY POINTS

7.44

- The law relating to company communications, shareholder meetings and resolutions and shareholder rights has been substantially changed by the CA 2006.
- The communications provisions are set out in ss 1143–1148 and Schs 4 and 5, and the meetings and resolutions provisions are set out in Pt 13 of the CA 2006.
- There are new generic provisions relating to communications by companies with shareholders and with any other third parties. In particular, these include general powers to communicate electronically. In relation to communications with shareholders there is a procedure for deemed acceptance of communications via a website if a shareholder fails to elect to continue to receive copies by post or email. This website route can only be used if the company has the consent of shareholders in general meeting or a provision in the articles. Shareholders must still be notified in hard copy (or by email if they have agreed to receive email) of the fact that the relevant document has been placed on the website.
- There is a new statutory written resolution procedure for private (but not public) companies which allows written resolutions to be passed with the same majority as a resolution passed at a meeting. There is no saving for written resolution procedures under a company's articles.
- The procedural requirements for meetings, including notice periods and rights of proxies and corporate representatives are substantially changed and in many cases override the provisions in a company's articles. Companies will need to change their meeting arrangements to comply with the new procedures.
- For quoted companies, there are new shareholder requisition rights in relation to accounting information and polls, which did not exist under the CA 1985.
- There are additional requirements for traded companies imposed by amendments made to Pt 13 with effect from August 2009, as a result of the implementation of the EU Shareholder Rights Directive.
- Shareholders of listed companies who hold shares on behalf of another person may nominate that person to have a right to receive all shareholder communications. Shareholders in all companies are given a right to exercise rights attaching to shares in different ways. Certain shareholder requisition rights are also extended to underlying owners.
- It is advisable for companies to amend their articles of association in order to reflect the provisions in the CA 2006 relating to communications, resolutions and meetings. In some cases, this will be in order to benefit from the relaxations provided by the CA 2006 (for example as regards notice periods) and in other cases it will be to ensure that the articles are consistent with the CA 2006 (for example as regards the new rights for proxies).
- The right to inspect and copy a company's share register has been limited by allowing the company to apply to court for an order that the request is not for a proper purpose.

Chapter 8

SHARE CAPITAL
AND MAINTENANCE

Ceri Bryant

OVERVIEW

8.1 The key changes to the law regarding share capital are:

- A new statutory procedure for private companies to reduce share capital by special resolution supported by a solvency statement from the directors and without an application to the court (ss 642–644).
- A new statutory procedure for all companies to redenominate the currency of share capital without an application to the court (ss 622–628).
- Abolition of the statutory prohibition on a private company giving financial assistance for the purpose of the acquisition of that company's own shares (ss 677–683).

8.2 In addition to these fundamental variations, there are other changes of a less dramatic kind to the law relating to share capital:

- Directors of private companies with a single class of shares do not need the authority of a resolution of the company to allot shares or to disapply the statutory pre-emption provisions (s 550).
- Companies have to communicate pre-emption offers to all registered holders with an address in an EEA State, rather than merely to those with a registered address in the UK (s 562).
- It is the directors rather than the company in general meeting which exercises the powers to alter share capital through subdivision and consolidation and so forth, provided the exercise of such powers has been authorised by a resolution of the members (s 618).

197

- The statutory procedures for varying members' class rights have been extended to the class rights of members of guarantee companies (s 631).
- Companies are able to redeem shares with payments made on more than one date although, curiously, they remain unable to purchase their own shares with payments made on more than one date (ss 686 and 691).
- New provisions regarding distributions in kind make it clear that a sale of an asset at an undervalue can constitute a distribution in kind, but also that a company can enter into a sale which must be characterised as a distribution in kind without a revaluation of the asset, so long as the company has distributable reserves to cover the difference between the consideration and book value (ss 845 and 846).
- Companies which refuse to register a transfer of shares or debentures must provide the reasons for the refusal and provide such further information about the refusal as is reasonably requested (s 771).

The share capital provisions are contained in Pt 17 which is in force from 1 October 2009. The provisions on distributions are set out in Pt 23 which came into force on 6 April 2008.

SHARE CAPITAL STRUCTURE

8.3 Companies need not have an authorised share capital. The Second Directive requires that the initial documentation provided by public companies which do not have an authorised share capital must state the amount of the subscribed capital. Instead of requiring companies to file information about the authorised share capital, the Act stipulates the occasions when all companies with a share capital, whether public or private, must provide the Registrar of Companies with a statement of capital.

There are no transitional provisions for the abolition of authorised share capital. Any provision in a company's memorandum as to the amount of authorised share capital that was in force before 1 October 2009 is treated on or after 1 October 2009 as a provision of the company's articles setting the maximum amount of shares that may be allotted by the company. Any such provision can be amended or revoked by ordinary resolution.[1] Companies which prefer not to run the risk of overlooking the restriction will choose to remove any such provision.

Applications to register companies having a share capital must contain a statement of capital and initial shareholdings which states the total number and aggregate nominal value of the shares taken on formation by the subscribers to the memorandum of association and gives for each class of shares the total number and aggregate nominal value of shares in that class (ss 9 and 10). Despite the abolition of the authorised share capital, companies must still denominate their share capital in shares of fixed nominal value (s 542). They can have shares denominated in any currency or in several currencies, although to obtain a trading certificate as a public company, or to re-register as a public company, a company must have share capital of a nominal value not less than the authorised minimum denominated either in sterling, or in euros, but not partly in one currency and partly in the other (s 765(1)). Once over either hurdle, a public company can redenominate its share capital into a currency other than sterling or euros, using the procedure described later in this chapter (see para 8.15). Regulation 3 of the Companies (Authorised Minimum) Regulations 2008, SI 2008/729, provides for a theoretical conversion, applying a theoretical exchange rate, to ascertain whether the allotted share capital is equivalent to the £50,000, or to the prescribed euro equivalent of €65,600, following a reduction of capital or redenomination of capital.

1 The Companies Act 2006 (Commencement No 8, Transitional Provisions and Savings) Order 2008, SI 2008/2860, Sch 2 para 42.

ALLOTMENT OF SHARES

8.4 Directors of private companies with a single class of shares have authority to allot shares of that class unless the articles prohibit them from doing so. Only if they wish to allot shares of a new class must they be authorised to do so by the articles or by a resolution of the company (s 550). Provisions in the articles of an existing company authorising the directors to allot shares in accordance with Companies Act 1985 ('CA 1985'), s 80, or added following an elective resolution under s 80A and authorising the directors to allot shares, are not to be treated as provisions prohibiting the directors from exercising the powers conferred by the Companies Act 2006 ('CA 2006'), s 550 in cases to which the authority does not extend.[1]

Although it is superficially attractive to use the existence of different classes of shares to decide whether the directors' power to allot shares should be subject to shareholder control, it provides a dividing line that is neither logical nor easy to operate. Some private companies may have preference shares with rights which have already specified that additional ordinary shares can be issued, and indicating that the shareholders had anticipated and given their approval to the allotment of ordinary shares and would not have considered it necessary to seek their approval afresh. In practice, it can be difficult to decide whether rights set out in a shareholders' agreement or debt instrument should be characterised as rights attached to shares. However, the Government, although it recognised that private companies will lose the ability to give authority to allot up to a maximum amount for an indefinite period enjoyed under s 80A of the Companies Act 1985 ('CA 1985'), considered it appropriate that the terms of approval for allotment given by private companies having more than one class of shares should be the same as those for public companies, and should therefore be limited to a period of not more than five years.

The directors of public companies and the directors of private companies with more than one class of shares can only allot shares if they are authorised to do so by the articles or by a resolution of the company (s 551). An authorisation in force before 1 October 2009 has effect on and after 1 October 2009 as if given under s 551.[2]

1   The Companies Act 2006 (Commencement No 8, Transitional Provisions and Savings) Order 2008, SI 2008/2860, Sch 2 para 44.
2   The Companies Act 2006 (Commencement No 8, Transitional Provisions and Savings) Order 2008, SI 2008/2860, Sch 2 para 45.

8.5 Companies are not only required to issue share certificates within two months of allotment, but must also register an allotment of shares as soon as practicable, and in any event within two months, unless the company had issued a share warrant in respect of the shares allotted. Failure to comply with the obligation to register an allotment is a criminal offence (s 554). The Act states that shares are taken to be allotted when a person acquires the unconditional right to be included in the register of members in respect of the shares (s 558), but leaves open questions as to when a person acquires such an unconditional right.

The disclosure obligations where shares are allotted fully or partly paid up otherwise than in cash are slightly lighter than before because it is no longer necessary for limited companies to deliver to the Registrar of Companies for registration the written contract with the allottee (or the details of the contract if it is not in writing). Instead, the information required in the return of allotment which must be delivered to the Registrar of Companies is limited to the number of shares allotted, the amount paid up (or unpaid) on the shares and a description of the consideration for the allotment of shares if it is not in cash (s 555 and reg 3 of the Companies (Shares and Share Capital) Regulations 2009, SI 2009/388). The delivery of a return of allotment is another occasion when a statement of capital is required.

Although now stated in a section dealing exclusively with unlimited companies (s 556), the details required to be provided by unlimited companies are the same particulars of the rights attached to a separate class of shares as unlimited companies had previously been required to provide under s 128 of the CA 1985.

Pre-emption rights

8.6 Companies are able to communicate pre-emption offers to shareholders in hard copy or in electronic form (s 562(2)).

Companies must communicate offers to all shareholders with a registered address in an EEA State, and not merely to those with a registered address in the UK (s 562(3)). Companies must give shareholders a period of at least 14 days within which a pre-emption offer can be accepted (s 562(6)).

Directors of a private company with only one class of shares can now be given power by the articles or by a special resolution to allot shares without complying with the statutory pre-emption provisions (s 569). As such, directors have authority to allot shares unless the articles restrict them from doing so under s 550. Their authority to allot shares without complying with the statutory pre-emption provisions does not depend upon a general authority to allot shares under s 551.

Directors of public companies and private companies with more than one class of shares can be given power by the articles or by a special resolution to allot shares pursuant to their general authorisation under s 551 without complying with the statutory pre-emption provisions (s 570). Alternatively, where such directors are authorised either generally or otherwise to allot shares under s 551, the company can by special resolution resolve that the statutory pre-emption rights should not apply to a specified allotment of shares, or that the statutory pre-emption rights should apply with modifications specified in the special resolution (s 571).

Allotment of shares by public company where issue not fully subscribed

8.7 The protection previously afforded to applicants for public company shares by s 84 of the CA 1985 is now embodied in s 578. The section ensures that if the increase in capital is not fully subscribed, the capital will only be increased by the amount of the subscriptions received if the terms of the issue had so provided. The section implements the policy of Art 28 of the Second Company Law Directive. Clearer boundaries are developing between those aspects of public offers such as the requirements relating to prospectuses that are dealt with by securities law, and are therefore within the scope of the Financial Services and Markets Act 2000, and those aspects of public offers that remain within the scope of the Act. It is now the date that an offer is first made, rather than the date that a prospectus is first issued, that starts the timetable for determining when money and interest must be returned to applicants for an issue which has not been fully subscribed and when directors become personally liable if repayment has not been made (s 578).

PAYMENT FOR SHARES

8.8 Any doubt on the question of whether an assured payment obligation under the CREST assured payment system would constitute 'payment in cash' has been resolved by the recognition that 'cash consideration' includes payment by any means giving rise to a present or future entitlement of the company or a person acting on the company's behalf to a payment or credit equivalent to payment in cash (s 583(3)(e) and, for Treasury shares, s 727(2)(e)). Regulation 4 of the Companies (Shares and Share Capital) Order 2009, SI 2009/388, provides that an obligation of a settlement bank to make payment in respect of an allotment of uncertificated shares to a system-member, payment up of shares by a system-member or transfer of uncertificated treasury shares by a company to a system-member by means of a relevant system would be regarded as giving rise to an entitlement to payment in cash for the purposes of s 583(3)(e) and s 727(2)(e).

Share premiums

8.9 Companies are more restricted in their use of share premiums than they were before 1 October 2009. Share premiums can still be used to pay up new shares to be allotted to members as fully paid bonus shares (s 610(3)), but share premiums from an issue of shares are otherwise only available for the expenses of the issue of those particular shares, and only to pay the commission paid on the issue of those particular shares (s 610(2)). Companies are not able to use share premiums to write off preliminary expenses incurred in the formation of the company or on the issue of debentures, or to provide for the premium payable on the redemption of debentures.

ALTERATION OF SHARE CAPITAL

8.10 For convenience, the powers to alter share capital (such as by increasing capital through the allotment of new shares, reducing share capital in accordance with Chap 10 of Pt 17, or subdividing or consolidating share capital) do not now have to be exercised by the company in general meeting, although their exercise must have been authorised by a resolution passed by the members (s 618(3)). The resolution authorising the exercise of a particular power might give authority to exercise one or more of such powers, or to exercise a power on more than one occasion or at a specified time or in specified circumstances (s 618(4)).

Companies must give notice of a subdivision or reconsolidation to the Registrar of Companies, together with an appropriate statement of capital (s 619).

The power to alter share capital includes the power to reconvert stock into shares. Although companies are no longer allowed to convert shares into stock, companies which have previously converted shares into stock are able to reconvert stock into shares. The power to reconvert stock into shares requires the same authority of a resolution passed by the members (s 620(2)), which can be given on the same terms as any other power to alter share capital (s 620(3)). Companies which reconvert stock into shares must give notice of the reconversion to the Registrar of Companies, accompanied by a statement of capital (s 621).

Regulations provide that the prescribed particulars of the rights attached to each class of shares required to be given for the purposes of s 621 and various other sections (notably, s 555, return of allotment) are the voting rights (including any that arise only in certain circumstances), dividend rights, capital rights, and rights of redemption (reg 2 of the Companies (Shares and Share Capital) Order 2009, SI 2009/388, Art 2).

CLASSES OF SHARE AND SHARE RIGHTS

8.11 The restrictions on variation of class rights which used to apply only to variations of the rights attached to a class of shares now apply also to variations of the rights of classes of members of a company without a share capital (s 631).

Under the heading 'Class Rights', the CA 1985 set out the procedures which must be followed where the rights attached to a class of shares were to be varied. The CA 1985 did not describe the kind of rights that might be attached to shares and which could constitute 'class rights'. The only guidance offered by the CA 1985 had been the grant of relief from any obligation to deliver a statement containing particulars of share rights if the shares were in all respects uniform with shares previously allotted, and the statement that shares were not to be treated as different from shares previously allotted by reason only that the former did not carry the same dividend rights during the 12 months immediately following their allotment (s 128(2) of the CA 1985).

Once again, and despite Chap 9 of Pt 17 of the Act being headed 'Classes of Share and Class Rights', the Act does not explain what is meant by 'class rights' or provide a universal method for determining when shares must be regarded as being in different classes. The Act provides that shares are to form a single class if the rights attached to them are in all respects uniform (s 629(1)), but this is a rule that applies only for the purposes of the Act and is not a universal rule. As was the case under CA 1985, the rights attached to shares are not to be regarded as different from the rights attached to other shares merely because they do not carry the same dividend rights in the 12 months immediately following their allotment (s 629(2)).

The question of whether there is a single class of shares is relevant to the directors' authority to allot shares (s 550) and to disapply statutory pre-emption rights on the allotment of shares (s 569), and to the information to be provided in the statement of capital on subdivision or consolidation (s 619).

The concept of an extraordinary resolution does not exist under the Act. Where previously the CA 1985 had provided for class rights to be varied by an extraordinary resolution passed at a separate general meeting of the class sanctioning the variation, the Act provides for class rights to be varied by a special resolution passed at such a meeting (ss 630(4) and 631(4)).

Alternatively, class rights can be varied by the consent in writing of the holders of at least three quarters in nominal value of the issued shares of the class concerned or, where the variation is of the rights of a class of members of a company which does not have a share capital, by the consent in writing of three-quarters of the members of the class concerned (ss 630(4) and 631(4)).

The general rules regarding voting on a special resolution in s 284 take effect subject to any provision of the articles, which could encompass weighted voting rights of the kind recognised as valid in *Bushell v Faith*.[1] The Act does not preclude the use of weighted voting on a special resolution to consent to a variation of class rights.

However, the statutory procedures for obtaining consent to a variation of class rights are subject to the provisions of the articles (ss 630(2) and 631(2)). The articles could incorporate an additional hurdle which must be overcome if the class rights are to be varied, such as a four-fifths majority. Alternatively, the articles could make it easier for class rights to be varied, by requiring, for example, a resolution passed by, or written consent provided by, a two-thirds majority.

It is open to a company to entrench class rights in its articles in accordance with s 22 of the Act. Entrenchment is discussed in paras 2.11–2.13.

The right to apply to the court for an order disallowing the variation, which had previously been enjoyed by shareholders holding in aggregate not less than 15 per cent of the issued shares of the class in question, has been extended to members amounting to not less than 15 per cent of the members of the class in question (ss 633 and 634).

Companies are not under an obligation to notify the Registrar of Companies of any new name or other designation, even if effected by a method already required to be notified to the Registrar of Companies, such as a resolution or agreement required to be notified under s 30 (s 636).

A statement of capital is not required, because a variation of rights does not change the aggregate amount of a company's subscribed capital.

[1]   [1970] AC 1099.

REDUCTION OF SHARE CAPITAL

Reduction of share capital supported by solvency statement

8.12 Subject to any provision of a company's articles restricting or prohibiting the reduction of the company's share capital (s 641(6)), a new procedure enables private companies to pass a special resolution to reduce their share capital without applying to the court for confirmation of the reduction, provided there will continue to be at least one member holding non-redeemable shares. All that is required is a solvency statement from the directors (s 641).

The solvency statement has to be in the form prescribed by regulations (s 643(3)) but Art 2 of the Companies (Reduction of Share Capital) Order 2008, SI 2008/1915, requires only that the solvency statement is in writing and signed by each of the directors and indicates that it is a solvency statement. It is likely to be the Registrar of Companies who formulates the rules as to form, authentication and delivery of the solvency statement under s1068.

The Registrar of Companies was apparently willing to accept multiple statutory declarations to whitewash financial assistance if they related to the same financial assistance, were in the same form, were sworn on the same date, and were submitted to the Registrar of Companies together, but the validity of such multiple declarations had not been tested in court. Perhaps the Registrar of Companies will clarify whether the requirement for 'a statement' can be met by more than one statement and, if so, whether the reference to 'the date of the statement' precludes statements made on more than one date. It might be considered too casual to take the approach adopted for written resolutions and to fix the date on which the last director signs as the date of the statement. Regulation 26 of the model articles for a public company (see SI 2008/3229) provides that an alternate director may sign a directors' written resolution in place of their appointor, suggesting that an alternate director should be able to sign the solvency statement in place of their appointor.

The reduction of capital cannot take effect any later than the date on which the special resolution for the reduction of capital will take effect (s 641(5)). The resolution does not take effect until the solvency statement and a statement of capital as reduced by the resolution have been registered by the Registrar of Companies (s 644(4)).

The solvency statement is a statement that each of the directors 'has formed the opinion, as regards the company's situation at the date of the statement, that there is no ground on which the company could then be found to be unable to pay (or otherwise discharge) its debts; and has also formed the opinion that (where it is intended to commence winding up within 12 months of that date), the company will be able to pay (or otherwise discharge) its debts in full within 12 months or the commencement of the winding up, or (in any other case) that the company will be able to pay (or otherwise discharge) its debts as they fall due during the year immediately following that date' (s 643(1)).

In forming their opinions, the directors must take into account all the company's liabilities, including any contingent or prospective liabilities (s 643(2)). However, the Government has said that the directors' opinion does not have to be directly linked to a company's accounts because to have only a balance sheet test might be a test which was too restrictive in some circumstances and open to abuse in others.[1]

Contrary to the position where a company purchases its own shares out of capital (s 714(6)), see para **8.18**, there is no need to have a report from the company's auditor stating that he has inquired into the company's affairs and is not aware of anything to indicate that the directors' opinion is unreasonable.

In contrast with the requirements when a company purchases its own shares out of capital (s 719), see para **8.18**, it is not necessary for a company effecting a reduction of capital supported by a solvency statement to publicise the proposed reduction in the Gazette or a national newspaper or by written notice to each creditor.

There is a further difference between the two procedures. Whereas any member or creditor of the company is entitled to apply to the court for the cancellation of a resolution approving a payment out of capital for the purchase of the company's own shares (s 721), there is no provision for a shareholder or creditor to apply to the court to cancel a resolution for a reduction of share capital supported by a solvency statement.

There are also subtle differences in the wording of the directors' statements required under the two procedures. To purchase shares out of capital, the directors must state that they have formed their opinion having made full inquiry into the affairs and prospects of the company, and that they have formed the view that the company will be able to continue to carry on business as a going concern (and will accordingly be able to pay its debts as they fall due) throughout that year, having regard to their intentions with respect to the management of the company's business during that year and the amount and character of the financial resources that will in their view be available to the company during that year (s 714(3)). Section 643(1) does not expressly state that, for a reduction of share capital supported by a solvency statement, the directors must have made a full inquiry into the affairs and prospects of the company before they form the opinion expressed in the solvency statement. However, it is probably implicit in a solvency statement for a reduction of capital that the directors have formed their opinion about the company's situation after making full inquiry into the company's affairs and prospects. The statutory declaration required to use the whitewash procedure for giving financial assistance under s 156 of the CA 1985 did not expressly state that the directors were required to make a full inquiry into the affairs and prospects of the company, but in *In a Flap Envelope Co Ltd*[2] the financial assistance was held unlawful because (amongst other things) the directors did not make sufficient inquiries into the financial affairs of the company to satisfy themselves that the statement required by s 156 could honestly be made.

Making a solvency statement without having reasonable grounds for the opinions expressed in it is a criminal offence (s 643(5)).

The solvency statement for a reduction of share capital cannot pre-date the resolution by more than 15 days (s 642(1)). The directors must deliver to the Registrar of Companies a statement confirming that the solvency statement was made not more than 15 days before the date of the resolution (s 644(5)).

The solvency statement must be available to be inspected at the meeting voting on the resolution, or must be sent or submitted to members at or before the time the proposed written resolution is sent to them (s 642(2) and (3)) and the directors must deliver to the Registrar of Companies a statement that the obligations to provide the members with the solvency statement were complied with (s 644(5)). To provide certainty for creditors inspecting the public register, a failure to make the solvency statement available to members, or to deliver to the Registrar of Companies a statement that it has been made available to members, will not affect the validity of the resolution to reduce share capital (ss 642(4) and 644(5)), although the failure to do either of these will be a criminal offence (ss 644(7) and 644(8)).

[1]   680 HL Official report (5th series) col GC13 (20 March 2006) per Lord Sainsbury.
[2]   [2003] EWHC 3047, [2004] 1 BCLC 64.

Reduction of share capital confirmed by the court

8.13 All companies proposing to reduce their share capital to zero must ask the court to confirm the reduction (s 641(2)).

There are a variety of other reasons why a private company might ask the court to confirm a reduction of share capital rather than rely upon a solvency statement:

(a) To draw as complete a line as possible under any questionable change in the share capital arising out of an invalid buy-back or redemption.

(b) To obtain the blessing of the court for an unusual reduction.

(c) To seek to proof the reduction against a subsequent challenge by providing a forum for raising objections to the reduction.

(d) To establish that a reduction which treats one group of a class of shareholders differently from another, but has been achieved without any objection from shareholders, is valid despite not having been effected by a scheme of arrangement under Pt 26 of the Act.

(e) To use the evidence that the company has complied with all the requirements for a valid meeting to obtain a ruling from the court that the special resolution has been properly passed.

(f) To obtain a ruling from the court that it is appropriate in the circumstances to have no regard to a particular creditor when considering the impact of the reduction on creditors.

(g) To have the blessing of the court for a reduction where the directors are faced with a difficulty in forming the opinion required for a solvency statement.

(h) To effect a reduction where the contingent and prospective liabilities preclude the making of a solvency statement, although for other reasons the court is willing to confirm the reduction.

When confirming a reduction of capital under the CA 1985, the court would approve a minute setting out the new share capital which would be registered by the Registrar of Companies. The reduction of capital would take effect upon registration of the minute. Under the Act, companies are obliged to seek the court's approval of a statement of capital to be registered by the Registrar of Companies, instead of seeking the court's approval of a minute for registration by the Registrar of Companies (s 649(1)).

The minute provided under the CA 1985 had stated only the total number of shares in each class and their nominal value before and after the reduction, together with the number of shares of each class currently in issue. By contrast, the statement of capital required under the Act must state the total number of shares and their aggregate nominal value; and then must also state for each class of shares the prescribed particulars of the rights attached to the shares,[1] the total number of shares of that class, and the aggregate nominal value of shares of that class, in addition to providing the amount paid up and the amount (if any) unpaid on each share, whether on account of the nominal value of the share or by way of premium. The information provided in the statement of capital put before the court must be transparently accurate if the court is to be satisfied that it should approve the statement of capital.

The creditors whose interests are required to be protected are those creditors who can show that there is a real likelihood that the reduction would result in the company being unable to discharge their debts or claims when they fell due (The Companies (Share Capital and Acquisition by Company of its Own Shares) Regulations 2009 reg 3).

1   See SI 2009/388, Art 2, and para 8.10 above.

All reductions of share capital

8.14 The reduction of share capital will take effect on the registrar of companies registering the order and statement of capital except where the reduction of share capital forms part of a compromise or arrangement under Pt 26 of the Act, when the reduction will take effect at the same time as the other aspects of the compromise or arrangement, on the delivery of the court order confirming the reduction and the statement of capital approved by the court, unless for some reason the court orders that it should take effect on registration of the order and statement of capital (s 649(3)).

The Act provides that the reserve arising from a reduction of capital is not distributable, subject to regulations specifying the cases in which the reserve is to be distributable and the cases in which the reserve is to be treated for the purposes of Pt 23 of the Act as a realised profit (s 654). Where the reduction is confirmed by the court, reg 3(3) of the Companies (Reduction of Share Capital) Order 2008, SI 2008/1915, makes the reserve distributable and also makes the reserve a realised profit unless the order of the court provides otherwise. Where the reduction is supported by a solvency statement, reg 3(2) makes the reserve distributable and makes the reserve a realised profit. In each case the regulations' treatment of the reserve as a distributable reserve and as a realised profit is without prejudice to any order of, or undertaking given to, the court, any relevant resolution, and to the company's memorandum and articles.

In the case of unlimited companies, reg 3(1) provides that the reserve is always distributable and, unless its articles provide otherwise, is a realised profit.

REDENOMINATION OF SHARE CAPITAL

8.15 Previously a company could only redenominate its share capital by cancelling the shares expressed in the old currency and issuing shares in the new currency, or by purchasing or redeeming shares in the old currency and replacing them with shares in the new currency. The Act provides a procedure for any company, whether public or private, to redenominate its share capital into any currency, or a multiplicity of currencies, without an application to court. Even a public company's authorised minimum share capital can be redenominated into a currency other than sterling or its euro equivalent, once the company has obtained its trading certificate.

Under the new procedure, a company can make the conversion using a spot rate specified in the resolution to redenominate the share capital. The spot rate can be a rate prevailing on a day specified in the resolution or a rate determined by taking an average of rates on consecutive days over a period specified in the resolution (s 622(3)).

The redenomination can be conditional upon conditions specified in the special resolution (s 622(4)), but the resolution will lapse if the redenomination has not taken effect at the end of the period of 28 days ending on the day before the resolution is passed (s 622(6)). The redenomination will take effect on the date that the resolution is passed unless the resolution provides for it to take effect on some later date (s 622(5)).

If redenomination produces a share capital with nominal values expressed in awkward fractions of the new currency, it is possible to renominalise the affected shares in order to have nominal values which are expressed in whole units of the new currency. Such adjustments can be achieved either by capitalising distributable reserves to increase the nominal value of the shares to a round number, or by reducing nominal values to a round number by reducing the share capital. Capitalisation can be done in accordance with the articles. Reduction can be done by special resolution and, since Chap 10 of Pt 17 of the Act does not apply to a reduction of capital in connection with a redenomination, it is not necessary either to have a solvency statement or to have the confirmation of the court (s 626(6)). A special resolution reducing share capital in connection with redenomination must be passed within three months of the redenomination resolution (s 626(3)) and cannot reduce the share capital by more than 10 per cent of the nominal value of the allotted share capital immediately after the reduction (s 626(4)). The amount of the reduction must be transferred to a 'redenomination reserve' which can only be used for paying up bonus shares, and is otherwise as non-distributable as if it were paid-up share capital (s 628).

The Registrar of Companies must be given notice of a redenomination (s 625) and notice of a reduction of share capital in connection with a redenomination (s 627), accompanied in each case by a statement of capital.

It is expressly provided that redenomination will not affect rights or obligations, or any restrictions affecting members, under the company's constitution, including the terms on which shares are allotted or held. It is said that, in particular, redenomination does not affect entitlement to dividends (including entitlement to dividends in a particular currency), voting rights or any liability in respect of amounts unpaid on shares (s 624(1)). Although references to the old nominal value in deeds, instruments and documents are to be read as references to the new nominal value (unless the context otherwise requires) such rewriting of documentation gives way to the express preservation of rights in s 624(1).

The amounts paid as dividends may depend upon whether the dividends payable are described as a percentage of paid-up capital expressed in the old currency, or as a percentage of the paid-up capital. The DTI Explanatory Notes to the Act posit a dividend of 20p payable on a £1 share which will continue to entitle the shareholder to be paid 20p after the share has been converted into a $1.50 share, although the company and the member might agree that the 20p dividend can be paid in cents or indeed in any other currency. However, a dividend which is expressed as 20 per cent of a member's paid-up share capital will entitle the shareholder to be paid 30 cents.

REDEEMABLE SHARES

8.16 The issue of redeemable shares by private companies ceases to require prior authorisation in the articles, although it is possible to use the articles to exclude or restrict the issue of redeemable shares (s 684(2)). Public companies still require authorisation in the articles for the issue of redeemable shares (s 684(3)).

It is open to directors to specify the terms, conditions and manner of redemption if they are authorised to do so by the articles or a shareholders' resolution (which can be an ordinary resolution even if it amends the articles, s 685). If the directors are so authorised it is essential that the directors do determine the terms, conditions and manner of redemption before the shares are allotted.

These provisions offer scope for directors to be given substantially more control over the issue of redeemable shares than had been permitted under the CA 1985.

If the articles or a shareholders' resolution has not authorised the directors to specify the terms, conditions and manner of redemption then these matters must be specified in the articles (s 685).

The terms of redemption no longer have to provide for payment on redemption, which precluded payment on more than one date.[1] The terms can now provide for payment on a date later than the redemption date (s 686(2)). Somewhat strangely, it is not open to a company to make payments on more than one date on a purchase of its own shares (s 691).

It would have been understandable if, as a matter of policy, a company had been prevented from entering into an arrangement committing it to make a payment in an uncertain future, when the company might be less able to afford to make the payment. Once it has been accepted that a company should be allowed to enter into a commitment to make a payment in the future and can redeem shares and pay for them later, there seems to be no good reason why a company should not be free to enter into a commitment to make several payments on several different dates in the future. Since companies can redeem shares for payment over several different dates, there is no need for companies which could not afford to be without the cash but which perceived it necessary for payment to be made on redemption to arrange for redemption money to be paid and immediately lent back to the company.[2]

The reference to 'the amount payable on redemption', and to the possibility of the amount being 'paid' on a date later than the redemption date, both support the view that the consideration for redeemable shares must continue to take the form of money and cannot take any other form. The doubts expressed by Park J in *BDG Roof-Bond v Douglas Ltd* as to whether references to 'payment' in the CA 1985 and, presumably, to shares being 'paid for' in s 686(3), remain unresolved. It was not necessary for Park J to reach a decision on whether consideration could only take the form of money because he decided that the agreement had provided for a money consideration of £135,000 and that there had been a bona fide set-off of the balance of £75,000 against £75,000 that he was satisfied would otherwise have been paid to the company for a property and a car.

Since the concept of authorised share capital has disappeared, it is no longer necessary to state that the cancellation of the redeemed shares on redemption does not reduce the authorised share capital. A company has one month to give notice to the registrar of the redemption of shares and to supply an appropriate statement of capital (s 689).

1   *BDG Roof-Bond Ltd v Douglas* [2000] 1 BCLC 401.
2   *Pena v Dale* [2003] EWHC 1065 (Ch), [2004] 2 BCLC 508.

PURCHASE OF A COMPANY'S OWN SHARES

8.17 It is no longer necessary for a company proposing to purchase its own shares to have the authority to do so in its articles, but the articles may restrict or prohibit the company's purchase of its own shares (s 690(1)). A company cannot purchase its own shares if as a result it would have only redeemable or treasury shares (s 690(2)).

In contrast to the relaxation of the position in relation to the redemption of shares, the shares must in all cases be 'paid for on purchase' (s 691(2)). The clear statement that the terms of redemption can provide for payment on a date later than the redemption date (s 686(2)) precludes any argument that the words 'paid for on purchase' in s 691(2) are sufficiently ambiguous to permit purchase monies to be paid in staged payments.

The fact that the shares must be 'paid for' on purchase favours the argument that the only permissible form of consideration is money, for the reasons explained in relation to the redemption of shares in para 8.16 above.

As was the case under the CA 1985, a contract must be approved by special resolution if it is a contract under which the company might become entitled or obliged to purchase shares if certain conditions are fulfilled, even if the contract does not itself amount to a contract to purchase shares. Significantly, it is now open to a company to enter into a contract for the purchase of its own shares before seeking approval from the shareholders for the purchase, provided the contract makes the purchase of shares under the contract conditional upon the terms of the contract being approved by special resolution (s 694(2)). This relaxation means that companies do not have to obtain a special resolution approving a contract before they can enter into binding agreements with prospective vendors.

Copies of the contract, or of the memorandum of terms, must still be available for inspection for a period of ten years after completion of the contract, but they may be kept at a place notified to the Registrar of Companies as an alternative inspection location instead of being kept at the registered office (s 702(3) to (5) and The Companies (Company Records) Regulations 2008, SI 2008/3006).

Purchase out of capital of a private company's own shares

8.18 A private company does not require authority under its articles to purchase its own shares out of capital. However, a private company's articles can prohibit or restrict a purchase of its own shares out of capital (s 709(1)).

Whereas a private company making a purchase out of capital can make the payment out of unrealised profits such as an amount standing to the credit of a revaluation reserve, a company reducing its share capital using the solvency statement procedure can resort only to share capital, share premium account, capital redemption reserve and redenomination reserve.

To achieve a degree of consistency with the procedure for a reduction of share capital supported by a solvency statement, it is no longer necessary for the statement made by the directors to be a statutory declaration.

There has been a change in the description of the contingent and prospective liabilities that must be taken into account in forming their opinion for the purposes of the statement under s 713. The directors must now take into account all of the company's liabilities, instead of having to take into account only such liabilities as would be relevant under s 122 of the Insolvency Act 1986 to the question whether a company is unable to pay its debts.

Article 5 of the Companies (Shares and Share Capital) Order 2009, SI 2009/388, requires only that the statement be in writing, indicate that it is a directors' statement, be signed by each of the directors, and state whether the company's business includes that of a banking company or that of an insurance company. As in the case of the solvency statement on a reduction of capital, the Registrar of Companies may clarify whether the requirement for 'a statement' can be met by having more than one statement and whether they can be signed on different dates. Regulation 26 of the model articles for a public company provides that an alternate director may sign a directors' written resolution in place of their appointor, suggesting that an alternate director should be able to sign the directors' statement in place of their appointor.

There remain significant differences between the requirements for a purchase of the company's own shares out of a capital and a reduction of share capital supported by a solvency statement.

First, a purchase of the company's own shares out of capital must be supported by a report from the company's auditor stating that he has inquired into the company's affairs and that he is not aware of anything to indicate that the directors' opinion in their statement is unreasonable (s 714(6)).

Second, a purchase of the company's own shares out of capital must be publicised by notice in the Gazette and notice in an appropriate national newspaper or written notice to each of the company's creditors (s 719).

Third, any shareholder or creditor can apply to the court for cancellation of the resolution approving the purchase of the company's shares out of capital (s 721).

The directors' statement and the auditor's report can be kept at a place specified in regulations made by the Secretary of State as an alternative to the registered office (s 720(2)), and the company must notify the Registrar of Companies of the place where the documents are kept if it is not the registered office (s 720(3)).

Treasury shares

8.19 Notice to the Registrar of Companies that treasury shares have been cancelled must be accompanied by an appropriate statement of capital (s 730).

FINANCIAL ASSISTANCE FOR THE PURCHASE OF SHARES

8.20 From 1 October 2009 the statutory prohibition on a company giving financial assistance is confined to:

- financial assistance given for the purpose of the acquisition of shares in a public company where such assistance is given by that public company or by one of its subsidiaries (the subsidiary being a company that could be either public or private) (s 678);
- financial assistance given for the purpose of the acquisition of shares in a company where such assistance is given by a subsidiary of that company if the subsidiary is a public company (the shares being acquired being in a company that could be either public or private) (s 679).

There has been no extension of the whitewash procedure to make it available to public companies.

For public companies and subsidiaries of public companies, the Act resolves one of the uncertainties in the scope of the statutory prohibition on a company providing financial assistance for the purchase of its own shares.

Under s 678, it is only a subsidiary of a public company which is itself a 'company' which is subject to the prohibition on giving financial assistance. A foreign subsidiary not formed and registered under the Act, and therefore not a 'company' under s 1, is outside the scope of s 678. The express exclusion of a foreign subsidiary from the prohibition is consistent with what Millett J, in

Arab Bank plc v Mercantile Holdings Ltd,[1] had presumed had been the legislative intention, which was a presumption that had gone unchallenged, and was implicitly approved by the CA, in *AMG Global Nominees (Private) Ltd v Africa Resources Ltd*.[2]

In s 677(1)(d) it is made plain that financial assistance is given by a company which has no net assets, even if the assets of such a company are not reduced to a material extent by the giving of the assistance, thereby removing the ambiguity which had arisen out of the wording of s 1521)(a)(iv) CA 1985.

Various other uncertainties remain.

First, the Act does not resolve the debate about whether s 678 can apply where the person acquiring shares is the company itself. The actual purchase or redemption of shares is specifically exempted from s 678 by s 681(2)(d), but those who argue that s 678 applies to an acquisition by the company itself contend that the exemption in s 681(2)(d) is required because otherwise, a purchase or redemption by the company itself could, for example, constitute financial assistance given for the purpose of an acquisition of shares on a transaction made between two shareholders. If a purchase or redemption is not exempted by s 681(2)(d) and the word 'person' in s 678 is capable of including the company itself, the scope of s 678 could be sufficiently broad to encompass financial assistance for a purchase or redemption of the company's own shares, if given in a form specified in s 677 and given for the purpose of the acquisition.

Second, there has been no attempt either to clarify or to replace the 'principal purpose' exemption stated in s 679(2). The suggestion that the 'principal purpose' test should be replaced by a test of 'predominant reason' or 'dominant reason' has been abandoned on the ground that it was unlikely to fare any better as a way of distinguishing between desirable and undesirable ulterior motives for giving financial assistance.

Third, there is no exemption for financial assistance for the purpose of a transaction that is itself the subject of a specific exemption from the prohibition, such as the giving of a charge to secure a bank loan of funds to be used to pay a dividend or to purchase the company's own shares. Such an exemption ought not to be required because it would merely be what was described in *Wellington Publishing Co Ltd*[3] as a normal application of funds towards something that was part of the normal functions of a company. However, the incorporation of a specific exemption would have removed any doubt on the matter.

Fourth, the Act does not expressly state that financial assistance given for the purpose of an acquisition of shares can only be unlawful if the acquisition did take place. Perhaps it is thought to be clear enough to everybody, as it was to Arden LJ in *Chaston v SWP Group plc*,[4] that an offence could be committed even though a person is only 'proposing' to acquire shares.

The Act does not add any extra exemptions from the prohibition on financial assistance.

The exemption for distributions continues to be confined to distributions by way of dividends lawfully made and distributions in the course of winding up. The Government rejected the proposal from the Institute of Chartered Accountants in England and Wales that the Act exempt any distribution permitted under Pt 23 of the Act in order to simplify group reconstructions, on the ground that the exemption should be confined to dividends which comply with both Pt 23 and relevant common law principles.

There is no exemption for lawful commissions and fees, indemnities and warrants for underwriting share issues, although the Second Directive envisages that shares will be issued and acquired, and costs incurred, in connection with new issues and acquisitions of shares, with exemptions for 'fully paid-up shares acquired free of charge or by banks and other financial institutions as purchasing commission' and 'transactions concluded by banks and other financial institutions in the normal course of business'.

The exemption for employee share schemes has not been widened to cover transactions between employees or employee trusts and outside investors.

The Act continues to be wider in scope than the Second Directive had required. The Second Directive does not expressly require the prohibition of 'assistance' given after the acquisition. The Act does not confine the prohibition on financial assistance to post-transaction financial assistance given pursuant to pre-acquisition understandings or arrangements to give post-transaction financial assistance, and instead retains a prohibition on financial assistance given for the purpose of reducing or discharging a liability incurred for the purpose of an acquisition of shares, whether or not it is given pursuant to a pre-acquisition understanding or arrangement (s 679(3)).

However, the Act only prohibits assistance given by a company or its subsidiary if the company in which the shares are acquired was a public company at the time the assistance is given (s 678(3)). It is therefore important to establish whether the company was a public or a private company at the time that the assistance was given. Financial assistance given by a public company is within the scope of the prohibition, even if it is given for an acquisition of shares that was made whilst the company was a private company.

The consequences of breaching the prohibition on financial assistance remain the same. Although the prohibition is perceived as providing necessary protection for the company in which the shares are acquired, the company has committed an offence. Transactions which have the potential for breach of the prohibition continue to be a source of anxiety for banks because such transactions, if found to have been in breach, are void rather than merely voidable. Until the statutory provisions can be made clearer, transactions will continue to be subject to uncertainty. Challenges will succeed, or will fail, depending upon whether the court considers that a transaction is one which exemplifies the court's own view of the mischief to which the financial assistance provisions are addressed. In the face of uncertainty, the court continues to take a robust approach to spurious allegations of financial assistance and to resist what it perceives as strained interpretations of the provisions (see *Anglo Petroleum Ltd v TFB (Mortgages) Ltd*).[5]

[1]   [1994] 2 All ER 74.
[2]   [2008] 1 BCLC 447.
[3]   [1973] 1 NZLR 133.
[4]   [2002] EWCA Civ 1999, [2003] 1 BCLC 675.
[5]   [2008] 1 BCLC 185.

Financial assistance for the purchase of a private company's own shares

8.21 Only public companies are prohibited from giving financial assistance for the purpose of the acquisition of their own shares. Private companies are only subject to the statutory prohibition when they are subsidiaries giving financial assistance for the purpose of an acquisition of a holding company's shares (s 678). The whitewash procedure, which had only ever been available to private companies, has not been retained.

Previously the prohibition applied to all companies, whether they were limited or unlimited. Since unlimited companies cannot be public companies, they are not subject to the prohibition on giving financial assistance for the purpose of acquisition of their own shares.

Any private company, whether limited or unlimited, is outside the scope of the statutory prohibition on giving financial assistance for the purpose of the acquisition of shares in itself.

In response to concerns that the abolition of the statutory prohibition on the giving of financial assistance and of the whitewash procedure for getting round the prohibition exposes private companies to common law constraints on companies giving financial assistance for the acquisition of their own shares, para 52 of Sch 4 to the Companies Act 2006 (Commencement No 5, Transitional Provisions and Savings) Order 2007, SI 2007/3495, states that the repeal of CA 1985, ss 151–153 and 154–158 would not cause anything to be rendered unlawful by reason of any rule of law which has ceased to have effect or been modified by the enactment of these provisions.

Although private companies cease to be subject to the statutory prohibition on financial assistance for the purchase of the company's own shares, they remain constrained by the statutory restrictions on distributions in Part 23 of the Act; by the prohibition on the return of capital known as the rule in *Trevor v Whitworth*;[1] by the provisions of the Insolvency Act 1986 and the duties in Part 10 of the Companies Act 2006.

[1]   (1887) 12 App Cas 409.

DISTRIBUTIONS IN KIND

8.22 In *Aveling Barford Ltd v Perion Ltd*,[1] the sale of an asset to an associated company for a price that was less than the asset's market value was characterised as a disguised distribution and, because the company had no distributable reserves, was held to be unlawful. A distribution of reserves by a company which did not have distributable reserves contravened the fundamental principle in *Trevor v Whitworth*[2] that no part of the company's capital could be paid out otherwise than in the legitimate course of its business or by a reduction of capital sanctioned by the court.

After *Aveling Barford*, there were different views on whether a sale of an asset for less than its market value would be lawful where the company had distributable reserves at least equal to the book value of the asset.

Some took the view that the company would be making a distribution of the difference between the sale price and the market value of the asset, and therefore that the company must revalue the asset before it enters into the sale in order that the company can treat the difference between the sale price and the revised book value as realised profit.

Others took the view that the amount of a distribution is determined by reference to an asset's book value rather than market value, and therefore that the company can enter into the sale provided it has sufficient distributable reserves to cover the difference between the sale price and the book value of the asset.

The Act resolves the debate by explaining how to determine the amount of any distribution where there is a distribution in kind.

The Act removes any doubt that a sale, transfer or other disposition of a non-cash asset can be characterised as a distribution. In s 845, the Act introduces a new provision for determining 'the amount of a distribution consisting of or including, or treated as arising in consequence of, the sale, transfer or other disposition of a non-cash asset' by reference to the book value of the asset (s 845(1)). In s 846, the Act uses the same terminology when describing the circumstances in which a company can treat an unrealised profit as a realised profit (s 846(1)).

The profits available for distribution are treated as increased by the amount (if any) by which the amount of the consideration exceeds the book value of the asset (s 845(3)).

Where the consideration for the disposition is not less than the book value, the amount of the distribution is zero. Where the amount of the consideration is less than the book value, the amount of the distribution is the amount by which the book value of the asset exceeds the amount of the consideration (s 845(2)).

The Act clarifies the interplay between the common law principles relied upon in *Aveling Barford* and the statutory rules in Pt 23 of the Act. Distributions in kind are to be governed by the statutory rules for determining the amount of any distribution (s 851).

1   [1989] BCLC 626.
2   (1887) 12 App Cas 409.

CERTIFICATION AND TRANSFER OF SECURITIES

8.23 Directors used to have the right to refuse to disclose their reasons for refusing to register a transfer in the absence of a provision in the articles compelling them to provide such information. In a switch to more open governance, directors are now obliged to register the transfer or to provide the transferee with reasons for their refusal to register a transfer (s 771(1)) and also with such further information about the reasons for refusal as the transferee may reasonably request, short of providing copies of minutes of directors' meetings (s 771(2)). The only exceptions to the directors' obligation to register a transfer or provide the reasons for a refusal to register are in relation to a transfer where the company has issued a share warrant in respect of the shares, and in relation to the transmission of shares by operation of law, such as transmission to a trustee in bankruptcy (s 771(5)).

There is a new obligation to issue a share certificate where a share warrant has been surrendered for cancellation, subject to any contrary provision in the articles (s 780).

The Secretary of State has the power to make regulations which can enable members of a company or of a designated class of companies to adopt arrangements under which title to securities can be required to be evidenced, or transferred, or both, without a written instrument. Only an ordinary resolution is required (s 785). However, the Government has indicated that it does not intend to use the power to make regulations at this stage.[1]

Any such arrangements must not cause a person who previously would have been entitled to have their name entered on the register of members to cease to be so entitled, or cause a person who would previously have been able to control the exercise of any rights in respect of the securities to cease to be so entitled (s 786).

1   DTI Consultative Document, *Implementation of the Companies Act 2006* (February 2007).

Chapter 9

TAKEOVERS, MERGERS AND RECONSTRUCTIONS

Alex Kay, James Palmer

INTRODUCTION

9.1 Parts 26 and 27 of the Companies Act 2006 ('CA 2006') contain the provisions previously in ss 425–427A of, and Sch 15B to, the Companies Act 1985 ('CA 1985'). Parts 26 and 27 largely restate the previous provisions, with a small number of changes. Part 28 of the CA 2006 provides the legislative framework for the implementation in the UK of the European Directive on Takeover Bids[1] (the 'Takeovers Directive') and for the broader regulation of takeovers by the Panel on Takeovers and Mergers (the 'Takeover Panel'). Part 28 also makes certain amendments to the existing law applicable to takeover offers, principally in connection with the rights of an offeror compulsorily to acquire residual minority shareholdings after making an offer and the right of such shareholders to require that they be bought out. Since the new provisions of Pt 28 are more significant in practice than the changes to Pts 26 and 27, Pt 28 is addressed first in this chapter.

[1] 2004/25/EC, adopted on 21 April 2004.

OVERVIEW OF JURISDICTION AND LEGAL STATUS OF THE TAKEOVER PANEL

9.2 Takeover regulation in the UK has been undertaken by the Takeover Panel since 1968 on a non-statutory basis by its development and application of the rules and principles contained in the City Code on Takeovers and Mergers (the 'Takeover Code'). Part 28 of the CA 2006 for the first time puts the whole of the Takeover Code and the Takeover Panel's activities on a statutory footing. Part 28 covers the implementation of the Takeovers Directive, completely superseding the Takeovers Directive (Interim Implementation) Regulations 2006 which first implemented the Takeovers Directive from 20 May 2006. The CA 2006 also provides the statutory regime for the regulation of takeovers outside the Takeovers Directive but historically within the scope of Takeover Panel regulation. The regime is in most respects the same for transactions which fall within the Takeovers Directive (offers (but not acquisitions by schemes of arrangement) for companies whose shares are traded on an EU regulated market ('Directive offers')) and for those which are outside the Takeovers Directive but over which the Takeover Panel continues to exert jurisdiction ('non-Directive offers').

9.3 It is worth noting that the Takeover Panel will have jurisdiction over Directive offers where the target company has its registered office in the UK and its sole or primary listing in the UK, as well as sharing jurisdiction with other regulators in certain circumstances.[1]

[1] Under the Takeovers Directive, where a company's shares are not traded on a regulated market in the member state in which it is incorporated, the regulator in the member state of incorporation regulates certain matters (such as the requirements for disclosure to employees, the rules on frustrating action and the setting of the mandatory bid threshold) while the regulator in the member state of trading regulates others (such as rules on consideration level and type, procedural matters, document contents and disclosure requirements): see Art 4(2) of the Takeovers Directive and s 3(d) of the Introduction to the Takeover Code.

9.4 The Takeover Panel and Takeover Code have statutory force pursuant to Pt 28 of the CA 2006. This provides the general jurisdiction of the Takeover Panel, covering Directive offers as well as non-Directive offers. A few distinctions in the regimes applicable to Directive offers and non-Directive offers remain, however. It is interesting to note that the Takeovers Directive did not require all takeovers to be regulated or all takeover rules to be made under statutory rules. However it was considered preferable to minimise the differences between the regulatory regime applicable to the implementation of the Takeovers Directive and the regime for other takeover regulation. This seems entirely sensible and avoids confusion, not least for the Takeover Panel itself.[1]

[1] See the DTI consultative document, Implementation of the European Directive on Takeover Bids of January 2005 (the 'DTI Takeovers Consultation Document'), ss 2.8–2.10.

9.5 Non-Directive offers include takeovers effected by scheme of arrangement (as to which, see the Code, Appendix 7), as opposed to contractual offer, takeovers of AIM listed or unlisted public limited companies and takeovers of certain private companies (in each case provided that the target company has its registered office in, and the Takeover Panel considers that it has its place of central management and control in, the UK, Channel Islands or Isle of Man): see s 3(a) of the Introduction to the Takeover Code. The place of central management and control is not relevant in identifying Takeover Panel jurisdiction as regards Directive offers.

9.6 CA 2006, s 942 provides, in sub-s (1), that the Takeover Panel is to have the functions detailed under Chap 1 of Pt 28, and sub-ss (2) and (3) provide the Takeover Panel with authority, respectively, to do anything it considers necessary or expedient in connection with its functions[1] and to delegate its functions to committees or officers or staff.[2] These allow the Takeover Panel Executive to continue much as it did before it obtained statutory authority and establish the authority for the key committees of the Takeover Panel. The Takeover Panel remains an unincorporated body, as constituted from time to time. As such it has rights and obligations under the common law which are supplemented by the provisions in the CA 2006. Included in these provisions is the obligation to co-operate with the Financial Services Authority ('FSA'), other designated EU takeovers supervisory authorities and any authority outside the UK that exercises public functions pursuant to statute that appear to the Takeover Panel to be similar to those exercised by it or by the FSA (s 950). The Takeover Panel's longstanding practice of publishing an annual report is the subject of a statutory obligation (s 963). The annual report must include the Takeover Panel's annual accounts, details of how the Takeover Panel's functions were discharged in the year to which the report applies and any other matters the Takeover Panel considers relevant.

1   This fulfils the obligation of the UK to designate an authority to supervise Directive bids: Art 4(1) of the Takeovers Directive.
2   Although the rules must be made by committees of the Takeover Panel and fees or charges must be set by a committee or the Takeover Panel itself, not individual officers or members of staff (ss 942(3), 943(4) and (5)).

9.7 Putting the regulation of takeovers under the Takeover Code and by the Takeover Panel on to a statutory basis was a source of considerable controversy for many years during the extended debate over whether the Takeovers Directive would be adopted. It is notable that the approach to implementation in the UK, which followed extensive consultation with both the Takeover Panel itself and other interested parties,[1] involved considerable efforts on the part of the Government to seek to preserve the strengths widely seen to exist in the pre-statutory operation of the Takeover Code. In particular, the flexibility of the Takeover Panel, its speed of response and its independence from other Governmental bodies were all elements that the statutory regime has sought to permit to continue. The degree of independent authority given to the Takeover Panel, even though it is now a creature of statute, is remarkable, but reflects the high degree of trust that the organisation has earned from those engaged in takeover activity in the UK.

1   See the DTI Takeovers Consultation Document, which was itself the product of extensive consultation.

9.8 The breadth of the Takeover Panel's powers to determine its own functions and constitution (s 942) and to make its own rules, as discussed more extensively below, are striking. The breadth of discretion and power was the subject of consideration both at the stage of the DTI Takeovers Consultation Document and subsequently in debate before Parliament. The Attorney-General gave specific assurance in the House of Lords that the Takeover Panel would not make changes to its constitution which could change its suitability as a rule-making body. The Attorney-General noted not only the support for the Takeover Panel being able to continue as it had done prior to its obtaining of statutory authority, but also both the inclusive make-up of the Takeover Panel's membership and the ultimate power of Government to replace the Takeover Panel as regulator.[1]

[1]   See 680 HL Official Report (5th series) cols GC285–286 (28 March 2006).

RULE-MAKING POWERS OF THE TAKEOVER PANEL

9.9   The Takeover Panel has an obligation to make rules giving effect to the Takeovers Directive (s 943(1)). In addition, the Takeover Panel has power to make rules which go beyond the scope of the Takeovers Directive (s 943(2)). In particular, it may exercise its rule-making power to provide for matters which were covered by the Takeover Code immediately prior to the passing of the CA 2006, or similar to such matters. This ensures that the Takeover Panel's statutory power is at least as broad as that required to allow it to regulate those matters which it regulated previously (subject of course to its duty to recognise the scope of regulation by other EU regulators of Directive offers). The Takeover Panel has vested its rule-making powers in the Code Committee of the Takeover Panel (the 'Code Committee'). The powers and functions of the Code Committee are set out in the Introduction to the Takeover Code. In addition, the rules are backed by a statutory-based sanctions regime.[1]

[1]   See paras 9.28–9.38 below.

9.10   It is interesting to observe that the Takeover Panel moved from making rules without any statutory authority, to making rules both under statutory authority and at the same time without statutory authority. From 6 April 2007, when Pt 28 came into force in the UK, the Takeover Panel continued to apply its rules, without a statutory basis, in relation to the Channel Islands and the Isle of Man pending those jurisdictions introducing equivalent statutory provisions, or until the relevant rule-making powers under the CA 2006 were extended to them. From 1 March 2009, Chap 1 of Pt 28, which includes the relevant rule making powers, was extended to the Isle of Man.[1] From 1 July 2009 Jersey and Guernsey will have equivalent statutory provisions to those contained in Chap 1 of Pt 28 in force.[2]

[1]   See the Companies Act 2006 (Extension of Takeover Panel Provisions) (Isle of Man) Order 2008, SI 2008/3122, which came into force on 1 March 2009 and extends Chap 1 of Pt 28 to the Isle of Man (with modifications reflecting the differences in the legal system and governmental and regulatory structures of the Isle of Man).
[2]   See the Companies (Takeovers and Mergers Panel) (Jersey) Law 2009 in respect of Jersey, and the Companies (Panel on Takeovers and Mergers) Ordinance, 2009 in respect of Guernsey.

9.11   That leads to the question of whether the Takeover Panel has any continuing power to make non-statutory rules in relation to offers generally. It is submitted that the effect and intent of Pt 28 is that, subject only to the necessary reserve power to regulate takeovers in the Channel Islands and the Isle of Man, the Takeover Panel's rules and accordingly the Takeover Code itself must be made under and subject to statutory authority, notwithstanding the common law status of the Takeover Panel. The Takeover Panel could not, it is suggested and despite the breadth of its authority, extend its rule-making powers to transactions beyond the scope specified in s 943.[1] One suspects it has no desire to do so in any event. Significantly, this also means that the Takeover Panel's rules may be challenged if they do not fall within or comply with the statutory scope or requirements.

[1] See 680 HL Official Report (5th series) col GC289 (28 March 2006). See also the DTI Takeovers Consultation Document, ss 2.10 and 2.25.

9.12 CA 2006, s 943 requires the Takeover Panel to make rules implementing those mandatory provisions of the Takeovers Directive not directly implemented elsewhere in Pt 28[1] and provides a further scope of matters in respect of which the Takeover Panel may make rules, covering takeovers, mergers and transactions which have or may have an effect on the ownership or control of companies.[2] It is made clear that such rules may cover not only the transactions themselves but also matters done in relation to or in consequence of such transactions,[3] together with regulating the position where such a transaction has not been announced but is in contemplation or apprehended or where an announcement is made denying that a transaction is intended.[4]

[1] CA 2006, s 943(1).
[2] Pursuant to s 943(6), 'companies' is not restricted to the definition set out in s 1 of the CA 2006.
[3] CA 2006, s 943(2)(b).
[4] CA 2006, s 943(2)(c).

9.13 The rule-making powers of the Takeover Panel are not limited to the scope of Takeover Panel regulation before it obtained statutory authority: this is to provide flexibility for the Takeover Panel to adapt its regulation as markets and transactions develop. Significantly, for example, the rule-making authority for non-Directive offers does not limit jurisdiction to companies with their place of central management and control in the UK, Channel Islands or the Isle of Man.[1] However the Takeover Code continues to maintain such jurisdictional limits. However, the scope of power to make rules must relate to the matters prescribed.[2] It is worth noting that these all relate to takeovers or mergers or other transactions that have or may have directly or indirectly an effect on the ownership or control of companies. It is suggested that this does not, for example, give the Takeover Panel authority to regulate transactions under which companies governed by the Takeover Code dispose of their underlying assets or acquire underlying assets, save where such transactions can reasonably be viewed as mergers affecting the ownership or control of the Takeover Code governed company.

[1] CA 2006, s 965 provides for the extension of the provisions of Chap 1 of Pt 28, which includes ss 942–965, to the Isle of Man or any of the Channel Islands by Order in Council. See para 9.10 above.
[2] See para 9.9 above and s 943.

9.14 CA 2006, s 944 seeks to clarify the breadth of the Takeover Panel's rule-making ability. It also authorises the Takeover Panel to dispense with rules or modify them in particular cases or circumstances (s 944(1)(d)). This is designed to retain the Takeover Panel's historic flexibility of approach.

However, where the power to dispense with or modify the application of a rule is exercised, the Takeover Panel must give its reasons. Rules must be made in writing and published (s 944).

9.15 The Takeover Panel is authorised to give rulings on the interpretation, application or effect of its rules and subject to rights of review or appeal, rulings are binding (s 945). The Takeover Panel may also take power under rules to issue directions in order to restrain someone from a breach of its rules or from acting prior to a determination of rules or otherwise to secure compliance with the Takeover Code (s 946). This once again is an example of the statutory framework seeking to preserve the approach of the Takeover Panel before it obtained statutory authority.

9.16 The Takeover Panel may make rules for the payment of fees or charges to meet its expenses (s 957). The Secretary of State is also given power to allow the Takeover Panel to levy charges as may be specified in regulations. The levy may be imposed on those capable of being directly affected by the exercise of the Takeover Panel's functions, or otherwise who have a substantial interest in such exercise (s 958).

INFORMATION RIGHTS AND DISCLOSURE RESTRICTIONS

9.17 Historically, the Takeover Panel expected 'full disclosure from those who are involved in its work'.[1] Such expectation covers those who are consulting the Takeover Panel on a voluntary basis to clarify an issue or clear a course of action, on a mandatory basis as required by the Takeover Code and those subject to a Takeover Panel investigation or involved in a Takeover Panel hearing or appeal process.[2] While certain persons have been obliged to co-operate with the Takeover Panel under other regulation,[3] the Takeover Panel did not have the power to compel those involved in takeovers to provide information. CA 2006, ss 947–949 provide the Takeover Panel with the power to require documents and information and detail certain restrictions on the information so required and the penalties for breach of such restrictions.

[1] See Takeover Panel Statement 1997/04 re purchases of shares in Northern Electric plc.
[2] See s 9(a) of the Introduction to the Takeover Code, which requires such a person to disclose any information known to them and relevant to the matter being considered by the Takeover Panel, and to correct or update the Takeover Panel if that information changes.
[3] Persons authorised under Financial Services and Markets Act 2000 are required by rules of the FSA to provide information and assistance to the Takeover Panel.

9.18 CA 2006, s 947 establishes the ability of the Takeover Panel to require, by notice in writing, a person to produce any documents which are specified or described in the notice[1] or to provide, in the form and manner specified in the notice, such information as is specified or described in the notice.[2] Such a notice must be complied with at a place specified in the notice and before the end of any period specified in the notice.[3] There is no restriction on the persons who may be subject to such a notice; there is no requirement that they be in contact with the Takeover Panel or involved, as principal or adviser, in the relevant activity or matter. The ambit of this power is restricted to 'documents and information [that are] reasonably required in connection with the exercise by the Panel of its functions'[4] and does not affect any lien that a person has on the relevant document.[5] The types of information and documents that the Takeover Panel may require to be produced are not restrictively defined and it is made clear[6] that this includes hard copies of information recorded otherwise than in hard copy form or information in a form from which a hard copy can be readily obtained. As well as covering email and other electronic data capture, the information that must be provided includes that which has not yet been recorded in hard copy (such as details of conversations and meetings.[7] The Takeover Panel can require any document produced to be authenticated and any information provided to be verified.[8] The Takeover Panel may delegate the exercise of this power[9] and take copies of or extracts from a document produced.[10] The power detailed in this section is subject to refusal of provision of documents or information on the grounds of legal professional privilege.[11] It is worth noting that at an earlier stage in the development of the proposed legislation a much broader right of the Takeover Panel to information was envisaged (see the DTI Takeovers Consultation Document) under which anyone subject to the Takeover Code would be required to disclose promptly to the Takeover Panel all information of which the Takeover Panel would reasonably expect notice. Such a wide obligation to volunteer information, without any request, was wisely dropped as a result of the concerns raised.[12]

1   CA 2006, s 947(1)(a).
2   CA 2006, s 947(1)(b).
3   CA 2006, s 947(2). The requirement to comply at a place specified in the notice implies that such a place must be specified for the notice to be valid, in contrast to the permissive wording of s 947(2)(b) which does not require a period for compliance, though does require that, if specified, the period must be reasonable.
4   CA 2006, s 947(3).
5   CA 2006, s 947(7).
6   CA 2006, s 947(9).
7   There is a separate recommendation, though not a requirement, in the Takeover Code in relation to maintenance of records by financial advisers of meetings between companies involved in a takeover (or their advisers) and shareholders, analysts or others involved in investment management or advice to ensure no material new information is forthcoming or no significant new opinions expressed: see Notes on Rule 20.1.
8   CA 2006, s 947(4). The Takeover Panel may also specify the manner of authentication or verification, subject to such specification being reasonable.
9   CA 2006, s 947(5), and any person exercising such power on the Takeover Panel's behalf must, if required to do so, produce evidence of his authority (s 947(6)). It would appear that such delegation need not be internal (ie persons other than members of Takeover Panel staff can be so authorised: see s 961(2)).
10 CA 2006, s 947(8).
11 CA 2006, s 947(10).
12 See s 2.49 of the DTI Takeovers Consultation Document.

9.19 CA 2006, s 948 imposes restrictions on the disclosure of information (in whatever form) provided to the Takeover Panel in connection with the exercise of its functions (ie whether provided on a voluntary basis or pursuant to a notice under s 947).[1] Where such information is not, and has not been, available from a public source[2] and relates to the private affairs of an individual or to a particular business, it may not be disclosed, during the lifetime of the individual or the currency of the business, without the consent of the individual or the person carrying on the business.[3] This prohibition on disclosure is subject to various exceptions:

- where the disclosure of the information 'is made for the purpose of facilitating the carrying out by the [Takeover] Panel of any of its functions';[4]
- if the disclosure is made to one of a defined list of regulatory authorities, Government departments, office holders or agencies in the criminal justice system;[5]
- disclosure for the purpose of enabling or assisting a defined list of investigations and regulatory processes or the functions of relevant regulators or authorities themselves;[6] and
- disclosure to persons or bodies outside the UK who appear to the Takeover Panel to have similar functions to the Takeover Panel or the FSA, where the disclosure is to enable or assist such person or body to exercise such functions.[7]

The CA 2006 permits the Secretary of State to amend Schedule 2 detailing the exceptions from the prohibition on disclosure by order subject to the negative resolution procedure.[8] Further, the prohibition on disclosure does not apply to:

- the FSA, an authority designated as a supervisory authority for the purposes of the Takeovers Directive or any other person or body which, under legislation in an EEA state, exercises functions similar to those of the Takeover Panel or the FSA ('Relevant Authorities'), where such authority received the information from the Takeover Panel pursuant to the above described exceptions;[9]
- disclosure by anyone who has obtained the information, directly or indirectly, from one of the Relevant Authorities.[10]

The above-described exceptions are without prejudice to any implications of disclosure pursuant to the Data Protection Act 1998.[11] A person who discloses information in contravention of the prohibition in s 948 is guilty of an offence[12] and liable, on conviction on indictment, to imprisonment for up to 2 years or a fine (or both),[13] and on summary conviction, to imprisonment for up to 12 months[14] or a fine not exceeding the statutory maximum. A defence is available if the person:

- did not know, and had no reason to suspect, that the information had been provided to the Takeover Panel in connection with the exercise of its functions; or
- took all reasonable steps and exercised all diligence to avoid the commission of the offence.

Where a company or body corporate commits such offence, an offence is also committed by every officer of the company or body corporate.[15] Prosecution of an offence under this section may only proceed with the consent of the Secretary of State or the relevant Director of Public Prosecutions.[16]

[1] This reflects the requirement under Art 4.3 of the Takeovers Directive that member states ensure that information received shall not be further divulged 'to any person or authority except by virtue of provisions laid down by law'.

2   CA 2006, s 948(8).
3   CA 2006, s 948(1) and (2).
4   CA 2006, s 948(3)(a). This exception is broadly cast – its use, like the functions themselves, is subject to review as further described at para 9.25.
5   CA 2006, s 948(3)(b) and Pt 1, Sch 2.
6   CA 2006, s 948(3)(c) and Pt 2, Sch 2.
7   CA 2006, s 948(3)(d) and Pt 3, Sch 2. In deciding whether so to disclose, the Takeover Panel must have regard to whether the likely use of the information justifies its disclosure and whether the relevant person or body has adequate arrangements to prevent the use or disclosure of the information otherwise than for its functions or for other purposes substantially similar to those for which information disclosed to the Takeover Panel could, pursuant to s 948(3)(a)–(c), be used or further disclosed.
8   CA 2006, s 948(4). The negative resolution procedure is detailed in s 1289, providing that the statutory instrument containing the order shall be subject to annulment in pursuance of a resolution of either House of Parliament. From 1 July 2009 The Companies Act 2006 (Amendment of Schedule 2) (No 2 Order) 2009, SI 2009/1208, replaced the previous version of Schedule 2. The effect of this Order was to include within Schedule 2 disclosures to specified persons and specified descriptions of disclosure relating to the Isle of Man, Jersey and Guernsey. The Order revoked The Companies Act 2006 (Amendment of Schedule 2) Order 2009, SI 2009/202, which was made in March 2009 to reflect the extended statutory jurisdiction of the Panel to offers for companies in the Isle of Man, see para 9.20 above.
9   CA 2006, s 948(6)(a) and 948(7).
10 CA 2006, s 948(6)(b). Note this exception is available regardless of whether the Relevant Authority obtained the information from the Takeover Panel.
11 CA 2006, s 948(9).
12 CA 2006, s 949(1).
13 CA 2006, s 949(2)(a).
14 Section 949(2)(b). Six months in Scotland or Northern Ireland.
15 CA 2006, s 949(3). Section 1121 applies in relation to provisions in the Companies Acts which impose liability on officers, and states that 'officer' includes any director, manager or secretary and any person so treated. An officer will be in default if he authorises or permits, participates in, or fails to take all reasonable steps to prevent, the contravention.
16 CA 2006, s 1126.

DISCLOSURE OBLIGATIONS IN ANNUAL REPORTS FOR TRADED ENTITIES

9.20 All companies whose voting shares are traded on an EU regulated market[1] at the end of the relevant year will need to include information on their share and control structures in their annual reports, regardless of whether the company is or has been involved in a takeover situation. This requirement is imposed by Art 10 of the Takeovers Directive, the Article's aim being to provide transparency for the market generally and for prospective bidders in relation to information which might impact the decision whether to make a takeover offer and how to structure any such offer. The relevant provisions are in The Large and Medium-sized Companies and Groups (Accounts and Reports) Regulations 2008, SI 2008/410, Sch 7 (Matters to be dealt with in directors' report), Pt 6, para 13[2], see para 6.19.

1   Note this is a subset of those companies subject to the Takeover Code.
2   For financial years beginning on or after 6 April 2008. For earlier financial years (commencing on or after 20 May 2006) the provisions (which are identical) are in Sch 7, Pt 7, para 13 of the CA 1985 which has been amended by CA 2006, s 992.

9.21 Paragraph 13(2) requires that detailed information on the following matters be disclosed in the annual report:

- share capital structure, including rights and obligations attaching to shares, or each class thereof, and the percentage of total share capital represented by each class (para 13(2)(a));
- any restrictions on transfer of securities, including limitations on holdings or transfer approval requirements (para 13(2)(b));
- the name of, and the size and nature of the holding of, each person with a significant direct or indirect[1] holding, so far as the company knows (para 13(2)(c));
- the name of any person who has securities with special control rights, and a description of such rights (para 13(2)(d));
- any control rights of securities subject to an employee share scheme which cannot be exercised directly by the employees (para 13(2)(e));
- any restrictions on voting rights (para 13(2)(f));
- any agreements between shareholders known to the company which may result in restrictions on transfer or voting rights (para 13(2)(g));
- any rules regarding the appointment or replacement of directors or amendments to the articles of association (para 13(2)(h));
- the powers of the company's directors, including in particular power to issue or buy back shares (para 13(2)(i));
- any significant agreements to which the company is a party that take effect, alter or terminate upon a change of control following a takeover bid and the effect of any such agreements (para 13(2)(j)). This does not apply to an agreement if disclosure would be seriously prejudicial to the company and the company is not under any other obligation to disclose it (para 13 (5)); and
- any agreements between the company and its directors or employees providing for compensation for loss of office or employment that occurs because of the takeover bid (para13(2)(k)).

[1] Paragraph 13(4) provides that a person has an indirect holding if they are held on his behalf or he is 'able to secure that rights carried by [them] are exercised in accordance with his wishes'.

9.22 Whilst much of the above information will feature in a traded public company's directors' report, or other public disclosures, there is still a need for an extensive disclosure exercise. This requires an assessment of which of the current contracts, not just those concluded in the relevant year, fall for disclosure as a 'significant agreement' which takes effect, alters or terminates on a change of control. The availability of the exception for agreements whose disclosure would be seriously prejudicial to the company is likely to be available only in a limited number of cases. As well as the information described above, the directors' report may need to contain explanatory material (where necessary) on such informatifon (para 14). Where a company sends out a summary financial statement pursuant to s 426 of the CA 2006,[1] the new provisions require that the report contain, or be accompanied by, such explanatory material.[2]

[1] For financial years beginning on or after 6 April 2008. For earlier financial years, the relevant provision is in s 251 of the CA 1985.
[2] The Companies (Summary Financial Statements) Regulations 2008, SI 2008/374, Pt 3, para 10(1) for financial years beginning on or after 6 April 2008. For financial years before that date the provisions are in CA 1985, ss 992(5) and 251(2ZB).

APPEALS PROCESS AND POTENTIAL FOR LITIGATION

9.23 The CA 2006 formalises the arrangements for appeals from Takeover Panel decisions, requiring that the Takeover Code provides for a decision of the Takeover Panel to be subject to review by a committee of the Takeover Panel (the 'Hearings Committee') at the instance of 'such persons affected by the decision as are specified in the [Takeover Code]'[1] and for there to be a right of appeal against a decision of the Hearings Committee to an independent tribunal (the 'Takeover Appeal Board') 'in such circumstances and subject to such conditions as are specified in the [Takeover Code]'.[2] The Takeover Code is also required to contain provisions:

- stopping a person who is or has been a member of the Code Committee[3] from being a member of the Hearings Committee or Takeover Appeal Board;[4]
- requiring the Takeover Panel to act in Hearings Committee/Takeover Appeal Board proceedings by one of its own officers or staff members,[5] other than someone who is a member of the Hearings Committee, the Takeover Appeal Board or the Code Committee.[6]

The rules and procedures of the Takeover Appeal Board are a matter for that board and are not determined by the Takeover Panel. The Takeover Appeal Board's rules are available on its website.[7] CA 2006, s 951 also provides that the Takeover Code may contain provisions about matters of procedure in relation to Hearing Committee proceedings (including as to time limits, the provision of evidence and the powers of the Hearings Committee in dealing with matters referred to it) as well as provisions regarding the enforcement of decisions of the Hearings Committee and the Takeover Appeal Board.[8]

1 CA 2006, s 951(1). The Takeover Panel has implemented this by requiring that the person affected by the decision must have 'sufficient interest in the matter' – Introduction to the Takeover Code, s 7(b).
2 CA 2006, s 951(3). The Takeover Panel has provided that any party to a hearing before the Hearings Committee (or any person denied permission to be such a party) may appeal – Introduction to the Takeover Code, s 7(e). This contrasts with the previous position, where there was only an absolute right of appeal in limited circumstances ((a) where a breach of the Takeover Code was found and disciplinary action proposed, (b) where it is alleged the Takeover Panel has acted outside its jurisdiction and (c) in respect of a refusal by the Takeover Panel to recognise a market maker, principal trader or fund manager as exempt from a presumption of membership of a concert party) and otherwise leave to appeal needed to be sought, it being noted that such leave would not generally be given against a finding of fact or a matter of interpretation of the Takeover Code. There were concerns that this could lead to an increase in the number of appeals being heard with no testing of whether the appeal has any merits: see response to Takeover Panel Consultation Paper 2005/5 by the Joint Working Party on Takeovers of the Law Society of England and Wales and the City of London Law Society. However, in the first two years of the new regime only one appeal was heard (relating to Eurotunnel plc, see Takeover Appeal Board statements 2007/1 and 2007/2). Although the Takeover Appeal Board dismissed the appeal and confirmed the decision of the Hearings Committee, it expressed 'great scepticism' on an (obiter) comment of the Hearings Committee that the Panel would have been entitled to waive an obligation on the offeror to make an offer to a separate class. The Takeover Appeal Board said 'in the context it would be a very strong and a surprising use of the Panel's undoubted power to derogate or waive in appropriate cases'. It is interesting that the Takeover Appeal Board was willing to publicly criticise the Hearings Committee on a point of interpretation and discretion and the ramifications for this could be considerable.
3 See s 943(5) and para 9.9 above.

4   CA 2006, s 951(5)(b). The general rules of natural justice preclude a person who has taken
    part in a decision from later considering a review or appeal in relation to that decision.
5   CA 2006, s 951(5)(a).
6   CA 2006, s 951(5)(c).
7   See http://www.thetakeoverappealboard.org.uk.
8   CA 2006, s 951(4).

No liability of the Takeover Panel in damages

9.24 CA 2006, s 961 provides that neither the Takeover Panel, nor any member of Takeover Panel staff[1] nor any person authorised by the Takeover Panel to require a third party to provide information or documents to the Takeover Panel,[2] is to be liable in damages for acts or omissions connected with the discharge of the Takeover Panel's functions. This immunity from damages is provided pursuant to the express discretion in Art 4(6) of the Takeovers Directive for member states to determine the legal position concerning the liability of authorities responsible for the supervision of takeovers. The immunity set out in the CA 2006 is subject to certain exceptions – it is not available if:

- the act or omission is in bad faith;[3] or
- it would prevent a damages award under the Human Rights Act 1998 for incompatibility with certain rights under the European Convention on Human Rights and its protocols.[4]

1   CA 2006, s 961(2)(a).
2   CA 2006, s 961(2)(b) and para 9.18 re s 947(5).
3   CA 2006, s 961(3)(a).
4   CA 2006, s 961(3)(b): see s 6(1) of the Human Rights Act 1998, ECHR, Arts 2–12 and 14,
    Arts 1–3 of the First Protocol and Arts 1–2 of the Sixth Protocol.

The Takeover Panel as party to proceedings: judicial review

9.25 The Takeover Panel has capacity to be a party to legal proceedings – this is confirmed by s 960, which provides that, despite being an unincorporated body, the Takeover Panel can bring proceedings under the provisions of Chap 1 of Pt 28 of the CA 2006 in its own name, and bring or defend any other proceedings in its own name. While it cannot be liable in damages to any third party, the Takeover Panel remains subject to judicial review as established in the *Datafin* case,[1] which also established the principles that the courts will ordinarily hear judicial review proceedings (for which permission is required) after a bid so as not to disrupt the bid timetable and will only make declaratory orders; they will not reverse Takeover Panel decisions unless the Takeover Panel has acted in breach of the rules of natural justice.[2] The Court of Appeal has described the judicial review jurisdiction as a 'supervisory or 'long stop' jurisdiction'.[3]

1   *R v Panel on Takeovers and Mergers, ex p Datafin plc* [1987] QB 815. Article 4(6) of the
    Takeovers Directive states expressly '... this Directive shall not affect the power which
    courts may have in a Member State to decline to hear legal proceedings and to decide
    whether or not such proceedings affect the outcome of a bid'.

² The courts have shown reluctance to review a decision of the Takeover Panel where other rights, such as an appeal to the Takeover Panel's Appeal Committee (now the Takeover Appeal Board), have not been exercised: *R v Panel on Takeovers and Mergers, ex p Guinness plc* [1990] 1 QB 146. This was reinforced in *Re Expro International Group Plc* [2008] EWHC 1543 in which Mr Justice Richards said 'I would not think it desirable that the court procedure involved in a scheme should allow in an undesirable level of certainty which the provisions of the [Takeover] Code have successfully reduced or eliminated in the case of ordinary offers'.

³ *R v Panel on Takeovers and Mergers, ex p Guinness plc* [1990] 1 QB 146 at 177, per Lord Donaldson MR.

9.26 Notwithstanding these well established principles, some difference of approach by the English courts cannot be discounted. Change of approach may stem from specific facts or from the long passage of time since the last challenges to the Takeover Panel before the courts, when combined with the increasingly technical and legal nature of the Takeover Panel's rules (and therefore the basis of its decisions).[1] Further, given that the Takeover Panel now derives its authority from a statute which implements, and the Takeover Panel is exercising functions determined by, a European directive which has primacy over national law, a claim based on a failure by the Takeover Panel to interpret the Takeover Code in accordance with the Takeovers Directive or on a failure of the CA 2006 to implement a requirement of the Takeovers Directive might well cause an English Court to disregard the *Datafin* principle that the relationship between the Takeover Panel and the courts should be historic rather than contemporaneous.[2] Similarly a case brought in the English courts under the auspices of the Human Rights Act 1998 (for example, for breach of the entitlement to a fair and public hearing within a reasonable time by an independent and impartial tribunal established by law) might cause the English Court to reconsider its unwillingness to intervene during the conduct of a bid. It must also be possible that a Takeover Panel decision which related to issues arising during the active stages of an offer, might justify challenge at that time given the significance of the consequences.

¹ The courts have historically demurred in judicial review cases from substituting their own judgement for that of a regulator where the regulator is exercising a commercial judgment; where decisions become more rules, as opposed to effects, based, the courts may be more willing to intervene (although see comment on *Re Expro* at para 9.25 above). The CA 2006 gives the Takeover Code the force of law, although it was already established (see *R v Spens* [1991] 1 WLR 624 at 632) that interpretation of the Takeover Code is a matter of law as opposed to a matter of fact.

² In the event of inconsistency with the Takeovers Directive itself, other avenues of challenge might also be available: see Arts 230 and 234 of the EC Treaty.

Actions between parties to a bid

9.27 CA 2006, s 956 confirms that a breach of the Takeover Code or a failure to comply with a notice from the Takeover Panel requiring disclosure of documents or information[1] does not give rise to a right of action for breach of statutory duty and that transactions or other matters cannot be set aside because of any such breach.[2] This was a key issue for debate in the DTI Takeovers Consultation Document. In addition to seeking to minimise the scope for additional legal challenge to the Takeover Panel during the course of takeover bids, the DTI, the Takeover Panel and others sought to avoid creating, through the statutory framework for takeover regulation, new bases of litigation between the various parties to a takeover bid.[3] The approach provided in s 956 seems likely on the whole to achieve this latter objective.

¹   Under s 947: see paras 9.17–9.18 above.
²   CA 2006, s 956(2).
³   See DTI Takeovers Consultation Document, ss 1.8 and 2.32–2.40.

ENFORCEMENT POWERS: SANCTIONS AND OFFENCES

Sanctions

9.28 Prior to the implementation of the Takeovers Directive, the Takeover Panel's ability to impose sanctions rested on the willingness of those participating in takeovers to accept Takeover Panel jurisdiction or on their recognition that they would be denied access to certain advisers or facilities of the UK financial markets if they did not accept such jurisdiction. The Takeover Panel's standing was reinforced by the FSA's support for the Takeover Code, so that FSA authorised persons could be sanctioned by the FSA for non-compliance. The Takeover Panel's principal sanctions have been private or public censure and on rare occasions, involved 'cold shouldering', whereby institutions would refuse to deal with the defaulting party[1] in certain contexts. Compensation has been ordered by the Takeover Panel, but on only one occasion.[2]

¹   Section 11(b)(v) of the Introduction to the Takeover Code. See, for example, the Takeover Panel decision in Panel Statement 1992/09 relating to Dundee Football Club plc.
²   Panel Statement 1989/13, relating to the Distillers Company plc.

9.29 Given the absence of any previous statutory power of sanction for the Takeover Panel, the breadth of its authority to impose sanctions is somewhat surprising. CA 2006, s 952 gives the Takeover Panel power to impose sanctions on those who breach its rules or fail to comply with its directions (s 952(1)). It is clear that it may create rules providing for sanctions which it has not utilised or reserved the right to impose under its pre-statutory existence (s 952(2)). The powers of sanction which the Takeover Panel could adopt include the power to fine (s 952(3)). However, if the Takeover Panel wishes to create rules allowing it to impose any sanction not provided for under the Takeover Code immediately prior to the passing of the CA 2006 (such as the power to fine), it must publish a policy statement in advance about the use of such sanction and the amount of any fine that may be imposed. Certain factors that the Takeover Panel must have regard to in any such policy are set out in s 952(4). These include the seriousness of the breach in relation to the rule or direction contravened, the extent to which any breach was deliberate or reckless and whether the subject of the sanction is an individual. The Takeover Panel must have regard to any relevant policy statement in exercising its power of sanction. It is not envisaged that the Takeover Panel will seek the power to levy fines.

Compensation orders

9.30 Even though the Takeover Panel already had rules providing for it to order compensation for breaches of certain rules which bear on the value of an offer, the CA 2006 specifically empowers the Takeover Panel to order compensation (s 954). Any such compensation must be in an amount the Takeover Panel thinks just and reasonable and must relate to the breach of a rule which has the effect of requiring the payment of money (s 954(1)).[1]

[1]   Rules 6, 9, 11, 14 15, 16 and 35.3 of the Takeover Code are rules which are likely to fall within this scope. Note also s 10(c) of the Introduction to the Takeover Code as regards compensation rulings.

Failure to comply with bid documentation rules

9.31 A criminal offence is created by s 953 in relation to default in complying with the rules for takeover documents (offer or response documents). The prospect of this offence was raised by the Government as a result of concerns that it might be said not to have implemented the Takeovers Directive properly, absent such an offence, as it could not show that Art 17 of the Takeovers Directive would have been complied with: that Article requires member states to put in place sanctions which are 'effective, proportionate and dissuasive'. It remains arguable that no such offence is needed in order to achieve effective implementation of the Takeovers Directive, but it was introduced in any event.[1]

[1]   See 680 HL Official Report (5th series) cols GC303–305 (28 March 2006).

9.32 Since the offence of failure to comply with rules about bid documenta-tion was only introduced to give effect to the Takeovers Directive, it only applies in the case of Directive offers (s 953(1)).[1] There was no policy concern that a general offence was required. An offence is committed where an offer document published in respect of the bid does not comply with offer document rules or where a response document does not comply with the relevant response document rules (s 953(2) and (4)).

[1]   The definition of 'takeover bid' has the same meaning as in the Takeovers Directive.

9.33 In each case, an offence may only be committed by a person if he:

- knew that the relevant document did not comply, or was reckless as to whether it complied; and
- failed to take all reasonable steps to secure that it did comply (s 953(3) and (4)).

9.34 The categories of persons potentially liable are expressed differently as between offer and response documents, reflecting the different types of entity that might be offerors. In the case of a response document, potential liability rests with the directors and officers of the company (and not with the company itself) (s 953(4)). Where a director or officer is itself a body corporate, liability may extend to a director, officer or member of the relevant body who had the relevant knowledge or recklessness. There is no need, in the case of response documents, to show that the relevant person caused the response document to be published (unlike the test for liability for offer documents).

In relation to the offence regarding offer document contents, those potentially liable include:

- the person making the bid; and
- where the person making the bid is a body of persons, any director, officer or member of that body who caused the document to be published.

Therefore, for liability to be imposed on any person other than the offeror itself for any default as regards the contents of an offer document, it must be shown that the relevant person caused the offer document to be published. This may be hard to establish in many cases. Furthermore, the drafting is unsatisfactory in connection with offer document liability: directors and officers of a target are clearly potentially liable to the criminal offence if a response document fails to comply with response document rules. However, s 953(2)(b) only purports to impose liability on the directors, officers or members of the bidder who caused the offer document to be published, 'where the person making the bid is a body of persons'. It is unclear what is meant by a 'body of persons'. It must be arguable that it does not mean a body corporate or company, which is a single legal person. However, it may also be argued (and perhaps prudently it should be assumed) that the phrase rather inelegantly seeks to include different forms of organisation, whether bodies corporate, partnerships or other unincorporated associations: this latter interpretation is consistent with the DTI Explanatory Notes to the CA 2006 at para 1208.

9.35 The scope of this offence was narrowed, helpfully, during the passage of the Bill from that originally proposed. In particular wording which would have left investment banks advising the parties to takeovers exposed to criminal liability was removed. Although there is no doubt that the Government intended to avoid investment bank advisers automatically falling within the category of those with potential criminal liability, some residual doubt remains as to whether, if the investment bank actually issues the offer document (albeit as agent for the bidder), that agency role could result in it still falling within the scope of persons making the bid (s 953(2)(a)). Whilst there is a good case to be made that a mere agent does not make the bid, to avoid any doubt general practice is now that investment banks and other advisers will not issue offer documents as agent for bidders (which is not required anyway).

9.36 An offence under s 953 is punishable by a fine. Prosecutions in respect of these offences may only be brought with the consent of the Secretary of State or the relevant Director of Public Prosecutions (s 1126).

Enforcement by the court

9.37 A power is created under s 955 for the Takeover Panel to apply to the court for an order requiring compliance with a rule-based requirement or a disclosure requirement of the Takeover Code. In essence this is a mechanism designed to allow the Takeover Panel to seek the support of the courts for its rulings and requirements. Application to the court for an order under this provision may only be made by the Takeover Panel. An order may be made by the court where it is satisfied that:

- there is a reasonable likelihood that a person will contravene a rule-based requirement, or
- a person has contravened a rule-based requirement or a disclosure requirement.

Disclosure requirements are those imposed under s 947 (exercise by the Takeover Panel of statutory powers to require documents and information). Those obligations do not stem from the Takeover Code, and so fall outside the concept of rule-based requirements.

9.38 The court may make any order it thinks fit to secure compliance with the relevant requirement. No person has a right to seek an injunction to prevent a contravention of a Takeover Panel rule or requirement (s 955(3)); this is to prevent new bases of litigation arising in connection with takeovers. There was some debate during the consultation stage and the passage of the Bill as to whether the power for the Takeover Panel to apply for an order to secure compliance with a 'rule-based requirement' might be construed as requiring the courts to re-examine the circumstances of the Takeover Panel's original ruling, to satisfy itself that there had indeed been a contravention of a Takeover Code rule. In practice, whilst the judge will of course not make an order if not persuaded that there is a contravention or likely contravention of the Takeover Code or the Takeover Panel's requirements under s 947, it must be likely in most cases where the Takeover Panel decides to seek such an order that the court will not require a full reconsideration of the facts.[1]

---

[1] See 680 HL Official Report (5th series) cols GC312–313 (28 March 2006) and para 1212 of the DTI Explanatory Notes to the CA 2006.

OPT-IN POSSIBILITY

The Takeovers Directive: background

9.39 Two of the most controversial elements of the Takeovers Directive were the 'passivity' or 'no frustrating action' rule, contained in Art 9 and the 'breakthrough' principle contained in Art 11.[1] In order to achieve political support for the Takeovers Directive, a compromise was proposed by the Portuguese presidency of the European Commission, whereby each of these Articles would be optional for member states, but in a member state which opted out of one or both of these provisions, an individual company could elect to opt back in to the relevant regime.[2] Articles 9 and 11 seek to achieve quite different objectives: Article 9 seeks to prevent boards and the management of companies from interfering with shareholder rights to decide on the success or otherwise of a takeover. Article 11 seeks to impose a consistent approach to the question of how shareholders arrange their affairs as amongst themselves, as regards rights to decide on the success or otherwise of a takeover. The UK opted in to Art 9 of the Takeovers Directive, so the Takeover Panel is required to make rules implementing that Article. Since the Article was largely based on the former General Principle 7 of the (pre-Takeovers Directive) Takeover Code and Rule 21 of the Takeover Code (no frustrating action), little change was required to the existing regimes in the UK. However, the UK, like almost all other EU member states has opted out of Art 11, so it has been required to legislate for companies' rights to opt in to Art 11.[3]

[1] In the debate around the development of the Takeovers Directive and in the DTI Takeovers Consultation Document the terms 'pre-bid' and 'post-bid' defences were generally used to differentiate the 'pre-bid' structures contained in constitutions or shareholders' agreements which Art 11 seeks to override and the 'post-bid' actions of management which Art 9 seeks to control. Whilst those terms generally reflect the way in which the different 'defence' mechanisms work, it is suggested they are unhelpful as they mask, first, the fact that certain matters covered by Art 11 could arise or be implemented 'post-bid' (for example a shareholders' agreement) and, second, the more substantive point that whilst Art 9 matters are generally 'defences', many arrangements caught by Art 11 have nothing to do with bid defences: that has been a significant factor in the widespread rejection of the Art 11 principles.

[2] Article 12 of the Takeovers Directive. See also the European Commission's report on the implementation of the Directive on Takeover Bids of 21 February 2007.

[3] Article 12 of the Takeovers Directive. See also the DTI Takeovers Consultation Document, s 3.

9.40 The effect of the 'breakthrough' rule, provided for in Art 11 of the Takeovers Directive, is to override certain constitutional or contractual restrictions on the transfer of control to a bidder. If a company elects to 'opt in' to the Art 11 regime, it must satisfy various conditions.

9.41 In implementing Arts 9 and 11 of the Takeovers Directive, Art 12 permits member states to implement such an Article subject to 'reciprocity' provisions: the reciprocity provisions allow companies to bind themselves to the Art 9 or 11 regime (as applicable) but, if the member state has elected to allow 'reciprocity', a company opting in can limit its opt-in so it only applies where the bidder or a company controlling the bidder is subject to the same Articles. This at first glance appears fair, but in practice it has been suggested that national protectionist motives were part of the rationale for such a regime, which makes it easier for opted-in companies to be acquired by other companies in their own jurisdiction, as the effect of the opt-in does not apply to, for example, bidders outside the EU (as the relevant Articles can only apply to EU companies). This has led to questions about the legality under the Treaty of Rome of the reciprocity element of the Takeovers Directive.[1]

[1] See Werdmuller, 'Compatibility of the EU Takeover Bid Directive reciprocity rule with EU free movement rules' (2006) 27 Bus L Rev 64 and also the European Commission's Report on the implementation of the Directive on Takeover Bids of 21 February 2007, SEC(2007) 268.

9.42 One might well wonder why any UK company would elect to opt in to the Art 11 regime, implemented in Chap 2 of Pt 28 of the CA 2006. The answer is that it is unlikely that any UK company will want to opt in: indeed some of the disadvantages are commented on further here. However, there is one circumstance in which a UK company might, in theory at least, consider opting in: that is where it is considering a takeover offer for another company in the EU which has opted in to the Art 9 or 11 regime in its jurisdiction (either because the member state in which it is incorporated has done so, or because it has chosen to opt in) and the company is in a jurisdiction, unlike the UK, which allows the reciprocity provisions to apply. In such a case the UK bidder might want to opt in, to avoid finding itself at a disadvantage compared with another bidder, in relation to a target which applies the reciprocity provisions. It is suggested that the likelihood of these circumstances arising is remote, but not inconceivable.

Procedure and conditions for opting in

9.43 There are three conditions to be satisfied if a company wishes to opt in. The first condition is that opting in only applies for companies incorporated in the UK and with voting shares admitted to trading on a regulated market.[1] A regulated market means a market treated as regulated for the purposes of the Directive on markets in financial instruments:[2] in other words, an EU regulated market, not just one in the UK: so a company incorporated in England and Wales but with voting securities listed on a regulated market in Germany, would need to follow these procedures to opt in.[3] Voting shares are defined as shares carrying voting rights; voting rights are rights to vote at general meetings of the company, including rights that arise only in certain circumstances.[4] Shares include securities convertible into shares or carrying rights to subscribe for shares.[5]

[1] CA 2006, s 966(2).
[2] CA 2006, s 1173(1).
[3] 2004/39/EC.
[4] CA 2006, s 971(1).
[5] CA 2006, s 971(2).

9.44 The second condition of opting in is that the relevant company's articles of association do not contain any constitutional restrictions of the type overridden (or subject to 'breakthrough') under the Takeovers Directive, or if they have such restrictions, the restrictions are disapplied when breakthrough would apply. In addition it is required that the relevant articles do not contain any other provision which would be incompatible with Art 11.[1] The scope of restrictions subject to the Takeovers Directive is arguably not entirely clear – Art 11 applies to 'restrictions on the transfer of securities' (Art 11(2)) and to 'restrictions on voting rights' (Art 11(3)). A requirement for a separate class of share or for a board to approve a particular transfer or vote is likely to be treated as a 'restriction' on the right of other voting shares even though each class understands the rights of the other and the creation of the class rights was subject to all necessary approvals. The fact that multiple voting securities are specifically dealt with suggests that securities holding enhanced rights may be distinguishable from those expressed to be subject to a specific restriction so weighted or enhanced voting rights are not overridden by breakthrough.

¹ CA 2006, s 966(3).

9.45 The approach adopted to the implementation of Art 12 effectively requires companies to provide for breakthrough of constitutional restrictions by obtaining the appropriate consents to remove the relevant restriction in advance, such that it does not need to be overridden or broken through. This is a pragmatic approach, as it recognises that a company seeking approval to override breakthrough might as well remove the restrictions which would be the subject of the breakthrough; however it does raise a theoretical question as to whether the Takeovers Directive has been fully implemented, as in theory the right to opt in should be available to a company without any precondition as to the form of its articles.¹

¹ See 680 HL Official Report (5th series) cols GC314–316 (28 March 2006).

9.46 The third condition to opting in is that the relevant company does not have a special 'golden share' held by Government, to avoid such share rights being the subject of breakthrough (and therefore overridden) (s 966(4)).

9.47 Opting in is by special resolution (s 966(1)). An opt-in may be revoked by special resolution (an opt-out) (s 966(5)). The relevant opt-in or opt-out resolution must specify an effective date, which cannot be retrospective (s 967(1) and (2)). An opt-in resolution can be passed (but not effective) before the company's shares are admitted to trading on a regulated market, to allow a company to list with an opt-in already in place. The other conditions must be satisfied before the opt-in resolution is passed (s 967(3)). An opt-out resolution may not become effective before the first anniversary of the opt-in. This latter requirement is not required by the Takeovers Directive, and given the limited circumstances in which a company incorporated in the UK might want to opt in, it seems a misconceived piece of 'gold-plating' by the Government.¹ Certain obligations to notify regulators and shareholders of an opt-in or opt-out are imposed under s 970.

¹ See 680 HL Official Report (5th series) cols GC316–317 (28 March 2006).

Effect of opting in

9.48 Since the mechanism for opt-in assumes that constitutional restrictions subject to breakthrough will be removed by consent (rather than themselves left but then overridden by breakthrough), the CA 2006 only addresses the consequences of opting in on contractual restrictions on transfers of shares or on voting. Where a takeover bid is made for an opted-in company, those contractual restrictions will be overridden to the extent they restrict the bidder from acquiring shares or voting them. This only relates to contractual restrictions entered into after the adoption of the Takeovers Directive. The theory of that cut-off date is that contracting parties after that date deal on risk of an opt-in resolution being passed, so should not suffer loss, so the

Takeovers Directive only applied breakthrough to such contractual restrictions.[1] However, in practice contracting parties in a range of situations do not contemplate their agreement being overridden: for example, an agreement between two shareholders under which one covenants to give a right of pre-emption to the other, or gives the other a call right over its shares, would both be contractual restrictions overridden in the case of an opted-in company. An irrevocable undertaking to accept one offer and not to accept another might also be ineffective in terms of its restrictions.[2] This is a significant disadvantage of opting in, as in practice confusion will exist if an opt-in override is involved after a takeover offer has been made. Companies will need to bear the potential consequences for shareholders in mind. If a person suffers loss as a result of any act or omission which would, but for the effect of breakthrough, give rise to a liability for breach of agreement, that person shall be entitled to just and equitable compensation from the person who benefits from what would otherwise have been a breach. This will in practice be very difficult to address and might well, if invoked, result in complex disputes as to the extent to which the bidder is the beneficiary of the default (or would-be default) and the extent the would-be defaulting contracting party – which is given no option by the opt-in but to find itself liable to compensation – should bear responsibility for compensation. It is not hard to see why most EU member states (except perhaps those which already have laws equivalent to breakthrough) have decided not to opt in to Art 11.[3]

1   Article 11(2) of the Takeovers Directive.
2   See 680 HL Official Report (5th series) cols GC319–320 (28 March 2006).
3   See the European Commission's Report on the implementation of the Directive on Takeover Bids of 21 February 2007, SEC(2007) 268.

9.49 The other consequence of opting in, if a takeover bid is made, is that whatever the target company's articles may say, the opted-in company must allow the bidder to require the directors to convene a general meeting, provided the bidder holds 75 per cent in value of all the voting shares in the company (s 969).

9.50 For the purposes of both ss 968 and 969 (contractual breakthrough and power to require general meeting), the offeror's rights to call a meeting and override restrictions, if it has 75 per cent in value of all voting shares, apply only to voting shares which carry rights to vote generally. This is helpful and avoids, for example, preference shares with contingent rights to vote in certain circumstances, counting towards the bidder's achievement of the 75 per cent threshold. Debentures are also expressly excluded. There was a suggestion that the concept of 75 per cent 'in value' of voting shares meant 'nominal value'. Whilst in most cases the value of shares will be proportionate to nominal value, in certain cases that could clearly be wrong and it is suggested that the section does not mean 'nominal value' where that gives rise to an illogical result.[1]

1   For example, a company with £1 ordinary shares, which subsequently issued new 10p ordinary shares, ranking *pari passu*. See 680 HL Official Report (5th series) cols GC317–319 (28 March 2006).

9.51 CA 2006, s 973 provides power for the opt-in provisions to be extended by Order in Council to the Channel Islands or the Isle of Man.

'SQUEEZE-OUT' AND 'SELL-OUT'

9.52 Chapter 3 of Pt 28 contains the provisions enabling an offeror, following a takeover, compulsorily to acquire the shares of the non-assenting minority on the same terms as the offer ('squeeze-out'). Chapter 3 also contains the corresponding 'sell-out' right for minority shareholders to require the offeror to purchase their shares on the terms of the offer. Chapter 3 was brought into force along with the other provisions relating to takeovers in Pt 28 on 6 April 2007.

9.53 The provisions in the CA 2006 restate ss 428–430F of the CA 1985, generally in a clearer form, and therefore the general concepts of and procedures relating to squeeze-out and sell-out are similar to the regimes in the CA 1985, but there are a number of changes of detail. Some of the changes were required to implement the Takeovers Directive. Other changes were made to implement the recommendations of the Company Law Review Steering Group's Final Report[1] which had identified some difficulties with the operation of ss 428–430F.

[1] The Company Law Review Steering Group's Final Report was issued in July 2001. See also Volume 8 of the Company Law Review, Completing the Structure, at Annex B and the DTI Takeovers Consultation Document.

Meaning of 'takeover offer'

9.54 The offeror's squeeze-out right (and the minority shareholders' sell-out right) applies only after a 'takeover offer' has been made to the target's shareholders. Takeover offers for both public and private companies fall within the scope of the compulsory acquisition provisions and it is irrelevant whether the bid or the company is one to which the Takeovers Directive or the Takeover Code applies.[1] There are, however, different deadlines for Directive offers and non-Directive offers as to the date by which offerors must send out their squeeze-out notices.[2] CA 2006, s 974 sets out two conditions which must be satisfied for the offer to be a 'takeover offer':

(a)   It must be an offer to acquire all the shares in a company (or where there is more than one class of shares in a company, all the shares of one or more classes) other than shares already held by the offeror at the date of the offer.

(b)   The terms of the offer must be the same in relation to all the shares to which the offer relates (or where the shares to which the offer relates include shares of different classes, in relation to all the shares of each class).

[1] Paragraph 1244 of the DTI Explanatory Notes to the CA 2006. See also paras 9.2–9.5 for further details of the companies and bids to which the Takeovers Directive and the Takeover Code apply.
[2] See para 9.69.

Meaning of 'an offer on the same terms'

9.55 CA 2006, s 976 clarifies an uncertainty arising from the interpretation of the CA 1985 and deems the offer to be on the same terms if the offeror offers to pay more for shares that carry a dividend than for those shares in the same class which do not, so long as the difference in consideration merely reflects the difference in entitlement to dividend. The other situation in which s 976 deems the offer to be on the same terms (which was also in the CA 1985[1] is where overseas laws preclude an offer of consideration in the form specified in the terms of the offer (or will only allow it if the offeror complies with conditions that it cannot comply with or which it regards as unduly onerous) and the overseas shareholders are able to receive a different sort of consideration that is of substantially equivalent value.

[1]   CA 1985, s 428(4).

9.56 The CA 2006 does not expressly provide that if some shareholders agree to accept more onerous obligations than other shareholders (for example, the target's management has agreed to give warranties), this will not prevent the offer from being on the same terms for compulsory acquisition purposes. The Company Law Review[1] had recommended that this clarification be included but it is suggested that the assumption by some shareholders, not the subject of squeeze-out or sell-out rights, of additional burdens (as opposed to receiving additional benefits) does not prevent the offer from being on the same terms, for these purposes, and never has done so.

[1]   At para 13.25 of the Final Report, Volume 1.

Effect of impossibility of accepting or communicating the offer

9.57 The CA 2006 makes clear that an offer is not prevented from being a takeover offer just because it is impossible or more difficult for overseas shareholders to accept it because of the laws of the country in which they reside (s 978(2)). Aside from this specific circumstance, there is no general provision in the CA 2006 providing that the offer will be treated as being on the same terms regardless of the relative ability or inability of shareholders to take it up, for example, if a particular form of consideration is only available to larger shareholders because of its terms, eg £X of loan notes for every £1m of target shares held.[1] However, s 978(3) states that it is not to be inferred that an offer which is impossible or more difficult for certain persons to accept for a reason other than its local laws cannot be a takeover offer.

[1]   The DTI Takeovers Consultation Document at s 4 and Annex C, indicated that such a change, consistent with the recommendations of the Company Law Review, be made. It is submitted that such a change was not necessary and that was and continues to be the correct position in any event.

9.58 The CA 1985 did not specify how a takeover offer should be communicated to shareholders in order for it to be a takeover offer for compulsory acquisition purposes. The CA 2006 specifically provides that the offer can still be a takeover offer if there are shareholders without a UK registered address and the offer is not communicated to those shareholders because it would contravene overseas law and instead either the offer is published in the Gazette[1] or there is a notice in the Gazette specifying a place in an EEA State or a website where the offer document can be obtained (s 978(1)).

[1] For companies registered in England and Wales, this will be the London Gazette; for companies registered in Scotland, the Edinburgh Gazette and for companies registered in Northern Ireland, the Belfast Gazette.

9.59 The commonly adopted approach under the CA 1985 where there were overseas target shareholders was for offerors to advertise the offer in a newspaper with domestic circulation (commonly the London edition of the *Financial Times*). The purpose of this advertisement route was to inform overseas shareholders to whom the offer document was not being sent of the existence of an offer (so that they could decide whether or not to accept the offer) but without the offeror contravening any laws of the jurisdiction in which the shareholder resided. This approach was confirmed by the Court of Appeal in *Winpar Holdings Ltd v Joseph Holt Group plc*[1] as generally constituting a valid communication of an offer to all shareholders for squeeze-out purposes.

[1] [2001] EWCA Civ 770, [2001] 2 BCLC 604, [2001] All ER (D) 165 (May).

9.60 The Gazette route aims to simplify matters for shareholders located outside the UK by providing a single point of information (the Gazette) on the existence of the offer. However, there is some doubt as to the usefulness of the Gazette route as it is only available where the offer was not communicated to the shareholders in the relevant overseas jurisdiction in order not to *contravene* the laws of that jurisdiction. This means that, for s 978(1) to apply, the offeror is still required to check whether sending the offer document into particular jurisdictions could contravene the laws of that jurisdiction. However, s 978(3) effectively confirms that *Winpar* is still valid and that even when the Gazette route has not been followed, the offer can still constitute a 'takeover offer'. It is slightly surprising that the modernisation of company law embodied in the CA 2006 should retain the use of the Gazette, a publication not generally read by those it is designed to inform. Accordingly some offerors may decide that in addition to complying with the requirements of the Gazette route, they will also place an advertisement in a national newspaper.

The bidder's right to squeeze-out

9.61 The offeror can serve notices on the minority shareholders compulsorily to acquire their shares if it has 'by virtue of acceptances of the offer, acquired or unconditionally contracted to acquire' (a) not less than 90 per cent in value of the shares (or class of shares) to which the offer relates and (b) not less than 90 per cent of the voting rights carried by those shares (or class of shares) (s 979).

Calculating the 90 per cent threshold

9.62 The dual 90 per cent test set out in s 979(2) is different to that set out in the CA 1985 under which only the first limb of the test applied; the second limb was added to the CA 2006 to implement the Takeovers Directive.[1] However, the dual 90 per cent test does not make much difference in practice since the percentage of the number of shares and the percentage of the voting rights will generally be the same. 'Voting rights' are defined in the CA 2006 as rights to vote at general meetings of the target, including rights that arise only in certain circumstances. In practice, this will often catch all non-voting shares since these will generally always have some residual voting rights (s 991(1)) but, as such shares will constitute a separate class from the shares carrying voting rights, this should not affect the 90 per cent threshold. The CA 2006 (like the CA 1985) does not define 'in value' and it is presumed to have its natural meaning, ie by value on the assumption that each share of the same class has the same value. Whilst this will usually be consistent with nominal value, it is clear these could differ[2] so nominal value is not the general test.

[1]   Article 15 of the Takeovers Directive.
[2]   See para 9.50 above.

Date of the offer

9.63 The date of the offer is relevant for a number of reasons under the compulsory acquisition procedure. First, any shares held by the offeror at the date of the offer are excluded from the 90 per cent calculation (ss 974(2) and 975). The date of the offer is defined in s 991(1) to mean either the date of publication of the offer or, where notices of the offer are given before the date of publication, the date when first notices of the offer are given. For takeovers governed by the Takeover Code, therefore, it is clearly the case that the relevant date is the date of publication of the offer document or other offer promulgation and not the date of announcement of a firm intention to make an offer.[1] The date of announcement is simply a notice of an offer still to be made.

[1]   Under Rule 2.5 of the Takeover Code.

9.64 The date of the offer is also relevant for determining whether market purchases can count towards the 90 per cent threshold. If a market purchase is made by the offeror or its associate at the offer price or below 'during the period beginning with the date of the offer and ending when the offer can no longer be accepted' then it can count towards the 90 per cent; if the market purchase is made earlier than the 'date of the offer' it cannot (s 979(8), (9) and (10)). The CA 1985 referred to 'the period during within which a takeover offer can be accepted' (s 429(8)) which clearly started when the offer document was posted. The Company Law Review had suggested this date be switched back to the date of announcement under Rule 2.5 of the Takeover Code. Whilst that had some logic and would have helped bidders, the rule in place is probably a clearer test.

Shares which the offeror holds or has contracted to acquire at the date of the offer

9.65   Shares which the offeror holds at the date of the offer are not treated as shares for which the offer is made (and so cannot be counted towards achieving the 90 per cent threshold) (s 974(2)). This includes shares that the offeror has contracted to acquire either conditionally or unconditionally (s 975(1)) except for shares the subject of irrevocable undertakings (see para 9.66 below). This clarifies an uncertainty in the CA 1985 which referred to shares which the offeror had 'contracted to acquire' and it was unclear whether this included conditional as well as unconditional contracts: in practice, the requirement in the CA 2006 was in any event assumed to be the requirement under the CA 1985.

Irrevocable undertakings

9.66   Under the CA 1985 irrevocable undertakings to accept a takeover bid could be counted towards the 90 per cent threshold (and were not treated as 'already held' by the offeror) so long as they were given either for no consideration and under seal or for no consideration other than a promise by the offeror to make the offer. The CA 2006 relaxes the provisions in two technical respects (s 975(2)). First, under the CA 1985 it was arguable (though it is thought the courts would have resisted such a consideration) that an irrevocable undertaking given by a beneficial holder who was not the registered holder would not satisfy the requirements (because it referred to 'the holder' of the shares[1] The CA 2006 provides that an undertaking given by a person who is not the registered holder of the shares but who can bind the registered holder is sufficient. This permits greater flexibility as to who can enter into irrevocable undertakings as it was often difficult in the short time frame normally available to arrange for the registered holder (rather than the beneficial owner or the fund manager on whose instructions the registered holder acts) to sign the irrevocable undertaking. Second, the CA 2006 also includes undertakings for negligible consideration.

[1]   CA 1985, s 428(5).

Shares that the offeror acquires during the offer period

9.67   Shares which the offeror acquires during the offer period otherwise than by acceptances of the offer at first sight appear to fall outside of the 90 per cent calculation, by being excluded from the shares to which the offer relates (s 977(1)). The same applies for shares so acquired by an associate of the offeror (s 977(2)). However, those provisions are subject to s 979(8) and (9). These provisions specify that shares so acquired during the offer period will still be treated as shares to which the offer relates, provided that:

- at the time the shares were acquired (or contracted to be acquired), the value of the consideration for which they were acquired or contracted to be acquired did not exceed the value for those shares under the offer, or

- if the offer terms are subsequently revised, the value of the consideration for the acquisition (whether paid or contracted to be paid) ceases
  to exceed the equivalent offer value.[1]

[1]   CA 2006, s 979(8), (9) and (10).

9.68 The provisions in the CA 2006 are clear that shares which the offeror
has contracted to acquire and which by virtue of s 979(8)–(10) are shares to
which the offer relates, may not be treated as counting towards the 90 per cent
target for squeeze-out to be implemented until the offeror or its associate has
acquired them or unconditionally contracted to acquire them. This is consistent with the approach generally taken under the provisions in the CA 1985.

Time limit for reaching 90 per cent threshold

9.69 There are different deadlines depending on whether the bid is a Directive
offer or a non-Directive offer (see paras 9.2–9.5). For Directive offers, no
squeeze-out notice may be served by the offeror 'after the end of the period of
three months beginning with the day after the last day on which the offer can
be accepted' (s 980(2)). This wording is copied directly from the Takeovers
Directive. All Directive offers will be governed by the rules of the Takeover
Code which does not set a deadline by which the offer must close. As a result,
offers are usually not formally closed and therefore, in practice, there will be
no statutory deadline for serving the squeeze-out notices for Directive offers
(although, in practice the offeror will wish to serve the notices as soon as
possible and, in any event, before the shareholders' sell-out right arises, in
order to avoid the logistical complexity of buy-out and sell-out rights being
exercised at the same time over the same shares). For non-Directive offers
(which include offers for AIM companies and unlisted public companies),
notices must be given within six months of the date of the offer, if this is
earlier than the three-month period (which, in practice, it almost always will
be because the offer will not generally be closed before the conclusion of the
squeeze-out). Both of these deadlines are a change from the CA 1985 which
provided that the 90 per cent threshold must be reached within four months of
the date of the posting of the offer document and notices had to be served
within two months of reaching 90 per cent. For Directive offers, this change
means that financial advisers will need to be particularly careful when
providing the cash confirmation statement required by the Takeover Code
(Rules 2.5(c) and 24.7) to ensure that the length of time for which they are
giving the cash confirmation has a definite end.

The 90 per cent test and exercise of options etc

9.70 If there are convertible shares in issue or outstanding options, the
offeror will normally extend the offer to any shares arising from a conversion
or exercise of an option while the offer is open. As the shares are converted or
options exercised, the pool of shares to which the offer relates increases and so
it is possible to reach 90 per cent and then subsequently fall below it. Legal
opinion has been divided in the past as to whether a subsequent drop below

the 90 per cent level invalidated a compulsory acquisition notice previously sent to a target shareholder if, on the date the notice is served, the 90 per cent test is met or indeed whether the offeror is actually allowed to commence the procedure if there is a risk that the 90 per cent level could drop as a result of share conversions or the exercise of share options. Section 979(5) of the CA 2006 provides that if the takeover offer includes among the shares to which it relates, shares that are allotted after the date of the offer, then the offeror's entitlement to serve a squeeze-out notice on any particular date shall be determined as if the shares to which the offer relates did not include any shares allotted after that date. The DTI Explanatory Notes to the CA 2006[1] clarify that: (a) the offeror need only consider issued shares when calculating the 90 per cent level; (b) if the offeror serves squeeze-out notices and more shares are subsequently allotted which take the percentage of acceptances then received below 90 per cent, that will not invalidate any notices already served; and (c) if the offeror wants to send out further notices it must ensure that it has at least 90 per cent at the time it sends the notices out (s 979(5)). It is suggested that this is a helpful clarification of what the previous law in fact intended and probably provided.

[1] Paragraph 1254.

Rights of non-assenting shareholders to sell-out

9.71 Under s 983 when the offeror has reached the dual 90 per cent threshold (which is calculated differently to the squeeze-out threshold – see below) the minority shareholders have the right to require the offeror to purchase their shares on the terms of the offer. The period within which the selling shareholder must exercise its rights has been extended by the CA 2006 (s 984(2)) so that it is the later of (a) three months from the close of the offer (as per the CA 1985); and (b) three months from when the offeror gives the shareholders notice of their rights. As offers are rarely closed before squeeze-out has concluded, this change should have no impact in practice.

Calculating the 90 per cent sell-out threshold

9.72 Mirroring the change that has been made to the squeeze-out threshold (see para 9.61), there is a dual test. A minority shareholder can require the offeror to acquire his shares when the offeror holds 90 per cent in value of all the shares in the company (or the class of shares) and 90 per cent of the voting rights in the company (or the class). Under the CA 1985 the test was that the offeror should have acquired 90 per cent in value of all shares in the company.

Conditional contracts

9.73 The CA 2006 clarifies that it is those shares which the offeror has acquired or unconditionally contracted to acquire by virtue of acceptances of the offer, together with those shares which the offeror has acquired or contracted to acquire (whether unconditionally or subject to conditions being met) which are relevant for the 90 per cent test (s 983(2)). The CA 1985 had referred to shares acquired or contracted (it was not clear whether this included conditional contracts) to be acquired in both instances. As a result, at first glance it appears that there may be circumstances where the 90 per cent threshold for sell-out is reached only because of shares that the offeror has conditionally contracted to acquire. However, if the conditions are never fulfilled the offeror is not forced to buy the minority's shares, as it has not actually acquired 90 per cent. In this case, the offeror does not have to purchase the shares unless it (or its associates) has acquired or unconditionally contracted to acquire 90 per cent by the end of three months from the end of the period within which the offer can be accepted or, if later, the date of the notice from the offeror notifying the holder of its sell-out right (s 983(6) and (7)).[1]

[1] Paragraph 1256 of the DTI Explanatory Notes to the CA 2006.

Dissenting shareholders' right to make an application to the court

9.74 A shareholder who receives a compulsory acquisition notice has a six-week period from the date of the sell-out notice to apply to the court for an order that the offeror shall not be entitled or bound to acquire the shares or to request the court to specify terms of acquisition different from those of the offer. The CA 2006 made two changes to the procedure in the CA 1985. First, the courts will not be able to reduce the consideration to below the consideration offered in the bid (s 986(4)). However, the dissenting shareholder will continue to be able to apply for consideration above the offer value if it can show that the offer value is unfair.[1]

[1] Although, in an offer governed by the Takeover Code, the offeror is generally prohibited from acquiring shares from a shareholder on more favourable terms than those under the offer for six months (Rule 35.3).

9.75 Second, the CA 2006 contains a provision requiring a shareholder who has made a court application to give notice of the application to the offeror. The DTI Explanatory Notes to the CA 2006[1] state that this must be done promptly. Under the CA 1985 the only method open to an offeror to check whether any application had been made was to make enquiries of all the district registries with Chancery jurisdiction, which was an onerous and uncertain procedure not in practice generally used. If the offeror receives such a notice, it must at the earliest opportunity inform the other shareholders who are being squeezed out or who are exercising their right of sell-out. The CA 2006 does not however specifically provide that the offeror is entitled to proceed with the squeeze-out without making any further enquiries if it has not received any notices within the statutory six-week period under s 981(6) (in fact the opposite is the case, if an application has been made the offeror is not permitted to proceed with the squeeze-out until the application has been dealt with regardless of whether it has actually received notice).

[1] Paragraph 1257.

MERGERS AND RECONSTRUCTIONS

Schemes of arrangement

9.76 Part 26 contains the provisions enabling companies to apply to the court for an order sanctioning an arrangement or reconstruction agreed with a majority of members or creditors. Part 26 restates with some amendments sections 425–427 of the CA 1985. The Company Law Review recommended important changes to the provisions of the CA 1985 regarding schemes of arrangement. In particular they recommended that:

- the court be given discretion to sanction a scheme of arrangement notwithstanding a technical defect in compliance with the statutory procedure, and
- the majority in number requirement for member or creditor sanction of a scheme be abolished (with just a 75 per cent majority by value required).

Neither of these changes were made and the justifications given by the Government when rebutting amendments to these effects were moved in relation to the Bill seemed not to recognise the rationale for the Company Law Review's suggestions which were widely supported by practitioners. It was suggested by the Government that the first amendment was not in practice needed as there was not evidence of schemes failing over technicalities; it was also suggested that the majority in number of registered holders requirement for approval of a scheme was an important investor safeguard. The Company Law Review and practitioners had argued that the risk of a scheme being rejected over a mere technicality was inappropriate, potentially costly and with no policy benefit. Similarly, the removal of the majority in number approval level had been strongly advocated (a) as it was not a protection provided elsewhere in the statutory framework and there is no logic in an exceptional approval process for schemes, (b) as it is open to abuse by the subdivision of registered holdings, and (c) as the widespread use of nominees makes the number of registered holders an arbitrary and irrelevant test. It is suggested that part of the reason for not proceeding with these changes was the Government's desire to avoid further expanding the scope of the CA 2006 (ie more pragmatic than policy oriented) and that accordingly these changes may return for debate in the future.

9.77 The provisions in the CA 2006, as well as redrafting the ones in the CA 1985, have clarified that an application for court sanction to a scheme may be made by any creditor or member (s 899(2)). This had previously been the general assumption. In addition, there is an obligation on the company to file with the Registrar of Companies any amended articles of association, if amended pursuant to the scheme. Further articles of association issued by the company thereafter must be accompanied by a copy of the relevant order, unless the amendment is already incorporated into them (s 901).

Provisions facilitating mergers and divisions of public companies

9.78 The provisions formerly in ss 425–427A of, and Sch 15B to, the CA 1985 are now contained in Pt 27 of the CA 2006. Apart from reordering the provisions, the main change has been the introduction of new independence requirements for experts and valuers providing reports or valuations under ss 909, 924 or 935. A person may not provide such a report or valuation if he is an officer or employee of any of the companies concerned, or a partner or employee of such a person, or has the same relationship with any associated undertaking of any of the companies concerned (s 936(1)). There is power for the Secretary of State by regulations to extend the independence requirements. However, an auditor is not for these purposes precluded from providing such a report or valuation (s 936(2)). The Companies (Mergers and Divisions of Public Companies) (Amendment) Regulations 2008, SI 2008/690,[1] have made a number of amendments to these sections. The Regulations provide an exception to the requirement for producing an independent expert's report for a merger of a public company if all the shareholders (and holders of other securities giving the right to vote) of each of the companies involved in the merger have agreed to dispense with the report (s 918A). They also bar transferor and transferee companies from being allotted any shares in a transferee company in the course of a merger or division (ss 914 and 930).

[1]   Which implement Directive 2007/63/EC (amending Council Directives 78/855/EEC and 82/891/EEC).

Index

Index

Index

Index

Index

Index

Index